Enjoy

Love,

Ivan & Loretta

A Bible! A Bible!

A Bible! A Bible!

Robert J. Matthews

With a Foreword by
Robert L. Millet
and Larry E. Dahl

Bookcraft
Salt Lake City, Utah

Material originally published by
The Church of Jesus Christ of Latter-day Saints
is here used by permission.

Library of Congress Catalog Card Number: 89-82695

ISBN 0-88494-727-0

First Printing, 1990

Printed in the United States of America

CONTENTS

FOREWORD

Robert J. Matthews has been our valued mentor, friend, and colleague for many years, and it is in the spirit of tribute and profound appreciation that we have obtained this humble scholar's permission to make the essays comprising this volume available for publication. As a beloved teacher and writer, Brother Matthews has had a marked impact upon gospel scholarship in the Church. He worked for many years in the Church Educational System as a seminary and institute instructor and a research and curriculum editor. In addition, for over twenty years at Brigham Young University he has given diligent service as chairman of the Department of Ancient Scripture, dean of Religious Education, and latterly as one of the senior editors of *The Encyclopedia of Mormonism.*

In his writings, his symposium addresses, his classrooms, and his life, Brother Matthews has borne fervent testimony of Jesus Christ and of the marvelous work and a wonder set in motion through the latter-day seer, Joseph Smith. Few persons in this dispensation have been as conversant with all of the standard works of the Church as Robert Matthews. He has written and spoken scores of times on subjects pertaining to the Old Testament, the New Testament, the Book of Mormon, the Doctrine and Covenants, and the Pearl of Great Price.

His life's work and consuming passion, however, have been Joseph Smith's translation of the Bible. It was in the summer of 1944 that Brother Matthews listened to a radio address given by Elder Joseph Fielding Smith, in which the Apostle quoted a passage of scripture from the King James Version (John 1:18), noted that the translation was incorrect, and then cited the same passage from the Joseph Smith Translation. At that point in his young life (he was eighteen years old), Brother Matthews had never heard of the Joseph Smith Translation. And yet there came a fascination—much more than a simple curiosity—with this work of the Prophet Joseph, a fascination which over the years ripened into a thorough, scholarly study of the translation. It was Robert J. Matthews who, for over fifteen years, persisted in his request to the Reorganized Church of Jesus Christ of Latter Day Saints to examine the original manuscripts of the Joseph Smith Translation. Permission was finally granted in 1968, and Brother Matthews was able to continue his important studies, now more richly informed through access to the original documents prepared by Joseph Smith and his scribes almost a century and a half earlier.

Much of what we know about the Joseph Smith Translation today—the accuracy of the printed editions made by the RLDS church, key dates for the Genesis chapters that appear in the Pearl of Great Price as the book of Moses, its tie to the ongoing history of the Church and the revelations in the Doctrine and Covenants, and the work of translation itself as a major branch of the Prophet's calling—much of this we know because of the labors of Robert J. Matthews. Years of earnest and detailed study resulted in the publication in 1975 of his significant volume, *"A Plainer Translation": Joseph Smith's Translation of the Bible, A History and Commentary*. In 1984 Elder Bruce R. McConkie referred to Brother Matthews as "the world authority on the Joseph Smith Translation."[1] On another occasion, to a group of religious educators, Elder McConkie said: "I am pleased to say that here at Brigham Young University we have the world's foremost authority on the Joseph Smith Translation. His contributions in this field of gospel scholarship rank with the best works published in our dispensation. He is of course Brother Robert J. Matthews, the dean of Religious Education. His published work, *'A Plainer Translation': Joseph Smith's Translation of the Bible, A History and Commentary*, is deserving of your careful study."[2] Because so much of what Brother Matthews has taught and written over the years has dealt with the clarifying and elevating influence of latter-day revelation upon the Bible, the title of this work, *A Bible! A Bible!* seemed most appropriate.

Though he has remained active in symposia and seminars, and though he has prepared articles for Church periodicals or chapters for others' books during the last two decades, Robert J. Matthews—largely because of his heavy administrative and editorial assignments—has not enjoyed those blocks of uninterrupted time so necessary for the organization, writing, and preparation of a book. Because we have found his insights into life and into the power of the gospel so seminal and life-changing, we have chosen

1. Bruce R. McConkie, "The Doctrinal Restoration," in *The Joseph Smith Translation: The Restoration of Plain and Precious Things*, ed. Monte S. Nyman and Robert L. Millet (Provo, Utah: Religious Studies Center, Brigham Young University, 1985), p. 22.

2. Bruce R. McConkie, "The Bible: A Sealed Book," *Supplement to the Eighth Annual Church Educational System Religious Educators' Symposium* (Salt Lake City: The Church of Jesus Christ of Latter-day Saints, 1984), p. 5.

to assemble for publication those writings that we believe represent some of his most pertinent and profound thinking. Brother Matthews's personal sense of modesty and humility would not have allowed him to do this himself. But we prevailed upon him to allow us to do so. We are grateful for the enthusiasm and encouragement of Russell Orton and Cory Maxwell at Bookcraft Publishers, and particularly for the sensitivity and keen editorial eyes of George Bickerstaff and Garry Garff.

Each person is responsible for what he says or writes. In that regard, this work is a private endeavor and not a production of or endorsed by either Brigham Young University or The Church of Jesus Christ of Latter-day Saints. We believe, however, that Brother Matthews's understanding and doctrinal interpretations are in harmony with the scriptural canon and the words of living Apostles and prophets.

Most of the chapters herein originated as talks given at different times, to different audiences, and in varying circumstances. They represent the teachings of a perceptive mind and a great man. It is our prayer that the doctrine taught and the expressions made in these pages will bring as much soul-satisfaction and depth of insight to the reader as they have brought to us.

ROBERT L. MILLET
LARRY E. DAHL

PART I

Ancient and Modern Scriptures

Chapter 1

A BIBLE! A BIBLE!

Consider for a moment the blessing of having the scriptures so readily available. Today Bibles are plentiful. Most of us have at least one copy written in our own language that we can read and study with little effort. But Bibles have not always been so accessible. In 2 Kings 22 and 23, written some time around 620 B.C., is the account of temple workmen finding an abandoned copy of the law of God. This discovery seemed to have been a surprise; copies of the scriptures were apparently hard to come by then. King Josiah read these writings, discovered that many religious practices of his people did not conform with the recorded commandments, and decided to make changes. He reemphasized the Passover feast, and conditions improved for a time in Jerusalem.

A few years later, Lehi and his family were commanded to leave Jerusalem and take with them a copy of the scriptures. Book of Mormon readers remember the efforts of Nephi and his brothers to obtain from Laban the plates of brass, which contained a record similar to our Old Testament down to that time (600 B.C.). Laban did not want to part with his copy of the scriptures even after he had been handsomely paid for it, but the Lord's interest was so keen on the matter that he explained to Nephi that it was "better that one man [Laban] should perish than that a nation should dwindle and perish in unbelief" (1 Nephi 4:13). As the account in 1 Nephi 4–5 implies, copies of the scriptures in any form were scarce.

King Benjamin, recognizing the importance of written scriptures, told his sons that without the brass plates the people would have suffered in spiritual ignorance, "for it were not possible that our father, Lehi, could have remembered all these things, to have taught them to his children, except it were for the help of these plates" (Mosiah 1:4).

In contrast, those who came with Mulek from Jerusalem to America about 589 B.C. did not bring any scriptures, and consequently they slipped into mental and spiritual darkness (see Omni 1:14–17). While it is possible that the Mulekites failed to take the scriptures with them primarily out of neglect, it is more likely that there were few copies of the scriptures around to take (see 1 Nephi 4–5).

In about 520 B.C., Ezra the scribe, after bringing the people of Judah back to the land of Judea from their seventy-year captivity in Babylon, gathered them together so he could read the Old Testament to them. He translated as he read because the scriptures were written in Hebrew and the younger Jews spoke only Aramaic, the language of Babylon. Probably for the first time in their lives these Jews heard and understood the scriptures in their own tongue, and they wept and rejoiced. (See Nehemiah 8.)

These examples lead us to believe that having the scriptures readily available and in our own language is a blessing that most people in bygone days have not enjoyed. And yet the Bible is recorded not only on paper for reading but also on tape for hearing, in braille for feeling, and even on microfilm. It has been translated into thousands of languages and is available in book form in a multitude of sizes and bindings.

The Lord said to Nephi that in our day, the last days, many would say, "A Bible! A Bible! We have got a Bible, and there cannot be any more Bible." To them, the Lord responded: "What do the Gentiles mean? Do they remember the travails, and the labors, and the pains of the [Jewish prophets], and their diligence unto me, in bringing forth salvation unto [them]?" (2 Nephi 29:3–4.)

The question seems to be, Do we appreciate what it means for each of us to have his own personal copy of the Bible?

The Latin Vulgate

The original languages of the Bible were Hebrew, Aramaic, and Greek. In A.D. 382, Pope Damascus persuaded Eusebius Sofronius Hieronymus (commonly known as St. Jerome), perhaps the most capable Bible scholar of the time, to translate the scriptures into Latin. This translation, called the Vulgate because it was in the "vulgar" or common tongue of the Latin people, was used in European countries where Catholicism was the dominant religion. Even with all his efforts and learning, however, Jerome could not avoid making some errors and misinterpretations. But of even greater importance, over the next thousand years more changes crept into the many versions of the Vulgate that were made.[1]

A Bible in English

During the Middle Ages few northern Europeans understood the Latin scriptures, and copies of the Bible were scarce. Sometimes even the local priests knew little of the Bible. The type of church service did not contribute to much reading anyway, as the emphasis was on celebrating the mass rather than preaching the word of God. Many of the poor people could not read at all; thus, concentrated, sustained, and regular study of the Bible was out of the question for most people.

Still, through the centuries, many wondered why the scriptures could not be translated into different languages so everyone could read and benefit. The ancient Hebrews had been taught by the prophets in their own language, and the Greeks had been taught by Paul in their native tongue. Why could it not be so with the English, the French, the Germans?

Let us now look at the momentous events that gave us the Bible in English—one of the most important of the instruments that helped to bring about the restoration of the gospel.

John Wycliffe (1320–84)

Although others had translated portions of the Bible into English, Oxford scholar John Wycliffe was the first to make the entire Bible available in an English translation. His efforts to translate and distribute the Bible have earned him the title "Morning Star of the Reformation."

A Bible in English had been Wycliffe's goal for years. Every leisure moment during his life was spent translating the scriptures into English. He said: "See [pointing to a table], it is there I sit not only by day, but often far into the night. Just a few lines only will sometimes cost me hours and days of study before I can satisfy myself as to the correct rendering. . . . If God spare my life another year, I hope to put the entire Bible in English into the hands of the copyists."[2]

Because Wycliffe had extensive knowledge of Latin, but not of Hebrew or Greek, he made his translation of the Bible from the Latin Vulgate and not from the original languages of the scriptures.

Handwritten Bibles

Since Wycliffe lived before the invention of movable-type printing, his translation was available in handwritten form only. This made copies very expensive. One historian reports that "a copy of the Bible cost from 40–60 pounds for the writing only. It took an expert copyist about 10 months to complete it."[3]

Since few could afford to own a hand-made Bible, Wycliffe and his followers traveled the countryside with Bible manuscripts for the people to read. Sometimes the people would borrow or rent the scriptures for a day, or even for an hour, because they could not afford to buy a copy. It is said that a load of hay was the going price to rent a Bible for an hour.[4]

Early copies of Wycliffe's Bible were written on large sheets of paper, but when authorities threatened to prosecute and even burn at the stake those who possessed them, Wycliffe made smaller copies so they could be more easily concealed.[5] The preface to the Wycliffe Bible contains a prayer that shows the spirit and circumstances under which Wycliffe and his associates labored: "God grant to us all, grace to know well and keep well the holy writ, and suffer joyfully some pains for it at the last."[6] Often when a brave soul was burned at the stake, he or she would go to the flames with a piece of the Bible dangling from a cord about his or her neck.

Although Wycliffe suffered ostracism and persecution for his work, he escaped martyrdom, died a natural death in 1384 at the age of sixty-four, and was buried at Lutterworth, England.

It is clear that Wycliffe's Bible, with its gracefully simple and direct language, was intended for the plain folk and not for scholars. He was not content merely to have the Bible translated; he wanted it to be understood, and he wanted multiple copies. It is reported that more than 150 copies of his small-sized, handwritten Bible survive today. When we consider that authorities burned as many copies as they could lay their hands upon, the survivors are evidence of the extensive circulation of the books and the value placed upon them by their owners.

William Tyndale (1492–1536)

A century passed between John Wycliffe's death and the coming of William Tyndale, the next great biblical translator. During that time Johannes Gutenberg invented movable-type printing and printed the Latin Vulgate Bible. It took Gutenberg and his associates about seven or eight years to print the first copy[7] and more than twenty years from their first experimentation with movable type and better kinds of paper and ink. Some reports say that Gutenberg died penniless and in debt, having devoted his life to developing a process that would change the course of the world forever.

It was into this changed world that William Tyndale, destined to become the "father" of our present English Bible, was born. As had Wycliffe, he became a scholar at Oxford. Trained in Latin, Hebrew, and Greek, Tyndale saw the need for and was able to make an English translation of the Bible directly from the Hebrew and Greek texts.

Tyndale was a popular teacher who often turned to his Hebrew and Greek texts to refute his opponents, showing that in some instances the Latin Vulgate Bible they used had been translated incorrectly. But he noticed that after he had taught a group and moved on, the priests would come and turn those people away from what he had taught them. The people generally did not have the scriptures in their own tongue and were at the mercy of the priests for their knowledge of religion.

Seeing that his teachings were being overturned, Tyndale decided to arm the common people with a Bible they could read, reasoning, "If [English] Christians possessed the Holy Scriptures in their own tongue, they could of themselves withstand these attacks. Without the Bible it is impossible to establish the people in truth. . . . Christians must read the New Testament [for themselves] in their own tongue."[8] He also said, "I had perceived by experience how that it was impossible to establish the lay people in any truth, except the scripture were plainly laid before their eyes in their mother tongue, that they might see the process, order and the meaning of the text."[9]

Once, when engaged in earnest debate with a learned clergyman over giving the common people a Bible they could understand, Tyndale said, "If God spare my life, I will take care that ere many years the boy that driveth the plow shall know more of the Scripture than thou dost."[10] Such bold expression caused clergy and state officials to intensify their opposition to Tyndale.

Seeing that he was opposed on every hand, Tyndale fled to various places in England to avoid arrest and possible death. He appealed to the bishop of London for official permission to translate the Bible into English but was denied. It soon became apparent that there was no place in England to make an English translation of the Bible from the original tongues, so in 1524 Tyndale went to Germany. There he lived very modestly and in seclusion. Soon he completed his translation of the New Testament and asked for publication of three thousand copies.

Because English-language Bibles could not openly be marketed in England, the first copies were smuggled into the British Isles from Belgium. When British government and church authorities learned that Tyndale's New Testament was being sold locally, they were furious. The bishop of London called the translation "a pestiferous and most pernicious poison."[11] The various bishops subscribed money to buy all available copies and conducted public burnings of Tyndale's Bible. This exercise was so thorough that only three copies of this first Tyndale New Testament are known to be in existence today.

Following publication of his translation of the New Testament, Tyndale commenced a translation of the Old Testament. The persecutions continued, and Tyndale was betrayed by a supposed friend, kidnapped, and put in prison near Brussels, where he suffered mentally and physically for eighteen months until 6 October 1536, when he was taken from his cell and tied to a stake. There he uttered a loud prayer: "Lord, open the King of England's eyes!"[12] referring to King Henry VIII, who had ignored efforts to grant his subjects personal and religious freedom. Tyndale was then strangled to death and burned.

The Reformation—a New Attitude about the Bible

As more and more people came to own and study the English translations of Wycliffe and Tyndale, the Bible became an increasingly powerful influence. Even in England, Tyndale's work became more accepted, and shortly after he died, copies of his Bible even found their way into the household of King Henry VIII.

For the next seventy years the political and religious complexion of England seesawed from Protestantism to Catholicism and back to Protestantism with changes of monarchs. Henry VIII had established the Church of England with himself, as king, the earthly leader and "defender of the faith." After Henry's death in 1547, his ten-year-old son, Edward VI, was king for a few years and Protestantism prospered. But Mary, Edward's successor, tried to restore Catholicism to England, and she ordered circulation of all English translations of the Bible to cease. Elizabeth I followed Mary, bringing with her a return to Protestantism. With the change in emphasis throughout the Protestant world, the preaching of the Bible became a major feature of church service. This influenced the architecture of church buildings, and the pulpit replaced the altar, upon which the mass was celebrated, as the focus of attention.

The King James Version

When James I followed Elizabeth to the throne in 1603, Tyndale had been dead sixty-seven years, and there had been several revisions of the English Bible. The principal versions were the Coverdale Bible (named after its translator), the Great Bible (named for its size), the Geneva Bible (named for its place of printing), and the Bishop's Bible (authorized by the Church of England clergy). All drew heavily from Tyndale's translation, but each favored different religious points of view. The Geneva Bible contained footnotes and marginal notes favoring Puritanism but was antagonistic toward the hierarchy of the Catholic Church, the Church of England, and the universities.

The Geneva Bible was the version used by Shakespeare and the Pilgrim fathers; it also came to America on the Mayflower. It was the first to use italics for words not in the manuscripts, to print each verse as a separate paragraph for convenience of concordances, and to use a ¶ sign to designate main concepts.[13]

The Geneva Bible was very popular with the people but was annoying to the bishops of the Church of England. The Bishop's Bible was the clergy's answer to the Geneva Bible, but it was so biased that it left the Puritans unhappy. No Bible translation was accepted by everyone.

As a consequence, in January 1604, King James I convened a conference to settle differences between these groups. A proposal was made for a new translation to be authorized by King James as the official Bible of England.

This new translation was eventually made by committees of scholars assigned to various parts of the Bible. The translation came off the press in 1611 and was called the Authorized Version in Britain and the King James Version in America, the latter reflecting the political differences of the American colonies and England.

Although the King James Version is the hallmark of English Bibles, it is in reality a revision of earlier English translations. In a lengthy introduction to the first edition, the translators explained: "We shouldn't need to make a new translation nor yet to make of a bad one a good one—but to make a good one better, or out of many good ones, [to make] one principal good one."[14] About 92 percent of Tyndale has survived in the King James Version. And Tyndale borrowed much from Wycliffe.

Not all editions of the King James Version have been identical to the first edition. For example, the number of words in italics (words not found in the original Hebrew and Greek manuscripts) increased considerably through the years until about 1870. The 1611 book of Matthew contained 43 italicized words; the present edition has at least 583.[15] There have also been modernizations in spelling, punctuation, and pronoun usage.

The King James Version of the Bible is recognized worldwide for its beauty of expression and general accuracy, given the limitations of the manuscripts from which it was translated. It is the version the English-speaking members of The Church of Jesus Christ of Latter-day Saints have used since the beginning of the dispensation of the fulness of times.

The Joseph Smith Translation of the Bible

With the restoration of divine priesthood authority and the reestablishment of the Church of Jesus Christ through the Prophet Joseph Smith, there came also the restoration of ancient scriptures. Not only were we to have a Bible, but also a Book of Mormon and other sacred records. The revelations received by the Prophet Joseph Smith made clear that the King James Version, great as it was, did not contain all that the ancient manuscripts had once contained. Many plain and precious things had been lost. (See 1 Nephi 13.) Being more than just a matter of translation of languages, the problem centered around a faulty transmission of the text. The King James Version is thus a remarkable vestige of an even more remarkable record of the gospel that was preached anciently.

With the Restoration, another revision of the English Bible was in order, not by a scholar but by a prophet. And it would come not from an ancient manuscript but from direct revelation of the same Lord from whom the Bible had originated. It was to be done at the Lord's commission rather than at the request of an earthly monarch or pope. This revision was to be an inspired version of the King James Bible, a divine restoration of ancient biblical knowledge. It is known today as the Inspired Version or, more properly, as the Joseph Smith Translation of the Bible. It should be seen in perspective as another step in the struggle to give mankind a Bible that not only can be read but also can be understood. The Prophet Joseph Smith made his translation during the years 1830 to 1844.

The LDS Edition of the Scriptures

In order to provide a Bible that would be the most helpful to members of the Church, the First Presidency in 1971 authorized a project to produce some study aids for the King James Version. This effort bore fruit in 1979 with a Bible that consists of (1) the text of the King James Version; (2) cross-references to latter-day scriptures—the Book of Mormon, the Doctrine and Covenants, and the Pearl of Great Price; (3) excerpts from Joseph Smith's translation of the Bible; (4) explanatory footnotes showing alternate readings from Greek and Hebrew; (5) footnotes showing clarifications of obsolete words and idioms in the English language; (6) new interpretive chapter headings; (7) a topical guide; (8) a Bible dictionary; and (9) a selection of maps.

Brought together in the LDS edition of the King James Bible is some of the best material available today from both scholarship and latter-day revelation. The genius of the LDS edition is to present this wealth of information about the Bible and latter-day revelation in a reference system that permits the reader to learn quickly what the scriptures say about a large number of subjects vital to eternal life.

In 1980 President Spencer W. Kimball invited us to become acquainted with the LDS edition of the Bible: "We now have a wonderful new edition of the King James Version of the Holy Bible with a topical index and a whole new reference system. . . . All of [this] should encourage further involvement with the scriptures, as individuals and as families."[16]

As the Lord promised centuries ago, his word has gone forth "unto the ends of the earth, for a standard unto my people" (2 Nephi 29:2).

Notes

1. See F. F. Bruce, *The Books and the Parchments* (London: Fleming H. Revel Co., 1955), pp. 191–200; also Frederic Kenyon, *Our Bible and the Ancient Manuscripts* (New York: Harper and Row, 1962), pp. 141–43, 242–44.

2. As cited in Bayly, *The Story of Our English Bible and What It Cost* (London: James Nisbet and Co., 1886), pp. 37–38.

3. Bayly, *Story of Our English Bible,* p. 58.

4. See Geddes MacGregor, *A Literary History of the Bible* (New York: Abingdon Press, 1968), p. 80.

5. See Josiah H. Penniman, *A Book About the English Bible* (Philadelphia: University of Pennsylvania Press, 1931), p. 341.

6. As cited in MacGregor, *Literary History of the Bible,* p. 80.

7. See Bayly, *Story of Our English Bible,* pp. 61–62.

8. As cited in Bayly, *Story of Our English Bible,* p. 90.

9. As cited in Harold L. Phillips, *Translators and Translations* (Anderson, Indiana: The Warner Press, 1958), p. 22. Tyndale's original spelling has been modernized.

10. As cited in Penniman, *A Book About the English Bible,* p. 348.

11. As cited in MacGregor, *Literary History of the Bible,* pp. 113–14.

12. See *The English Hexapla* (London: Samuel Bagster and Sons, 1846), p. 18. Spelling has been modernized.

13. See MacGregor, *Literary History of the Bible,* pp. 143–45; also S. L. Greendale, ed., *The Cambridge History of the Bible: The West from the Reformation to the Present Day* (Cambridge: Cambridge University Press, 1963), p. 156.

14. As cited in Penniman, *A Book About the English Bible,* p. 394.

15. See P. Marion Sims, *The Bible in America* (New York: Wilson-Erickson, 1936), p. 97.

16. Spencer W. Kimball, "We Feel an Urgency," *Ensign* 10 (August 1980): 3.

Chapter 2

THE BIBLE AND ITS ROLE IN THE RESTORATION

The Church of Jesus Christ of Latter-day Saints has always been a Bible-believing church, holding that the Bible contains the word of God as delivered to ancient prophets. The Prophet Joseph Smith stated that one can "see God's own handwriting in the sacred volume: and he who reads it oftenest will like it best, and he who is acquainted with it, will know the hand [of God] wherever he can see it."[1]

Of course Joseph Smith also stated that the Bible had not been preserved in its original purity: "We believe the Bible to be the word of God as far as it is translated correctly" (Articles of Faith 1:8). The word *translated* as it is used here must be understood to include the idea of *transmission*. That is, error has occurred not only in the translation from one language to another but also in the transcription of the text from manuscript to manuscript, even in the same language. The Bible has apparently suffered mostly from omissions—it is not particularly erroneous, but many important items are missing, and this in turn leaves some parts unclear. Joseph Smith explained this further when he said, "I believe the Bible as it read when it came from the pen of the original writers. Ignorant translators, careless transcribers, or designing and corrupt priests have committed many errors."[2]

The Book of Mormon identifies the Bible as the record of the Jews and makes several assertions concerning the Bible: prophets wrote it through inspiration; originally, it was easily understood; through the centuries many plain and precious things have been lost from it. The Book of Mormon also records prophecy that the lost parts of the Bible would be restored. Indeed, many of the "plain and precious things" have again been made known through heavenly manifestations to Joseph Smith; through the coming forth of the Book of Mormon, the Doctrine and Covenants, and the Pearl of Great Price; and through Joseph Smith's translation of the Bible.

Clearly, the Restoration did much to make the Bible understandable and complete, but the converse is also true. The Bible played a unique and indispensable role in the Restoration. This is particularly evident in the restoration of many fundamental doctrines of the gospel.

The Bible and the First Vision

The story of the Restoration itself begins with an important reference to the Bible: "I was one day reading the Epistle of James, first chapter and fifth verse, which reads: *If any of you lack wisdom, let him ask of God, that giveth to all men liberally, and upbraideth not; and it shall be given him.* Never did any passage of scripture come with more power to the heart of man than this did at this time to mine. It seemed to enter with great force into every feeling of my heart. I reflected on it again and again. . . . I at length came to the determination to 'ask of God.' " (Joseph Smith—History 1:11–13.)

In response to his prayer, Joseph experienced one of the greatest spiritual manifestations of all time, in which he saw and talked with both the Father and the Son. Among other things the First Vision taught Joseph that there is a God who hears and answers prayers, that the Father and the Son are separate beings, and that each is in the form of a man. He also learned that the true Church of Jesus Christ was not at the time upon the earth. All of these fundamental principles of the restored gospel are linked historically and theologically with the Bible through James 1:5 and the First Vision.

The Bible and the Angel Moroni

About three years after the First Vision, the Prophet received several visits from the angel Moroni. Although the central theme of Moroni's message to Joseph Smith appears to be the coming forth of the Book of Mormon, Moroni also quoted and explained numerous passages from the Bible. This appears to have been primarily for the purpose of orienting the young prophet in the Lord's plan for the last days.

Some of the passages Moroni quoted, as identified by the Prophet, were from the third and fourth chapters of Malachi, the eleventh chapter of Isaiah, the third chapter of Acts, and the second chapter of Joel. However, Joseph Smith also said that Moroni quoted and explained many other passages. (See Joseph Smith—History 1:36–41.) Although these "other passages" are not identified in the Prophet's account, they are the subject of a series of letters written by Oliver Cowdery and published in the *Latter Day Saints' Messenger and Advocate* during the months of February and April 1835. In these letters Brother Cowdery stated that a major purpose of the angel Moroni's instruction was to inform the young prophet of the work of God on the earth in the last days and to give him a perspective of the magnitude of his calling so as to prepare him for the work. Old Testament scriptures played an important part in Moroni's instruction. Oliver Cowdery cited Psalms 100, 107, and 144, Isaiah 1 and 2, and Jeremiah 31 as being among the passages Moroni quoted and explained to Joseph Smith.[3] In his own account Joseph Smith stated that Moroni quoted some passages differently than they appear in the King James Version (see Joseph Smith—History 1:36–39).

The First Vision and the instruction of Moroni thus greatly enlarged Joseph Smith's understanding of the Bible—he knew it was divinely inspired, but he also knew that certain passages should be rendered differently in order to convey the original meaning.

The Bible and the Translation of the Book of Mormon

In the task of translating the Book of Mormon, the Prophet had firsthand experience with the difficulty of rendering a passage accurately from one language into another. It was only by the influence of the Spirit and through the "gift and power of God" that a correct translation could be made—and considerable effort and thought were still required of the translator.

This difficulty in conveying the true intent of scripture may account, in part at least, for the frequent use of King James Version language in the Book of Mormon translation. The Bible was not the *source* of the information in the Book of Mormon, but apparently the literary style of the Bible was used as a *vehicle* to convey many of the concepts in the Book of Mormon. The hundreds of verses in the Book of Mormon that are similar in language and style to the King James Version illustrate the Bible's influence in this phase of the Restoration.

The Bible and the Doctrine and Covenants

The word *Bible* appears only once in the Doctrine and Covenants (42:12); however, there are many allusions and references to the Bible in the latter-day book of scripture, and much that is in the Doctrine and Covenants is allied closely to the Bible.

The Doctrine and Covenants contains instructions about Joseph Smith's translation of the Bible—when to begin the translation, when to stop, who is to be scribe, how to get it printed, and so on. It also contains revelations which were not intended as part of the Bible text but grew out of the translation experience, such as sections 76, 77, 86, 91, and probably 132.

Many verses in the Doctrine and Covenants are unintelligible to a reader unless he knows that the subject of those verses is the translation of the Bible. Just as some early sections of the Doctrine and Covenants revolve around the translation of the Book of Mormon (sections 3, 5, 8, 9, 10, and 17), some later sections revolve around the translation and intended printing of the Bible—parts of 35, 37, 41, 42, 45, 73, 74, 93, 94, 104, and 124, and all of sections 76, 77, 86, and 91.

There is also much biblical phraseology in the Doctrine and Covenants; for example, section 133 is similar in content and language to Isaiah 63 and 64. One cannot be familiar with the Doctrine and Covenants and the Bible without being aware that both books support each other and are tied together at key points by subject matter and phraseology. Indeed, the revelations contained in the Doctrine and Covenants are a strong witness for the truth and worth of the Bible.

The Bible and the Pearl of Great Price

Two major portions of the Pearl of Great Price, the book of Moses and Joseph Smith—Matthew, are actually extracts from Joseph Smith's translation of the Bible (discussed below). Thus, sizable portions of this standard work are also closely related to the Bible.

The New Translation and Doctrinal Development

Early in the Prophet's ministry the Lord instructed him to make a revision, or as he termed it, a "translation" of the Bible. This was not to be a translation in the usual sense, employing a knowledge of biblical languages, use of ancient manuscripts, and the usual procedure and paraphernalia of the scholar, but rather a translation in which Joseph Smith would discern the true intent of the Bible through revelation. It is now known as the Joseph Smith Translation, or JST.

A major purpose of the new translation seems to have been the spiritual understanding that came to the Prophet as a result of his effort. The process brought him a new knowledge of doctrine and principle. This is possibly one of the most important aspects of the Prophet's work with the Bible, and seems to be consistent with the purpose for the translation as stated by the Lord: "And now, behold, I say unto you, it shall not be given unto you to know any further concerning this chapter, *until the New Testament be translated, and in it all these things shall be made known;* wherefore I give unto you that ye may now translate it, *that ye may be prepared* for the things to come. For verily I say unto you, that great things await you." (D&C 45:60–62, italics added.)

It is evident from this passage that the Prophet's translation of the Bible was not to be limited to a correction of passages based on revelation and knowledge he had already received, but was to be the means by which he would receive new revelation on matters that had not yet been made known to him. Plain and precious things were to be restored. This concept gives an importance and a dignity to the Prophet's work with the Bible that is frequently overlooked, and it forms an inseparable link between the translation of the Bible and the restoration of gospel doctrine in this dispensation.

The following topics are fundamental elements of the restored gospel that were revealed to the Prophet as he translated the Bible.

The Visions of Moses

The exact date the Prophet began his translation of the Bible is not known, but it is clearly associated with the revelation received in June 1830 concerning the visions of Moses, now printed as Moses 1 in the Pearl of Great Price. The importance of the doctrinal, philosophical, and historical content of this chapter is well known to students of the gospel, since it gives considerable information about Moses, Satan, Deity, and the purpose of God's creations.

This revelation reaches a sublime philosophical note when Moses, overwhelmed by the creations of the Lord, asks: "Tell me, I pray thee, why these things are so, and by what thou madest them." The Lord then explains the mission of the Only Begotten and of the first man, Adam, and points out that His work and glory is "to bring to pass the immortality and eternal life of man." (Moses 1:30–39.) This answers the *why* of creation; the early chapters of Genesis explain the *how*. Thus this revelation is an introduction to Genesis, and without it Genesis loses some of its perspective.

Adam

Adam holds a special place in the theology of the Latter-day Saints, and much of the particular information about Adam, his immediate family, and his introduction to the gospel is found in the Prophet's translation of Genesis. This is now published as Moses 3–7 in the Pearl of Great Price and Genesis 2–7 in the Joseph Smith Translation. Adam's faithfulness in offering sacrifice, his diligence in teaching his children, his pure language, his baptism, and other important doctrinal and historical points are made known in the Joseph Smith Translation of the Bible.

Cain and Satan

The Prophet's Bible translation brought forth revelations not only about God and about the righteous patriarchs of the early ages, but also about Cain's rebellion and Satan's secret oaths with Cain and many of the children of Adam. Much of our present knowledge of Cain came to us through the Prophet's translation of the fourth chapter of Genesis, which can be found also in Moses 5.

Zion and Enoch

The concept of Zion, both as an ancient city built by the patriarch Enoch and also as a prominent part of the work of the Lord yet to be accomplished in this dispensation, is paramount in the theology of the Church. Much of what we know concerning Enoch and his city comes to us through the revelations given to Joseph Smith while he was translating the early chapters of Genesis in November and December 1830. These currently appear as Moses 6 and 7 in the Pearl of Great Price and as Genesis 6 and 7 in the Joseph Smith Translation. This information about Enoch and his city forms a general background for the more detailed instruction about Zion given in February through August 1831 and recorded in the Doctrine and Covenants (see D&C 42–59).

The Age of Accountability of Children

One of the fundamental and best-known doctrines in the Church today is that little children do not begin to be accountable before God until they reach the age of eight. The Book of Mormon is very clear in specifying that little children are innocent before the Lord, but it does not specify at what age they begin to become accountable. Section 68 of the Doctrine and Covenants (dated November 1831) mentions the age of eight years for the beginning of accountability (see verses 25 and 27) and is the reference usually referred to for information on the subject.

However, Genesis 17:11 in the Prophet's translation of the Bible (dated between February 1831 and 5 April 1831) also gives the time of accountability as eight years of age.[4] The information appears in the context of the Lord's instructions to Abraham, and the passage is as follows:

King James Version	**Joseph Smith Translation**
Genesis 17:7: And I will establish my covenant between me and thee and thy seed after thee in their generations for an everlasting covenant, to be a God unto thee, and to thy seed after thee.	Genesis 17:11: And I will establish a covenant of circumcision with thee, and it shall be my covenant between me and thee, and thy seed after thee, in their generations; *that thou mayest know for ever that children are not accountable before me until they are eight years old* (italics added).

The relationship between circumcision and baptism is not explained, but the Prophet's translation definitely states what the age of accountability is.

Of special importance is that the date upon the Prophet's manuscripts for this particular passage in the Bible shows that the concept of an eight-year-old accountability was known to the Prophet at least as early as 5 April 1831, or at least five months before it is mentioned in the revelation now identified as Doctrine and Covenants 68. This very significant doctrine of the gospel, then, was apparently first made known to the Prophet while he was translating the seventeenth chapter of Genesis and is another example of the Bible's significant role in the restoration of the gospel in this dispensation.

The Three Degrees of Glory

Another well-known revelation given to the Prophet Joseph Smith describes the conditions of mankind after the bodily resurrection from the dead, and is frequently spoken of as the vision of the three degrees of glory, although it also includes a description of a state without glory. The written account of this vision is identified today as Doctrine and Covenants 76 and records a great spiritual manifestation given to Joseph Smith and Sidney Rigdon on 16 February 1832, while they were engaged in the translation of the Bible. The brethren had progressed in the work to the fifth chapter of John, at which point they received the heavenly vision. Their report of the event, as given in Doctrine and Covenants 76:15–19, is as follows:

> For while we were doing the work of translation, which the Lord had appointed unto us, we came to the twenty-ninth verse of the fifth chapter of John, which was given unto us as follows—
>
> Speaking of the resurrection of the dead, concerning those who shall hear the voice of the Son of Man:
>
> And shall come forth; they who have done good, in the resurrection of the just; and they who have done evil, in the resurrection of the unjust.
>
> Now this caused us to marvel, for it was given unto us of the Spirit.
>
> And while we meditated upon these things, the Lord touched the eyes of our understandings and they were opened, and the glory of the Lord shone round about.

The revelation that follows is one of the subjects that Church members most frequently discuss and constitutes one of the great visions of this dispensation. In fact it is frequently designated as "The Vision" in Church literature. The Prophet called it "a transcript from the records of the eternal world."[5] It is noteworthy that the setting for this revelation was the Prophet's translation of the Bible.

The Celestial Order of Marriage

Another significant feature of the restored gospel that appears to be directly associated with the Bible is the doctrine of celestial marriage. It is a well-attested fact that this subject was known to the Prophet Joseph several years before it was committed to the written document now identified as Doctrine and Covenants 132. Several of the early brethren testified that they heard the Prophet speak of this subject as early as 1831 or 1832. Since this is the same period that the Prophet was translating Genesis, and since the beginning verses of the revelation on marriage speak of the Prophet's inquiry of the Lord about Abraham, Isaac, and Jacob, it seems likely that the revelation on celestial marriage was associated with Joseph Smith's translation of the Bible.

Thus we see that several significant doctrines revealed in this dispensation are inseparably connected with Joseph Smith's translation of the Bible. Few subjects are more prominent in the gospel than the age of accountability, the building of Zion, Adam's role in the gospel plan, the degrees of glory, and the doctrine of celestial marriage.

It is likely that other important items also were revealed to the Prophet in connection with his work in translating the Bible. There is some evidence that much of what the Prophet knew about the ancient patriarchs, ancient councils and Church organizations, and other topics were revealed to him in the context of this work.

The real product of the Prophet's work with the Bible, then, is not only the manuscript that constitutes the Joseph Smith Translation but also the many revelations and spiritual experiences that came to him—and from him to the Church—as a result of his work with the Bible. Both the manuscript of the Joseph Smith Translation and the additional revelations are important, but of these it would seem that the multitude of the specific revelations on doctrine are of the greatest significance. These give increased knowledge and clarity to such items as the priesthood, the resurrection, and the premortal existence, and also enrich our understanding of the ministries of Jesus, Adam, Enoch, Melchizedek, Abraham, Paul, Peter, and John the Baptist. One can hardly have a clear perspective of the biblical record without these revelations.

Without doubt the Bible played an essential role in the restoration of the gospel.

Notes

1. *Teachings of the Prophet Joseph Smith,* comp. Joseph Fielding Smith (Salt Lake City: Deseret Book Co., 1976), p. 56. Hereafter cited as *TPJS.*

2. *TPJS*, p. 327.

3. See *Latter Day Saints' Messenger and Advocate* 1 (April 1835): 109–12.

4. The dating of the translation of this passage is obtained from the original manuscript prepared by the Prophet and his scribes, courtesy of the historian, Reorganized Church of Jesus Christ of Latter Day Saints, Independence, Missouri.

5. *TPJS*, p. 11.

Chapter 3

LATTER-DAY REVELATION ON OLD TESTAMENT PATRIARCHS

This chapter will discuss the contribution of latter-day revelation to a correct understanding of what the ancient patriarchs were like and of what they taught. The Bible gives us a great amount of historical information about these things, but it is often vague in doctrinal content. It is a cardinal principle of the Church that many plain and precious things have been removed deliberately from the text of the Bible since the time it was originally written. The most serious things that were removed were the doctrinal things. The angel in 1 Nephi 13 said that "many plain and precious things" were "taken away from the book," and also "many covenants of the Lord" were "taken away" (vv. 26–28). It appears that most of the extractions occurred in the first century A.D.; thus, since that time the Jewish and the Christian worlds have not had a completely adequate Bible. Even so the Bible is wonderful and is a force for good and for righteousness in the earth. But think of how marvelous it must have been and of the added message it must have contained when it was complete and doctrinally much richer than it is now.

Consequences of the Removal of Portions from the Bible

Two problems arise when information is taken out of a record. First, there is the loss of that which is removed. Second, and in some cases more significant, when one piece of information is lost it often renders some of the remaining information unintelligible or even misleading. Many of the parts now missing from the Bible were vital to a correct understanding of the historical, intellectual, and doctrinal milieu in which the ancient prophets and patriarchs lived. Without those missing parts the picture is fragmented and vague, if not distorted. My purpose is to discuss a number of things that are found only in latter-day revelation that nevertheless pertain to the biblical story. These are things that we would not know if we had only the Bible.

Some may feel that these things are not important, since the Bible provides a general outline of Old Testament events and concepts. But, to illustrate how the incomplete biblical record, standing alone, has led to some less-than-adequate interpretations, let us consider some entries from two standard reference sources on the Bible. First, from the dictionary section of an edition of the Bible published by Cambridge University Press, we have the following under the entry "Fall":

> This word denotes the first entrance of sin into the world, as described in Gen. 3. The story which is there told should probably be regarded as allegory rather than as literal history. The Bible does not teach that man was originally created perfect, i.e., with all his moral faculties perfectly developed, but that at a certain point in the history of the race the development took a wrong turn, which was not in accordance with God's original purpose. Man consciously set himself to act in opposition to the will of his Creator. This deliberate act of self-assertion produced in the race a natural inclination towards what is wrong, a taint which is handed on from one generation to another, and which is generally called "original sin"; we are all "by nature born in sin."[1]

The second reference source, *Harper's Bible Dictionary,* offers this definition of the Fall: "The lapse from innocence and goodness, the first apostasy: the loss of Adam's position of integrity, virtue, and innocence, after his sin, as related in the Genesis accounts of the Eden tragedy. . . . There is no Old Testament doctrine of the Fall. But the Fall and the atoning grace of Christ are the core of the New Testament theology of Paul."[2]

And now, on the subject of the offering of sacrifices, the dictionary in the Cambridge edition of the Bible states: "No Divine command can be quoted for the institution of sacrifice; the desire to offer some thank-offering was instinctive in man. . . . The earliest sacrifices [were] those of Cain, Abel and Noah. . . . The idea of propitiation became prominent later on, after the Mosaic Law had brought in a fuller knowledge of sin, and had produced a deeper sense of guilt."[3]

In contrast to the above statement about the origin and purpose of sacrifice, the Lord has revealed that he commanded Adam to offer sacrifice and told him to use the firstlings of his flock for this purpose. An angel later came and explained to Adam that this animal sacrifice was a similitude of the forthcoming sacrifice of Jesus Christ. (See JST, Genesis 4:5–8; Moses 5:4–10.) Furthermore, latter-day revelation speaks of the Fall as an actual event, not as an allegory, and presents it as a necessary part of the eternal plan. No doubt the scholars who prepared the two dictionaries cited above were good, God-fearing Christian men, but they simply did not have the benefit of a complete Bible or of latter-day revelation.

It is true, as *Harper's Bible Dictionary* states, that the Old Testament, as it has come down to us, contains virtually no doctrine of the Fall, but that is because almost all traces and doctrinal discussions of it have been removed from that record. Latter-day scriptures attest that at one time the Old Testament, especially the book of Genesis, had a very clear doctrine of the Fall, beginning with God's revelation to Adam on the subject. We know from these scriptures that the ancient biblical prophets taught the concept of the fall of Adam and the atonement of Christ. This is especially evident in the Book of Mormon and in the Joseph Smith Translation.

While it is true that nearly all of the doctrines of the gospel are at least mentioned in the Bible, they are not presented in an organized form or in logical proximity to one another; rather, they are scattered throughout the Bible in such a manner that they are not easily recognized nor properly associated. After a person has learned the gospel and become acquainted with the plan of salvation from latter-day revelation, he can then see traces of the plan and discover references to it in the Bible; but he can't construct the plan and fit it together initially from the Bible alone.

Twenty-five years ago another teacher and I were standing along a roadway in Washington State with plans to photograph Mount Rainier, which stood in the distance. There was a considerable amount of mist in the air, and the view was hazy and obscured. This other teacher told me he could put a filter on his camera that would remove much of the haze from the scene as it would appear in the photograph, providing us with a clearer shot of the mountain. That was a new idea to me, but I liked it. In a similar way, as we look through the lens of latter-day revelation, we can see the ancient patriarchs with much of the mist and obscurity removed. I believe we can filter out some of the accumulated fog, and smog, and distant haze—the fog of mistranslation, the smog of neglect or unbelief, and the haze of fragmentary records.

Sources of Information on Ancient Patriarchs

The chief sources of information on the ancient patriarchs, as well as on other gospel matters, are the standard works of the Church and the writings and teachings of the Prophet Joseph Smith. A brief comment about each of these is in order.

The Bible

The Bible is an old book and has been available to man over many years. The prophets who wrote it made it plain and doctrinally strong. They made it clear that they knew of and worshipped Jesus Christ as their Redeemer. The prophets are dead, the original manuscripts are gone, and all the copies have suffered many changes and losses at the hands of men. Some losses were unintentional, but some were intentional. The intentional losses are the most serious because they involved the systematic removal of basic doctrinal passages.

The Book of Mormon

The Book of Mormon is also an old book, as old as the Bible, but the plates upon which it was written were kept hidden in the ground, out of the reach of man for over fourteen hundred years; therefore it did not suffer the kinds of changes and alterations that occurred to the Bible. One of its values is that it demonstrates that the same doctrines known by the biblical writers were known by the Book of Mormon writers and compilers. In fact the Book of Mormon says that God speaks the "same words unto one nation like unto another" (2 Nephi 29:8). Likewise, both records mention many of the same important persons and events. The Book of Mormon has come forth as a second witness for Jesus Christ, as a companion to the Bible, making known many of the things that have been taken away from the Bible (see 1 Nephi 13:39–40).

The Doctrine and Covenants

The Doctrine and Covenants is a new book, containing revelations from the same Lord who gave revelations to the prophets who wrote the Bible and the Book of Mormon. In addition to new and important divine information, this latter-day book of scripture contains many of the same doctrines that the two older books contain, and it speaks often of the ancient biblical prophets.

The Pearl of Great Price

The Pearl of Great Price contains, among other things, two translations by Joseph Smith of ancient material. The first is taken from his translation of Genesis and is called the book of Moses. The second is a translation of records containing the writings of Abraham and is called the book of Abraham.

The Joseph Smith Translation

The Joseph Smith Translation of the Bible is a document containing thousands of additions to and clarifications of the King James Version. In his calling as a prophet and seer Joseph Smith began and carried forth this work of translation under the express direction of the Lord. Many of the doctrinal revelations now in the Doctrine and Covenants were received as a consequence of the Prophet's work on this Bible translation.

Joseph Smith's Writings and Teachings

The writings and teachings of Joseph Smith are also valuable for our study at hand because this man was such a great prophet and restorer, the recipient of so much direct revelation from God. Many of the ancient biblical prophets visited him personally, and he understood the work of the Lord that has taken place on this earth from the beginning. The Lord said of Joseph Smith: "I have given unto him the keys of the mystery of those things which have been sealed, even things which were from the foundation of the world" (D&C 35:18). Joseph Smith's teachings about the work of God and the history of the prophets back to Adam are very important to us, if we want to know about things as they really were.

Latter-day Sources Provide Greater Understanding

An interesting phenomenon of gospel study is that the more you know, the more you want to know. Abraham said he wanted to be a "greater follower of righteousness" and to possess a greater knowledge (Abraham 1:2). Likewise, Moses yearned for another chance to commune with God, for, said he, "I have other things to inquire of him" (Moses 1:18). Once a person is awakened to a basic knowledge of the doctrine and laws of God, his soul thirsts for gospel knowledge even more vigorously than his body craves food.

A second interesting aspect of studying the gospel is that the more a man or woman learns, the more he or she is able to learn. Thus the latter-day revelation contained in our standard works and in the teachings of Joseph Smith opens up the vistas of understanding and spiritual joy like nothing else can.

In providing this understanding, our modern scriptures are fulfilling ancient prophecies. In 2 Nephi 3:12 we read that the writings of the fruit of the loins of Judah (the Bible) and the writings of the fruit of the loins of Joseph (the Book of Mormon) shall come together in the last days. That is a parallel passage to Ezekiel 37:15–17, which states that the stick of Judah and the stick of Ephraim shall become one in our hands. But notice the special wording of the Book of Mormon passage: these writings "shall grow together, unto the confounding of false doctrines." The growing together of these records consists of more than their being placed together under one cover or in a zippered carrying case. The word *grow* implies action. Something that grows is dynamic. Thus, these scriptural records grow and get better in the sense that studying them together yields a greater understanding of vital gospel subjects. That is what happens when we use latter-day revelation to understand the Bible.

I have come to the firm conclusion that the Lord wants us to know the doctrines of the gospel, and to know them well. One purpose of the coming forth of the Book of Mormon is to bring us to a knowledge of "the very points of his [the Redeemer's] doctrine" (1 Nephi 15:14). And in the Doctrine and Covenants we read that "the true points of [the Lord's] doctrine" are to be brought forth "that there may not be so much contention" (D&C 10:62–63). Those who have only the Bible in its imperfect, altered condition are, in the words of the angel in Nephi's vision, in an "awful state of blindness" (1 Nephi 13:32), because they lack the greater gospel knowledge that latter-day scriptures can offer them.

We will now take a specific look at what latter-day revelation tells us about Adam (and Eve, his companion), Enoch, Noah, Melchizedek, Abraham, and Moses.

Adam and Eve

It seems only proper that we begin with Adam and Eve. We cannot enter into an extensive biography; rather, we will deal with a few specific items of historical and doctrinal importance.

Location of the Garden of Eden

The existence of the Garden of Eden is taught in each of the standard works and is a frequent topic in Joseph Smith's teachings. The Bible does not indicate where it was located, and the popular conclusion is that the garden, if it existed at all, was somewhere in the Near East or Asia. Latter-day scripture does not categorically pinpoint the location of the Garden of Eden, but it does place Adam in the Western Hemisphere—stating that he dwelt at Adam-ondi-Ahman—and speaks particularly of Spring Hill in Daviess County, Missouri, as the place where Adam shall come to a future council meeting (see D&C 78:15; 116:1; 117:8–11). Drawing on this information, early Latter-day Saints concluded that the area now called the state of Missouri is the place where Adam and Eve dwelt after their expulsion from the garden.

I do not know of an existing document containing a specific declaration in the words of Joseph Smith in which he gave the exact location of the Garden of Eden, but several secondary sources report that he did so. Presidents Brigham Young, Heber C. Kimball, and Joseph Fielding Smith all said that Joseph Smith taught that the Garden of Eden was located in Jackson County, Missouri, where the city of Independence now is.

According to Wilford Woodruff, President Brigham Young once said: "Joseph, the Prophet, told me that the Garden of Eden was in Jackson County, Missouri. When Adam was driven out he went to the place we now call Adam-ondi-Ahman, Daviess County, Missouri. There he built an altar and offered sacrifices."[4]

Speaking in Provo, Utah, in 1863, Heber C. Kimball discussed several things about Adam and about the redemption of the earth. As one of his points he said: "The spot chosen for the garden of Eden was Jackson County, in the state of Missouri, where Independence now stands; it was occupied in the morn of creation by Adam and his associates who came with him for the express purpose of peopling this earth." President Kimball further commented that "the Prophet Joseph frequently spoke of these things in the revelations which he gave, but the people generally did not understand them."[5]

An interesting scriptural maxim, or formula, states that the "first shall be last; and the last shall be first." Of course that has a lot of meanings and can be applied to a number of things. However, when applied to the establishment of the city of New Jerusalem, the idea can be quite instructive. The Lord revealed that the New Jerusalem and its temple should be located where Independence now is (D&C 57:1–3; 84:1–3). On the basis of the "first last, and last first'' principle, we can reason that the Lord's City in the last dispensation should be located where the work of saving men on earth all began, in the Garden of Eden—that the first place should also be the last place.

President Joseph Fielding Smith taught that the Garden of Eden was located where the New Jerusalem will be established: "In accord with the revelations given to the Prophet Joseph Smith, we teach that the Garden of Eden was on the American continent located where the City Zion, or the New Jerusalem, will be built. When Adam and Eve were driven out of the Garden, they eventually dwelt at a place called Adam-ondi-Ahman, situated in what is now Daviess County, Missouri."[6]

The Family of Adam

As to the family of Adam and Eve, Genesis gives the names of Cain, Abel, and Seth as though these were the earliest children. It does not explicitly say they were the first; it simply does not mention any before them, which leads the reader to assume they were the first. Later, Genesis 4:17 mentions Cain's wife, with no explanation of who she is. This has been a problem to some students, since no daughters of Adam and Eve are mentioned in the record before this. However, in the Joseph Smith Translation (JST, Genesis 4:1–3; Moses 5:1–3) we read that Adam and Eve had many sons and daughters and that these had children also, making Adam and Eve grandparents before either Cain or Abel was born. Whom did Cain marry? The Joseph Smith Translation identifies her as a daughter of one of Cain's brothers (JST, Genesis 5:27; Moses 5:28).

In the King James Version of Genesis, no mention is made of how Adam and Eve felt about the Fall and their having been cast out of the Garden of Eden. But the Joseph Smith Translation (JST, Genesis 4:9–12; Moses 5:10–11) records that both of them rejoiced because of the great new life and spiritual opportunities available to them as a result of the Fall. We don't know how they felt about their situation immediately after they were cast out, but after they were taught the gospel they rejoiced because of the Fall.

It is only from latter-day revelation that we learn that Adam and Eve would have had no children without the Fall. The Bible does not explain this, and therefore many have looked upon the transgression of Adam as a bad thing, believing that, if Adam had not transgressed, the earth would have kept its paradisiacal status and the entire human family could have lived in paradise without sin and death. These theorists do not realize that none of the human family would have been born if Adam and Eve had not fallen. (See 2 Nephi 2:23; Moses 5:11; 6:48.)

Furthermore, we learn from latter-day scripture that Adam could read and write, that he had a perfect and pure language, and that a book of remembrance was kept. Adam and his immediate posterity kept this record, and they taught their children to read and write in the "pure and undefiled" language. (JST, Genesis 6:5–6; Moses 6:5–6.)

Enoch, seven generations and nearly a thousand years later, made reference to this book of remembrance (JST, Genesis 6:49–50; Moses 6:45–46), as did Abraham another thousand years after that (Abraham 1:28–31). Abraham reported that he had in his possession detailed and informative written records kept by his ancestors back to Adam. Those records contained information not known to mankind today.

There is nothing in the King James Bible that would suggest the existence of such a set of records, or of such a highly developed and literate society among Adam and his immediate family. Yet in latter-day revelation these subjects are not simply alluded to or hinted at; they are a major thrust of the revelation about Adam.

Adam and the Gospel

Latter-day Saints have the opportunity to view Adam in a much clearer light than do those who are dependent on the Bible alone. We read in chapters 4 and 5 of Joseph Smith's translation of Genesis (Moses 5–6) that Adam offered animal sacrifice with faith toward the coming Messiah, was visited by angels, was taught the doctrines of the Fall and the Atonement, was baptized with water, and held the priesthood.

We learn from the teachings of the Prophet Joseph Smith that Adam was visited by Christ and that Adam possesses the keys of every dispensation as the father and patriarch of the human race. None of this is discernible from the present biblical record. The Prophet taught that Adam "is the father of the human family, and presides over the spirits of all men. . . . He . . . is the head, and was told to multiply. The keys [of the priesthood] were first given to him, and by him to others. He will have to give an account of his stewardship [to God], and they [those who have held keys] to him. . . . Christ is the Great High Priest; Adam next."[7]

Joseph Smith also provided the following significant information concerning Adam:

> I saw Adam in the valley of Adam-ondi-Ahman. He called together his children and blessed them with a patriarchal blessing. The Lord appeared in their midst, and he (Adam) blessed them all, and foretold what should befall them to the latest generation.[8]

> [Adam] is Michael, . . . the first and father of all, not only by progeny, but the first to hold the spiritual blessings, to whom was made known the plan of ordinances for the salvation of his posterity unto the end, and to whom Christ was first revealed, and through whom Christ has been revealed from heaven, and will continue to be revealed from henceforth. Adam holds the keys of the dispensation of the fullness of times; i.e., the dispensation of all the times have been and will be revealed through him from the beginning . . . to the end of the dispensations that are to be revealed. . . .
>
> . . . [God] set the ordinances to be the same forever and ever, and set Adam to watch over them, to reveal them from heaven to man, or to send angels to reveal them. . . .
>
> These angels are under the direction of Michael or Adam, who acts under the direction of the Lord.[9]

> This, then, is the nature of the Priesthood; every man holding the Presidency of his dispensation, and one man holding the Presidency of them all, even Adam; and Adam receiving his Presidency and authority from the Lord.[10]

None of these concepts taught by the Prophet Joseph Smith could be discerned from the biblical record alone, yet these teachings constitute basic, indispensable information about Adam that we need to know if we are to understand much about him and the plan of God for this earth.

In a modern revelation Adam's son Seth is spoken of as a "perfect man," in the express likeness of Adam's person, and as being so much like Adam that he "could be distinguished from [Adam] only by his age" (D&C 107:43). This certainly attests to the physical perfection and beauty of Adam and Seth. However, there is more that we can learn about this. In January 1843 the Prophet Joseph, speaking of his brother Alvin (whom he regarded very highly and who had died some years before), said he "was a very handsome man, surpassed by none but Adam and Seth."[11] I do not know Alvin's exact physical dimensions, but several members of the Smith family were tall. Joseph Smith, Sr., was six feet three; Hyrum and Joseph were six feet; and their brother William is said to have been six feet four. We have every reason to believe, therefore, that Alvin was tall and long limbed like the other men in the family. *Handsomeness* is, of course, a relative term; yet Joseph Smith believed Alvin to be, by nineteenth-century standards, a handsome man, and by those same standards he judged Adam and Seth, who the Lord said were perfect men, to be even more handsome than Alvin. If by relatively modern standards, then, Adam and Seth were very handsome—and this is speaking of their whole appearance—it follows that they did not have caveman physiques, only one step removed from the apes. Joseph never would have thought a Neanderthal type was more handsome than his beloved brother Alvin. I think we are safe to conclude that, by our standards today, Adam and Seth were upright, straight, tall, and well proportioned.

Furthermore, Joseph Smith was not guessing at Adam's appearance, for in 1839 he had said, "I saw Adam in the valley of Adam-ondi-Ahman."[12] And Oliver B. Huntington's diary quotes the Prophet as having said that Adam was "such a perfect man, great and stout, that he never stumbled or fell a joint [*sic*] to the ground."[13] Elder John Taylor, who knew about Joseph Smith's acquaintance with Adam, said: "If you were to ask Joseph what sort of a looking man Adam was, he would tell you at once; he would tell you his size and appearance and all about him. You might have asked him what sort of men Peter, James and John were, and he could have told you. Why? Because he had seen them."[14]

Enoch

Enoch is a famous patriarch, frequently spoken of in the Church, yet the Bible gives very little information about him. Today we speak of Enoch and his city of Zion, which was translated and taken from the earth nearly five thousand years ago. We also know that Enoch's city will return to the earth in the last days to be joined with the New Jerusalem, which will be built upon the earth in Jackson County, Missouri. We speak of Enoch's city having the ideal social and economic system, whereby there were no poor among them. None of this information is given in the Bible; all of it is dependent upon latter-day revelation. The Bible tells us that Enoch was translated, but it says nothing about a city of Enoch and nothing of Enoch's ministry as a preacher of the gospel of Jesus Christ.

In addition to the information above, we learn from Joseph Smith that Enoch, after his translation, became a ministering angel to people on other planets of a terrestrial order. The Prophet also said that Enoch came as a ministering angel and instructed Paul.[15]

Enoch's Ministry

Although the Bible gives us to understand that Enoch was a righteous man, a man of faith, it does not tell us categorically what Enoch did. From the Joseph Smith Translation we learn that Enoch was a missionary and a successful expounder of the gospel of Jesus Christ, including the fall of Adam, and that he had great visions of eternity, the spirit world, the Judgment, and related things.

One of the greatest statements concerning the fall of Adam and the atonement of Jesus Christ—and the effect of the Atonement in freeing little children from so-called original sin—was given by Enoch and is found in the Joseph Smith Translation or in the book of Moses. Here we learn from Enoch that Adam was taught that, for a remission of any sins he committed after he became mortal, he would have to exercise faith in Jesus Christ, repent, and be baptized in water. But for the transgression in the Garden of Eden, apparently Adam was forgiven without these things. The passage reads as follows:

> But God hath made known unto our fathers that all men must repent.
>
> And he called upon our father Adam by his own voice, saying: I am God; I made the world, and men before they were in the flesh.
>
> And he also said unto him: If thou wilt turn unto me, and hearken unto my voice, and believe, and repent of all thy transgressions, and be baptized, even in water, in the name of mine Only Begotten Son, who is full of grace and truth, which is Jesus Christ, the only name which shall be given under heaven, whereby salvation shall come unto the children of men, ye shall receive the gift of the Holy Ghost, asking all things in his name, and whatsoever ye shall ask, it shall be given you.
>
> And our father Adam spake unto the Lord, and said: Why is it that men must repent and be baptized in water? And the Lord said unto Adam: Behold I have forgiven thee thy transgression in the Garden of Eden.
>
> Hence came the saying abroad among the people, that the Son of God hath atoned for original guilt, wherein the sins of the parents cannot be answered upon the heads of the

> children, for they are whole from the foundation of the world. (JST, Genesis 6:51–56; Moses 6:50–54.)

There is no other passage or reference that surpasses this for clarity. Since these are the words of the Lord to Adam, cited by Enoch and contained in the writings of Moses, we know that all three of these prophets were acquainted with the doctrine of Christ relative to the Fall and the status of little children.

Latter-day revelation also tells us that Enoch was present at a great conference held at Adam-ondi-Ahman three years before the death of Adam. The proceedings of the meeting, including the prophecies of Adam uttered at that time, were all written at the time in the book of Enoch and are yet to be revealed to us. (D&C 107:53–57.)

We learn further that Enoch saw many things in vision, the breadth of which extended from the premortal spirit world, through mortality, up to and including the Millennium, and beyond. Among the many things he saw were Noah and the Flood, the crucifixion of Jesus, the resurrection, and the restoration of the gospel in the last days. (See Moses 6–7.)

Enoch was the great-grandfather of Noah, and in his vision of Noah and his family he saw that Noah built the ark and that the Flood came "upon the residue of the wicked" (Moses 7:43). Enoch received a promise that his (Enoch's) posterity would never be completely destroyed but would continue on the earth as long as the earth should stand. "And the Lord showed Enoch all things, even unto the end of the world" (Moses 7:67). None of these critical items is in our present Bibles.

An interesting and highly spiritual event in which Enoch witnessed the God of heaven weeping is recorded in Moses 7:28–41. At first the patriarch was surprised and expressed his astonishment that the Lord, who had so many creations and so much power, should weep. The Lord explained that he wept because of the wickedness of his children: they were without natural affection; they hated one another; they would not receive him to be their Father and God; and their wickedness would bring about their own suffering and the sorrow of heaven. Then Enoch also wept with the Lord. This is a most touching and spiritual scene, and we are indebted to the Prophet Joseph Smith's translation of Genesis (part of which can be found in the book of Moses) for the account of this remarkable event.

Enoch was translated—which means his life in the flesh was extended in such a way that he did not die—some three thousand years before Christ's mortal ministry. We learn from modern revelation that Enoch underwent a change equal to death and was resurrected at the time of Jesus' resurrection. Such a change, although occuring "in the twinkling of an eye," was a real and necessary step in Enoch's progression, and that great patriarch—as is the case with all those translated before the time of Christ—is now a resurrected being.

It was with Enoch as with all of the patriarchs and prophets: he was baptized, confirmed, ordained, and endowed in the regular order of the gospel and its ordinances.

Noah

We have already spoken somewhat of Noah, but there are a few other things we should note concerning this patriarch.

Noah's Ministry

The Genesis story of the Flood is well known to Bible readers. It is mentioned in both the Old Testament and the New Testament; it is also spoken of in the Book of Mormon, the Doctrine and Covenants, and the Pearl of Great Price. However, strange as it may seem, our present book of Genesis does not give a single word of what Noah preached to the people for the 120 years he warned them of the coming deluge. Not one word! Chapters 6 through 8 of Genesis tell the story but say nothing about what Noah preached. These chapters recount what the Lord said to Noah but fail to tell us what Noah said to the people.

However, we learn from the Joseph Smith Translation (Moses 8:23–24) that Noah preached faith in Jesus Christ, repentance, baptism, and the reception of the Holy Ghost. He also warned the people that if they did not accept the gospel of Christ the floods would come upon them. This is an important item to bear in mind. It was not for rejecting a weather report that the people were destroyed, but for rejecting the first principles of the gospel of Jesus Christ. Noah was not merely a weather prophet; he was a prophet of the Lord Jesus Christ.

The New Testament compensates only slightly for this deficiency of information in Genesis. We read in an epistle of Peter that Noah was "a preacher of righteousness," but we find no direct word about his preaching the gospel of Christ (2 Peter 2:5).

Because of latter-day revelation we know that Noah—like all the other prophets—was baptized, confirmed, ordained, and endowed according to the same gospel and the same ordinances found among us in the Church today. We don't know who baptized Noah, but we learn from the Doctrine and Covenants that Noah was ordained at the age of ten years by his grandfather Methuselah (D&C 107:52).

Noah and the Restoration of All Things

We learn from the Prophet Joseph Smith that Noah is Gabriel and that this patriarch stands next to Adam in the hierarchy of the priesthood. In saving things through the Flood and repopulating the earth, Noah was like a second Adam.[16]

Since we know that Noah is Gabriel, we also know that Noah was the angel who came to Zacharias and to Mary and announced the forthcoming births of John the Baptist and of Jesus (Luke 1). We learn further from modern revelation that this same person, who also bears the title of Elias, has an assignment to bring to pass "the restoration of all things" in the last days (D&C 27:6–7). No doubt he is second to Adam in this function. Adam, you recall, presides over all dispensations. Thus, Noah seems to have a special responsibility under Adam to help bring about the restoration of all things, and consequently both patriarchs have a special relationship to The Church of Jesus Christ of Latter-day Saints.

Melchizedek

Like Enoch, Melchizedek has been almost lost from the pages of the Bible, yet he is and was one of the greatest of prophets and patriarchs. Alma says of him, "There were many before him, and also there were many afterwards, but none were greater" (Alma 13:19).

Melchizedek's Ministry

In Genesis little is said of the ministry of Melchizedek, but from the Joseph Smith Translation we learn that he was valiant even as a youth and that he wrought great miracles by faith. Latter-day scripture indicates that he had the same priesthood, the same covenant, and the same faith as Enoch, and suggests that he was translated, even as Enoch. (JST, Genesis 14:25–40.)

We also know from modern revelation that in the ancient Church the priesthood of the Son of God was named the Melchizedek Priesthood, and this because of his great faith and righteousness and in order to avoid the too frequent use of the name of Deity (D&C 107:1–4).

Latter-day revelation makes it clear that Melchizedek believed in Jesus Christ and preached His gospel. For example, Alma says that Melchizedek was a high priest after the order of the holy priesthood. Alma also explains that high priests were ordained "after the order of the Son, the Only Begotten of the Father." (Alma 13:7–9, 14; see also D&C 107:2–3; JST, Genesis 14:25–40.) Because of latter-day revelation we know that Melchizedek, like the other ancient patriarchs, had faith in Christ, was baptized, received the gift of the Holy Ghost, was ordained, and was endowed in accordance with the same gospel and the same ordinances we know in the Church today.

In the old, sixth-century church of Saint Apollinare Nuovo in Ravenna, Italy, there is an interesting mosaic showing Melchizedek at an altar with bread and wine. This is a depiction of Genesis 14:18. However, the mosaic goes beyond this: on one side of the altar is Abel offering a lamb; on the other side is Abraham with his son Isaac; above the whole scene is the rainbow, reminiscent of Noah and his ministry; and through the clouds, reaching down from heaven, is the hand of God. This unique piece of art brings together many notable prophets in a redemptive motif that points to Christ. The fact that this mosaic exists shows that somebody in Ravenna in the sixth century A.D. had ideas about Melchizedek. It suggests a unity of purpose in the ministries of Abel, Noah, Abraham, and Melchizedek. Christianity and Judaism have all but lost sight of Melchizedek today, probably because the Bible now contains so very little about him. Later Christian art does not emphasize Melchizedek; therefore, we have to go back to the earliest centuries to find evidence of a tradition about him.

The Prophet Joseph explained that it was Melchizedek who taught Abraham the gospel of Jesus Christ and who also ordained Abraham to the priesthood (D&C 84:14).[17]

Genesis 14:18 reports that Melchizedek brought forth bread and wine for himself and Abraham. However, the Joseph Smith Translation rewords this verse as follows: "Melchizedek . . . brake bread and blest it; and he blest the wine, he being the priest of the most high God." This wording suggests that there were two blessings, one for the bread and one for the wine. That would be unusual procedure for a regular meal. It almost suggests a prefigurement of the sacramental emblems of the atonement of Jesus Christ, which would take place many centuries later.

There can be no mistaking the evidence from latter-day scripture and from Joseph Smith's teachings that Melchizedek was a prophet of Jesus Christ.

Abraham

I have repeatedly pointed out in this paper that Adam, Enoch, Noah, and Melchizedek each had the gospel of Christ, with the same baptism, the same priesthood, and the same endowment that are found in the Church today. There are several ways to establish this in the case of Abraham, but let us focus on the following statement from the Prophet Joseph Smith:

> According to Paul, (see Gal. iii:8) the Gospel was preached to Abraham. . . . Our friends may say, perhaps, that there were never any ordinances except those of offering sacrifices before the coming of Christ, and that it could not be possible for the Gospel to have been administered while the law of sacrifices of blood was in force. But we will recollect that Abraham offered sacrifice, and notwithstanding this, had the Gospel preached to him. That the offering of sacrifice was only to point the mind forward to Christ, we infer from these remarkable words of Jesus to the Jews: "Your Father Abraham rejoiced to see my day: and he saw it, and was glad" (John viii:56.) So, then, because the ancients offered sacrifice it did not hinder their hearing the Gospel; but served . . . to open their eyes, and enable them to look forward to the time of the coming of the Savior, and rejoice in His redemption.[18]

It would be difficult to find words any clearer than these to show that, indeed, Abraham and all the ancient patriarchs knew of the great gospel plan.

Moses

The New Testament leaves no question that Moses knew of the coming of Jesus Christ and wrote of him (see John 5, 6, 7; Luke 24:25–27). However, the Old Testament references regarding such things are not that clear. Even so, our present Old Testament offers at least some evidence that Moses knew of Christ, more evidence than it offers in the case of the earlier prophets. Latter-day revelation's account of the glorious vision of Moses makes it clear that this great prophet knew of Christ (see Moses 1). In this vision Moses learned much about the work of Jesus Christ as creator; he learned that Jesus is the Savior, the Only Begotten of the Father (Moses 1:6–21, 32–33). Just as Genesis is an introduction to the Old Testament, chapter 1 of Moses is an introduction to Genesis.

In addition, we learn from a revelation to the Prophet Joseph Smith that Moses was ordained to the Melchizedek Priesthood by his father-in-law, Jethro. This same revelation gives a priesthood lineage from Adam to Moses. (D&C 84:6–17.)

The Continuity of the Lord's Work

From our examination of how latter-day revelation contributes to an understanding of the Old Testament patriarchs, we can clearly discern the continuity and unity of purpose in God's work among his prophets from Adam's time down through the centuries. This is one of the most significant contributions of latter-day revelation.

Common Elements Among the Ancient Patriarchs

Modern scriptures teach us that, beginning with Adam, all of the prophets and patriarchs had the gospel of Jesus Christ and that it was the same gospel then as it is now. Adam received the same gospel, the same ordinances, the same endowment, the same celestial marriage, and the same covenants that members of The Church of Jesus Christ of Latter-day Saints receive today. Furthermore, these prophets knew of each other. The earlier ones met together, and the later ones knew they were engaged in the same divine work that the earlier ones were, and for the same purposes. This continuity and unity are no longer evident in the Bible. I have no doubt they were there in the beginning, but they have become obscured.

The patriarchs from Adam to Methuselah were all on the earth together and knew one another, and they were all in the meeting at Adam-ondi-Ahman mentioned earlier in this chapter. An unbroken line of ordination existed from Adam to Methuselah, from Methuselah to Noah, and from Noah to Moses.

The Joseph Smith Translation informs us that when the Lord called Noah, instructed him concerning his ministry, and commanded him to build an ark, he also told him that he (Noah) had the same priesthood and covenant that was given to Enoch (see LDS edition footnotes for Genesis 6:18; 9:9, 11, 16).

The Prophet's Bible translation also tells us that later, when the priesthood and covenant were given to Melchizedek, this patriarch was told that these were the same that Enoch possessed (JST, Genesis 14:25–40). Still later, modern revelation informs us, as Abraham was called and ordained, the Lord told him: "And remember the covenant which I make with thee; for it shall be an everlasting covenant; and thou shalt remember the days of Enoch thy father" (see LDS edition footnote for Genesis 13:14).

These passages from the Joseph Smith Translation, plus the priesthood genealogy lists of Doctrine and Covenants 84:6–17 and 107:40–52, contribute the following to our understanding: (1) they certify the credentials of the ancient patriarchs, showing that they were called of God and ordained under the hands of living priesthood bearers; (2) they certify that the patriarchs all received the same covenant and were engaged in the same sacred work and purposes of God; and (3) they demonstrate that the work of God is standardized and unified, that there was unity and organization anciently as there is today. These concepts cannot be discovered by examining our present book of Genesis alone, for it tends to treat each patriarch and prophet independently as well as scantily.

Every Dispensation was Governed by the Gospel Law

To appreciate the continuity of the Lord's work throughout time, we should understand that everything is governed by a law that was formulated and existed in the premortal life before the world was created. The plan of salvation existed then, and the same plan is still operating; nothing has been added, nothing taken away. We read in the Doctrine and Covenants: "There is a law, irrevocably decreed in heaven before the foundations of this world, upon which all blessings are predicated—and when we obtain any blessing from God, it is by obedience to that law upon which it is predicated" (D&C 130:20–21).

We read further in that same modern book of scripture:

> For all who will have a blessing at my hands shall abide the law which was appointed for that blessing, and the conditions thereof, as were instituted from before the foundation of the world. . . .
>
> Behold, mine house is a house of order, saith the Lord God, and not a house of confusion.

> Will I accept of an offering, saith the Lord, that is not made in my name?
>
> Or will I receive at your hands that which I have not appointed?
>
> And will I appoint unto you, saith the Lord, except it be by law, even as I and my Father ordained unto you, before the world was?
>
> I am the Lord thy God; and I give unto you this commandment—that no man shall come unto the Father but by me or by my word, which is my law, saith the Lord. (D&C 132:5, 8–12.)

Once we know the laws of the gospel, it is not necessary that every point about each prophet's calling be repeated in the scriptures. The following excerpts from the Prophet Joseph Smith's teachings illustrate his understanding of these matters:

> The gospel has always been the same; thc ordinances to fulfill its requirements, the same, and the officers to officiate, the same; and the signs and fruits resulting from the promises, the same; therefore, as Noah was a preacher of righteousness he must have been baptized and ordained to the priesthood by the laying on of hands, etc.[19]
>
> He [God] set the ordinances to be the same forever and ever.[20]
>
> It was the design of the councils of heaven before the world was, that the principles and laws of the priesthood should be predicated upon the gathering of the people in every age of the world. . . . Ordinances instituted in the heavens before the foundation of the world, in the priesthood, for the salvation of men, are not to be altered or changed. All must be saved on the same principles.[21]

If a person wishes to have a clear perspective of the work of God on the earth, he should understand these concepts taught by the Prophet Joseph Smith. This perspective on the nature and the cohesiveness of the Lord's work is no longer found in the biblical record. We should be grateful for latter-day scripture, which puts all the aspects of God's work together for us in a comprehensive package.

Conclusion

What, then, are some of the contributions of latter-day revelation to our understanding of the Old Testament and the ancient patriarchs? Among the contributions mentioned in this chapter are the following concepts:

1. The ancient prophets were real people. Although they lived and died, they are alive in eternity now, many of them having returned to earth as angels to visit the Prophet Joseph Smith.
2. All of these ancient prophets had the gospel of Jesus Christ; therefore they had the same priesthood, the same covenants, the same ordinances, the same endowment, and the same celestial marriage that are known among us in the Church today.
3. The plan of salvation—the work of God on the earth in every age—has been and is a standardized and unified objective.
4. The ancient patriarchs were intelligent; they were effective gospel preachers and record keepers. Moreover, they had a highly literate society with a written and spoken language that exceeds any on earth today, and their records contained information not known among mankind today.

These and other important doctrinal concepts are now known among us through modern revelations that add to and clarify the biblical record.

Notes

1. Holy Bible (Cambridge: Cambridge University Press, 1950), dictionary section, p. 56.
2. *Harper's Bible Dictionary* (New York: Harper and Row, 1961), p. 185.
3. Holy Bible, dictionary section, p. 134.
4. As found in Matthias F. Cowley, *Wilford Woodruff: History of His Life and Labors* (Salt Lake City: Bookcraft, 1964), p. 481; see also

pp. 545–46. Compare George Q. Cannon, in *Journal of Discourses* 11:336–37; John Taylor, *The Mediation and Atonement* (Salt Lake City: Deseret News Co., 1882), pp. 69–70.

5. Heber C. Kimball, in *Journal of Discourses* 10:235. Hereafter cited as *JD*.

6. Joseph Fielding Smith, *Doctrines of Salvation*, comp. Bruce R. McConkie, 3 vols. (Salt Lake City: Bookcraft, 1954–56), 3:74.

7. *Teachings of the Prophet Joseph Smith*, comp. Joseph Fielding Smith (Salt Lake City: Deseret Book Co., 1976), pp. 157–58. Hereafter cited as *TPJS*.

8. *TPJS*, p. 158.

9. *TPJS*, pp. 167–68.

10. *TPJS*, p. 169.

11. *History of the Church* 5:247. Hereafter cited as *HC*.

12. *TPJS*, p. 158.

13. Diary of Oliver B. Huntington, part 2, p. 207, Harold B. Lee Library, Special Collections, Brigham Young University, Provo, Utah; also cited in Hyrum Andrus, *Joseph Smith, the Man and the Seer* (Salt Lake City: Deseret Book Co., 1960), p. 92.

14. John Taylor, in *JD* 18:326.

15. *TPJS*, p. 170.

16. *TPJS*, p. 157.

17. *TPJS*, pp. 322–23.

18. *HC* 2:17.

19. *TPJS*, p. 264.

20. *TPJS*, p. 168.

21. *TPJS*, p. 308.

Chapter 4

ALL THINGS BEAR WITNESS OF CHRIST: AN OLD TESTAMENT PERSPECTIVE

The essential character of scripture is that it bears witness of Jesus Christ. Scripture may deal with history, doctrine, prophecy, administration, government, or other topics; but it is all directed toward the work and ministry of Jesus Christ. The scriptures were written by the prophets, "holy men of God [who] spake as they were moved by the Holy Ghost" (2 Peter 1:21; see also D&C 68:2–5; 2 Timothy 3:16). These prophets had testimonies of Jesus Christ, for "the testimony of Jesus is the spirit of prophecy" (Revelation 19:10). Our underlying purpose for studying a book of scripture such as the Old Testament, therefore, is not just to read the book, but to obtain a perspective on those things that God revealed in ancient times about the life and mission of Jesus Christ.

Imperfect Transmission of the Biblical Text

We are slightly handicapped in a study of the Old Testament because the oldest available manuscripts are hundreds of years removed from the originals. What we have are translations of copies of copies of copies. Yet the fundamental problem is not one of translation but of transmission. There are able scholars today who could translate correctly the ancient texts into English or any other language, but they lack an accurate and complete manuscript from which to work.

It is easy to understand that a manuscript at the end of a long line of copies and translations has probably suffered at the hands of scribes; such would be the case even in the hands of the most careful workmen. The problem with the biblical record, however, is more serious. According to modern revelation the text of the Old Testament has suffered also at the hands of copyists and translators who deliberately altered the text with the intent to deceive future readers (1 Nephi 13:23–42; Moses 1:40–41; JST, Luke 11:53–55). Planned departures are in a different category than mistakes caused by the frailty of man. When perpetrated willfully, huge errors and omissions can occur in a very short time. Thus our present text of the Bible has suffered from changes of all kinds, both planned and unplanned.

Fortunately, in our biblical studies we have not only the Masoretic or traditional Hebrew text but also the Septuagint, or Greek text, of the third century B.C. and the Dead Sea Scrolls of about the same time. Comparing these helps us to discover and correct some of the unplanned variants. But even more fortunate, we as Latter-day Saints have the Book of Mormon, which contains the text of certain portions of the Old Testament taken from the plates of brass as early as 600 B.C., predating the Dead Sea Scrolls and the Septuagint by more than three hundred years. We have also the book of Abraham from a text written much earlier. In addition we have other latter-day scriptures, such as the Doctrine and Covenants and the Joseph Smith Translation of the Bible, which are not translations of ancient documents but are revelations from the God of Israel; these scriptures correctly manifest the spirit and content of the Old Testament and also supply many passages and concepts lost from all known texts. Thus, one who believes in latter-day revelation not only has the benefit of all that the world has in the way of multiple Bible manuscripts but also has the reliable documents of latter-day scripture to supplement, interpret, and add to the available sources.

The Old Testament Testifies of Christ

We should not be surprised that there are many things in the Old Testament that speak of or point to Christ. After all, that is the purpose of scripture, and the Old Testament was written by prophets who knew that Jehovah was not only the Creator but also the Redeemer and future Messiah. Jesus said to the learned but unbelieving Pharisees: "Search the scriptures; for in them ye think ye have eternal life: and they are they which testify of me" (John 5:39). On the day of his resurrection, as Jesus walked to Emmaus with the two disciples, he chided them for their failure to understand and "believe all that the prophets have spoken." Then, the scriptural account tells us, "beginning at Moses and all the prophets, he expounded unto them in all the scriptures the things concerning himself." (See Luke 24:25–27.) The soul craves knowledge of the gospel as the body craves food; and after Jesus had left them, the two disciples reflected upon their meeting with the Savior and said, "Did not our heart burn within us . . . while he opened to us the scriptures?" (Luke 24:32.) That evening Jesus appeared to the eleven and said: "These are the words which I spake unto you, while I was yet with you, that all things must be fulfilled, which were written in the law of Moses, and in the prophets, and in the psalms, concerning me." The record goes on to say that "then opened he their understanding, that they might understand the scriptures." (Luke 24:44–45.) Paul said that he taught the Corinthians, first of all, the things he had received of first importance, "how that Christ died for our sins according to the scriptures . . . and that he rose again the third day, according to the scriptures" (1 Corinthians 15:3–4).

The scriptures referred to in the passages above are from the Old Testament, and these expressions make it plain that the Old Testament contained numerous passages that referred to Jesus Christ. We will examine some of the passages that Jesus and Paul may have used in their explanations.

Animal Sacrifice

Adam was the first to offer animal sacrifice. It was explained to him that not just any animal would serve; only a firstling could be used. A firstling is the first offspring of its mother, the one "that openeth the matrix" (Exodus 13:12, 15). An angel explained to Adam that animal sacrifice was in similitude of the sacrifice of the Only Begotten Son, which was necessary because of the fall of Adam (see Moses 5:7–9). Jesus was the firstborn of Mary, and thus a firstling was used anciently as a symbol for Christ.

The Passover lamb was designated as a male of the first year, without spot or blemish, and it had to be slain without breaking any of its bones (see Exodus 12:46; Numbers 9:12; John 19:36). All of these provisions pointed toward Jesus; and thus Paul, knowing the meaning of these things, said that "Christ our passover is sacrificed for us" (1 Corinthians 5:7), and likewise John the Baptist referred to Jesus as "the Lamb of God" (John 1:29, 36).

Abraham and Isaac

The Lord commanded Abraham to offer his son Isaac, the child of promise, as a sacrifice. This was a heartrending trial for Abraham; yet he was willing and proceeded to make the offering, believing that "God was able to raise him up, even from the dead" (Hebrews 11:19). As recorded in Hebrews, Isaac is called Abraham's "only begotten son" (v. 17); thus, Abraham's offering of Isaac as a sacrifice was a figure or a symbol of the great and eternal sacrifice to come. As Jacob the Nephite prophet explained, the figure of Abraham and Isaac was "a similitude of God and his Only Begotten Son" (Jacob 4:5).

Melchizedek

We read in modern revelation that Melchizedek was such a great high priest that the priesthood was called after his name to avoid too frequent use of the name of Deity (see D&C 107:1–4). Before that time the priesthood was called "the Holy Priesthood, after the Order of the Son of God" (v. 3), which indicates that the priesthood itself is a type of the Son of God. The faulty text of Hebrews 7:3 states that Melchizedek was "without father, without mother," and that he was "made like unto the Son of God." This passage is corrected in the Joseph Smith Translation to read: "For this Melchizedek was ordained a priest after the order of the Son of God, which order was without father, without mother. . . . And all those who are ordained unto this priesthood are made like unto the Son of God, abiding a priest continually."

The name Melchizedek typifies Christ and means "my king is righteous." According to the scriptures Melchizedek was "King of righteousness" and "King of peace" (Hebrews 7:2), titles we would ordinarily reserve for Jesus. Yet all those on whom the priesthood is conferred and who honor the priesthood become representatives or types of Christ, "for which cause he is not ashamed to call them brethren" (Hebrews 2:11), and they become joint-heirs with Christ.

David

King David was a symbol for Christ. He united Israel and obtained a promise that the Messiah would come through his lineage. When Christ comes, he will reign as the "second David."[1]

Old Testament Allusions to Christ

We include here a few of the instances in which the Old Testament alludes to the Messiah.

Genesis 3:15. The Lord said to the serpent (Lucifer): "I will put enmity between thee and the woman, and between thy seed and her seed [Christ]; it shall bruise thy head, and thou shalt bruise his heel." The Hebrew word translated "bruise" actually means to "crush," and thus the seed of the woman (Christ) will crush the head of the serpent, and that is a fatal wound. This prophecy of Christ's victory over the devil is also mentioned in a Latter-day Saint hymn: "He seized the keys of death and hell / And bruised the serpent's head."[2]

Genesis 49:10. "The sceptre shall not depart from Judah . . . until Shiloh come." That this is a prophecy of Christ is shown in the Joseph Smith Translation of Genesis 50:24, wherein Shiloh is identified as the Messiah.

Leviticus 16:21–22. Part of the revealed ceremony of the law of Moses involved the use of a scapegoat. On the Day of Atonement the high priest laid his hands on the head of a live goat, which then bore the sins of the community and was sent outside of the camp. This clearly points to Christ's taking upon himself the sins of all mankind.

Numbers 24:17. Balaam, the non-Israelite prophet from the land of the Euphrates, prophesied of the Messiah, saying, "I shall see him, but not now: I shall behold him, but not nigh: there shall come a Star out of Jacob, and a Sceptre shall rise out of Israel."

Deuteronomy 18:15, 18–19. To the Israelites Moses prophesied that "the Lord thy God will raise up unto thee a Prophet from the midst of thee, of thy brethren, like unto me; unto him ye shall hearken." He declared further that the Lord had told him: "I will raise them up a Prophet from among their brethren, like unto thee, and will put my words in his mouth; and he shall speak unto them. . . . And it shall come to pass, that whosoever will not hearken unto my words which he shall speak in my name, I will require it of him." Peter identified this prophet as Jesus Christ (Acts 3:22–26), as did the angel Moroni (Joseph Smith—History 1:40).

Psalms. Many are the passages in the psalms that allude to some specific aspect of Jesus' mortal existence. Psalm 22:1 contains the words, "My God, my God, why hast thou forsaken me?" which Jesus spoke while on the cross (Matthew 27:46). Psalm 22:16 speaks of his pierced hands and feet. Psalm 22:18 says, "They part my garments among them, and cast lots upon my vesture," a messianic prophecy whose fulfillment is recorded in Matthew 27:35. A messianic statement can be found in Psalm 34:20 to the effect that not one of his (the Messiah's) bones would be broken, as prophesied in Exodus 12:46 and acknowledged in John 19:36. Psalm 69:21 speaks of one thirsting being given gall and vinegar, which were offered to Jesus on the cross (Matthew 27:34). Psalm 118:22 says that "the stone which the builders refused is become the head stone of the corner," a statement which Jesus identified with himself (Matthew 21:42; see also Jacob 4:15–17).

Psalm 41:9. "Yea, mine own familiar friend, in whom I trusted, which did eat of my bread, hath lifted up his heel against me." This was cited by the Savior as foreshadowing Judas's betrayal of his Master (John 13:18).

Isaiah. This prophet spoke of the coming Messiah more than any other in our present Old Testament. In both subject matter and expression, little else can equal the transcendent beauty of Isaiah's description of Jesus as the son of a virgin (Isaiah 7:14), as the child who would be called the mighty God, the Prince of Peace (Isaiah 9:6–7), and as the man of sorrows wounded for our transgressions (Isaiah 53:1–12).

Micah 5:2. Micah prophesied of the Messiah by saying: "But thou, Bethlehem Ephratah, though thou be little among the thousands of Judah, yet out of thee shall he come forth unto me that is to be ruler in Israel." This passage is referred to in Matthew 2:6 as a prophecy of the birth of the Messiah.

Zechariah 11:13. This passage speaks of thirty pieces of silver, reminding us of Judas's arrangement with the Jewish priests as recorded in Matthew 26:15 and 27:3. Zechariah 13:6 tells of Christ's being "wounded in the house of [his] friends," as Jesus certainly was and as he will testify to the Jews on the Mount of Olives at his second coming (D&C 45:51–53).

The Ancient Prophets Knew of Jesus' Future Ministry

Even though four thousand years passed between the fall of Adam and Christ's mortal advent, all of the major aspects of Jesus' ministry were revealed to the prophets during those intervening years. We have already noted many of the prophecies and types found in the King James Version of the Old Testament; many more are found in the Book of Mormon and in the Joseph Smith Translation of Genesis.

The prophetic vision of Enoch (about 3000 B.C.), as revealed through Joseph Smith's translation of the Bible (JST, Genesis 7:61–63; Moses 7:54–56), foretold such events as the Savior's being lifted up on the cross, the groaning of the earth, the rocks' being rent, and the Saints' arising from their graves. Enoch also spoke of Jesus' being "lifted up" as a "Lamb . . . slain from the foundation of the world" (JST, Genesis 7:54; Moses 7:47; see also 1 Peter 1:19).

The Book of Mormon records many of the details of Jesus' mortal ministry, which were known by prophecy hundreds of years before they occurred. For example, the Book of Mormon reports that Neum, an Israelite prophet living before 600 B.C., testified of the crucifixion of Jesus. This book of scripture also tells us that Zenos, another Israelite prophet, testified of Jesus' burial in a sepulcher and also of the three days of darkness that would be a sign of Christ's death to the inhabitants of the isles of the sea. Both of these prophets were of Old Testament time, place, and lineage, but their writings are not in our current Old Testament. Fortunately, they were recorded on the plates of brass, and we are made aware of them through the Book of Mormon. (See 1 Nephi 19:10, 12, 16; Jacob 5; 6:1–10; Alma 33:3–17; 34:7; Helaman 8:19–20; 15:11; 3 Nephi 10:15–16.)

In several passages the Book of Mormon states that all of the prophets, from the very beginning of the world, knew of Jesus Christ and wrote of his ministry. Following are a few of those Book of Mormon passages:

> We knew of Christ, and we had a hope of his glory many hundred years before his coming; and not only we ourselves . . . but also all the holy prophets which were before us (Jacob 4:4).
>
> They [the scriptures] truly testify of Christ. Behold, . . . none of the prophets have written, nor prophesied, save they have spoken concerning this Christ. (Jacob 7:11.)
>
> For behold, did not Moses prophesy unto them concerning the coming of the Messiah . . . ? Yea, and even all the prophets who have prophesied ever since the world began—have they not spoken more or less concerning these things? (Mosiah 13:33.)
>
> And now behold, Moses did not only testify of these things, but also all the holy prophets, from his days even to the days of Abraham. . . .
>
> Yea, and behold I say unto you, that Abraham not only knew of these things, but there were many before the days of Abraham who were called by the order of God; yea, even after the order of his Son; and this that it should be shown

> unto the people, a great many thousand years before his coming, that even redemption should come unto them. (Helaman 8:16–18.)

In addition, the Book of Mormon prophets knew the exact year in which Jesus would be born (1 Nephi 10:4; 19:8); that his mother would be called Mary and would be a virgin from Nazareth (Mosiah 3:8; Alma 7:10; 1 Nephi 11:13–21); that Jesus would be baptized (1 Nephi 11:27); that he would teach the people, heal the sick, and cast out devils; that he would experience pain, sorrow, hunger, thirst, and fatigue; and that he would bleed at every pore, die upon the cross, be buried, and rise from the dead after three days (1 Nephi 11:27, 31–33; Mosiah 3:5–10).

Although the Old Testament gives us many prophetic glimpses of the Savior, it does not offer the extensive detail that the Book of Mormon does. Apparently this is the result of two conditions: (1) the Old Testament has suffered at the hands of copyists and editors who have deliberately removed many plain and precious parts; and (2) the ancient Jewish people were not especially receptive to the words of the prophets, and therefore the Lord may not have permitted them to have the word in detail and clarity. Chapter 15 of 3 Nephi provides an example of this second condition in relation to the "other sheep." In this chapter Jesus explains that the Jews in the Old World were not given as much information about the "other sheep" as the Nephites were because the first group did not have sufficient faith. However, we can be sure that on both continents, those called as prophets had great knowledge, in plainness and detail, about Christ's forthcoming ministry—even if they were not permitted to reveal all of it to the people.

All Things Bear Record of Christ

The scriptures say that all things are the "typifying of" Christ (2 Nephi 11:4); that "all things have their likeness, and all things are created and made to bear record of [him]" (Moses 6:63). The law of Moses was a type and "shadow of things to come" (see Colossians 2:16–17; Mosiah 3:15; 13:31). The ordinances and ceremonies of the tabernacle—and even the tabernacle (or temple) structure itself—were a "shadow of heavenly things," typifying Christ (see Hebrews 8:5; 10:1). They were, in the words of the scriptures, "patterns of things in the heavens" (Hebrews 9:23).

It should not be thought incredible that the plan of salvation, along with so many details concerning the mortal life of the Messiah, could be revealed to the prophets centuries before Jesus came into mortality. Jesus was chosen in the pre-earth life to atone for the fall of Adam. He is the Lamb slain from before the foundation of the world, and the entire plan of salvation was known even in that premortal life. Therefore there is no difficulty in understanding how any or all of this information could be revealed to Adam, or to Enoch, or to Isaiah, or to any other prophet. There is no alternate plan, and there is no other Savior—there never was and never shall be. If Jesus had not accomplished the Atonement, nothing mankind could do, collectively or individually, could make up for the loss. Therefore it is imperative that people in every age of the world know of their Redeemer that they might exercise faith in him unto salvation.

Notes

1. See Bruce R. McConkie, *The Millennial Messiah* (Salt Lake City: Deseret Book Co., 1982), pp. 602–11.
2. "We'll Sing All Hail to Jesus' Name," *Hymns,* no. 182.

Chapter 5

MOSES: PRINCE OF EGYPT, PROPHET OF GOD

The prophet Moses is prominent in the literature and belief of millions of people. He is revered by three large segments of the religious world: Judaism, Islam, and Christianity. The New Testament record tells us that at the Jerusalem Conference, James, the brother of the Lord, observed that Moses' writings were "read in the synagogues every sabbath day" (Acts 15:21). In fact, according to Jewish custom, in the synagogue service it was not permissible to read anything from the prophets (such as Isaiah or Jeremiah) or from the writings (such as Psalms or Kings) until after a reading from the law written by Moses.

In the Old Testament Moses is mentioned 657 times; in the New Testament, 65 times; in the Book of Mormon, 26 times; in the Doctrine and Covenants, 21 times; and in the Pearl of Great Price, 29 times. This is a total of 798 times. The Pearl of Great Price contains writings of three of the greatest prophets who ever lived. That Moses is one of them (the other two are, of course, Abraham and Joseph Smith) illustrates how important he is to Latter-day Saints.

Volume ten of the *Catholic Encyclopedia* offers two large pages in small print on the subject of Moses; and volume nine of the *Jewish Encyclopedia* devotes fourteen large pages in small print to that ancient prophet.

There are a lot of things about the ancient world in which Moses lived that we do not know. We do not know all we would like to about ancient Egypt; this is especially true of precise dates in that nation's history. And there is much about the culture of the ancient Israelites that we do not know. We do not know the date of the exodus of Israel from Egypt—probably not within a hundred years. Nor do we know the name of the pharaoh who enslaved and oppressed Israel, nor that of the later pharaoh at the time of the Exodus. Furthermore, in all the available records of Egypt no mention is made of Abraham, Jacob, Joseph, or Moses. They say nothing about the Israelites' being in Egypt and therefore nothing about their being led out of Egypt by the hand of God through a prophet. Here we have four hundred years of our ancestral history, including mighty works of God such as the ten plagues and the dividing of the Red Sea, and the records of Egypt are as silent about them as the great stone sphinx.

Yet we do know some crucial things concerning this ancient period; and as we learn and use latter-day revelation as our scope, filter, and key, we are able to see the purposes of God as they were unfolded among the ancient Israelites in the land of Egypt under the leadership of Moses.

Birth and Early Life of Moses

In the Bible the first mention of the name Moses occurs in the story of his birth (Exodus 2:10). But in the Bible translation given by revelation through the Prophet Joseph Smith, the patriarch Joseph, in his prophecy, mentions Moses' name at least three hundred years before his birth. Joseph spoke to his brothers about their future condition in Egypt and told them that the house of Israel would come into "bondage" and "affliction," but he had obtained, he said, a promise of deliverance from the Lord: "The Lord God will raise up . . . unto thee, whom my father Jacob hath named Israel, a prophet; (not the Messiah who is called Shilo;) and this prophet shall deliver my people out of Egypt in the days of thy bondage" (JST, Genesis 50:24). As Joseph continued, he declared the Lord had told him: "A seer will I raise up to deliver my people out of the land of Egypt; and he shall be called Moses. And by this name he shall know that he is of thy house; for he shall be nursed by the king's daughter, and shall be called her son." (JST, Genesis 50:29.) This inspired scriptural account also informs us:

> The Lord sware unto Joseph that he would preserve his seed forever saying, I will raise up Moses, and a rod shall be in his hand, and he shall gather together my people, and he shall lead them as a flock, and he shall smite the waters of the Red Sea with his rod.
>
> And he shall have judgment, and shall write the word of the Lord. And he shall not speak many words, for I will

> write unto him my law by the finger of mine own hand. And I will make a spokesman for him, and his name shall be called Aaron.
>
> And it shall be done unto thee in the last days also, even as I have sworn. Therefore, Joseph said unto his brethren, God will surely visit you, and bring you out of this land, unto the land which he sware unto Abraham, and unto Isaac, and to Jacob.
>
> And Joseph confirmed many other things unto his brethren, and took an oath of the children of Israel, saying unto them, God will surely visit you, and ye shall carry up my bones from hence.
>
> So Joseph died when he was an hundred and ten years old; and they embalmed him, and they put him in a coffin in Egypt; and he was kept from burial by the children of Israel, that he might be carried up and laid in the sepulchre with his father. And thus they remembered the oath which they sware unto him. (JST, Genesis 50:34–38.)

When the proper time came (about three hundred years after Joseph), Moses was born. He was of the tribe of Levi and was a son of Amram and Jochebed. Josephus, the great Jewish historian, points out that Moses was a very special child, the seventh generation from Abraham.[1] No doubt Josephus mentions this because the ancient Jews considered a person's being the seventh son, or the seventh generation, to be very significant. The numbers three and forty were also important anciently, and the scriptures speak of three forty-year periods in Moses' life: the first he spent in Egypt, the second, in Midian and Sinai, and the third, in leading Israel in the wilderness.

The book of Exodus account of Moses' birth and the first forty years of his life is very brief. It tells us that a pharaoh arose who "knew not Joseph" (Exodus 1:8) and that the children of Israel were enslaved and forced to work at hard labor: "And they [the Egyptians] made their [the Israelites'] lives bitter with hard bondage, in morter, and in brick, and in all manner of service in the field: all their service, wherein they made them serve, was with rigor" (Exodus 1:14). They were employed also in the building of two "treasure cities, Pithom and Raamses" (Exodus 1:11).

Because the Israelites were so numerous, the Egyptian king began to fear and gave command that every Israelite boy that was born should be cast into the river, but every daughter should be saved alive (Exodus 1:22).

When Moses was born, his parents kept him three months and then put him in a basket among the reeds along the banks of the river Nile, while Miriam, his older sister, watched nearby. Moses also had a brother, three years older, named Aaron.

The pharaoh's daughter found the baby, had compassion on him, recognized him as a Hebrew child, and took him out of the basket. Miriam, standing by, offered to find a woman who could care for the baby, to which the princess agreed. Miriam ran home and got Moses' mother; thus his mother nursed her own son, with the permission of the royal household, and was even paid wages to do so. (Exodus 2:1–9.)

"And the child grew, and she brought him unto Pharaoh's daughter, and he became her son" (Exodus 2:10). It is an interesting paradox that the king's own command to destroy the sons of the Israelites led to the bringing up in his own household and court the very man who would take the Israelites away from Egypt.

Moses, a Mighty Man in Egypt

The Old Testament gives us little else about Moses' boyhood or life in Egypt. We learn that when he was forty years old he saw an Egyptian smiting an Israelite and came to the rescue. In the struggle the Egyptian was slain (Exodus 2:11–12). The ancient record also tells us that the next day, Moses saw two Israelites fighting and "said to him that did wrong, Wherefore smitest thou thy fellow?" (Exodus 2:13.)

At this point in the record we find the only allusion or hint in the Old Testament to Moses' being a great man in the Egyptian government, for the Israelite to whom Moses spoke replied: "Who made thee a prince and a judge over us? intendest thou to kill me, as thou killedst the Egyptian?" At least those words imply that Moses was looked upon as a prince and a judge of the Egyptians, and maybe a future pharaoh—an heir to the throne. "Now when Pharaoh heard this thing [the slaying of the Egyptian], he sought to slay Moses. But Moses fled . . . and dwelt in the land of Midian." (Exodus 2:14–15.)

Moses stayed in Midian forty years, married the daughter of Jethro, and tended Jethro's flocks in the area we know as the Sinai Peninsula, the approximate area in which he later led the children of Israel for forty more years.

Thus, in that brief account from our current Old Testament, we have but little information about Moses' life during his boyhood and young manhood. We cannot help but wonder if he knew that he was an Israelite, not an Egyptian, and if he did know this, when and how he learned it. We wonder also if, during those first forty years in Egypt, he knew what his mission was and what significance his name had. We do not know how much his mother told him; if he was with her enough years, she probably informed him that he was an Israelite, but we do not know if she knew what his mission was to be. Finally, we cannot help but wonder if it was a difficult thing for Moses to give up the splendor and prestige of the palace to live in the desert with the sheep. But there is absolutely no mention in our present Old Testament of Moses' activity and training as a prince of Egypt. We are left, then, without answers to these questions, unless we turn to other sources.

As the New Testament clearly demonstrates, both Paul and Stephen knew things about Moses beyond what is in our current book of Exodus. They must have had a better Exodus account, had other sources, or had both. Consider this excerpt from Stephen's address to the Sanhedrin, as recorded in the book of Acts:

> But when the time of the promise drew nigh, which God had sworn to Abraham, the people grew and multiplied in Egypt,
>
> Till another king arose, which knew not Joseph.
>
> The same dealt subtilly with our kindred, and evil entreated our fathers, so that they cast out their young children, to the end they might not live.
>
> In which time Moses was born, *and was exceeding fair,* and nourished up in his father's house three months:
>
> And when he was cast out, Pharaoh's daughter took him up, *and nourished him for her own son.*
>
> And Moses *was learned* in all the wisdom of the Egyptians, *and was mighty in words and in deeds.*
>
> And when he was full forty years old, it came into his heart to visit his brethren the children of Israel.
>
> And seeing one of them suffer wrong, he defended him, and avenged him that was oppressed, and smote the Egyptian:
>
> *For he supposed his brethren would have understood how that God by his hand would deliver them: but they understood not.* (Acts 7:17–25, italics added.)

We can see from this passage that Moses did know of his own identity and of his mission, and that he was also learned and active in things Egyptian.

Paul, as recorded in the book of Hebrews, says more about Moses. Note that Moses, according to Paul, made a conscious and deliberate choice to serve the Lord:

> By faith Moses, when he was born, was hid three months of his parents, because they saw he was a proper child; and they were not afraid of the king's commandment.
>
> By faith Moses, when he was come to years, *refused* to be called the son of Pharaoh's daughter;
>
> *Choosing* rather to suffer affliction with the people of God, than to enjoy the pleasures of sin for a season;
>
> Esteeming the reproach of Christ greater riches than the treasures in Egypt: for he had respect unto the recompense of the reward.
>
> By faith he forsook Egypt, not fearing the wrath of the king: for he endured, as seeing him who is invisible. (Hebrews 11:23–27, italics added.)

Clearly, Stephen and Paul had more information about Moses than we have in our present Old Testament. From them we learn, among other things, that Moses, years before being called at the burning bush, knew of his own identity and of his mission.

That brings us back to the aforementioned prophecy of Joseph recorded in the Joseph Smith Translation. How did Moses learn who he was and what his mission was? Joseph's prophetic report of the Lord's words has considerable bearing on this point, especially in conjunction with the words of Stephen and Paul: "A seer will I raise up to deliver my people out of the land of Egypt; and he shall be called Moses. And by *this name* he shall know that he is of thy house; for he shall be nursed by the king's daughter, and shall be called *her* son." (JST, Genesis 50:29, italics added.)

Since Moses was prince of Egypt and was educated "in all the wisdom of the Egyptians," could it be that perhaps one day in the royal archives he came across the writings of Abraham and of Joseph and there read this prophecy of Joseph? If so, he would have read about the precise circumstances of his being in the Pharaoh's household; he even would have read his own name and also the name of his brother, Aaron. All of this would have been rather impressive to a bright young man.

Josephus reports still other dimensions of Moses' life during those first forty years in Egypt. Of particular interest is the historian's mention of Moses' being a military leader in Egypt. No hint of this is given in any portion of the Bible, but Josephus says that, Ethiopia having conquered much of Egypt all the way down to

Memphis, Moses led an Egyptian army against them and freed Egypt from Ethiopian domination. According to Josephus, Moses took his army up the Nile into Nubia and Ethiopia, besieging the Ethiopian city of Saba, and even brought back the Ethiopian king's daughter as his wife.[2]

The Bible informs us that Moses, while in Midian for forty years, became the son-in-law of Jethro and the keeper of the sheep; but this record is silent about any spiritual activities of Moses during this period. In fact it says only that Jethro was the priest of Midian. However, from modern revelation we learn that it was Jethro (a descendant of Abraham through Abraham's wife Keturah and thus a non-Israelite) who ordained Moses to the Melchizedek Priesthood (D&C 84:6). This was done through a priesthood line outside of Israel. We are accustomed to thinking of ancient priesthood holders such as Abraham, Isaac, Jacob, Joseph, Ephraim, and so on, but here we learn that others also had the holy priesthood of God. As the modern missionary effort spreads the gospel wider across the earth, it may be a great plus in the presentation for it to become known that Moses, the great prophet of ancient Israel, obtained the priesthood not through the house of Israel, but through another Semitic lineage.

Egypt's Ancient Religion Contained an Imitation of the Temple Endowment

It appears that the religion of ancient Egypt—at least the religion of the pharaohs, the royal families, the priests, and the nobles of Egypt—contained a form of the temple endowment presumably borrowed from other ancient sources.[3] Evidence of this endowment and its ceremonies and anticipations can be seen today in the paintings on the walls of Egyptian tombs and the carvings on the walls of Egyptian temples. We cannot say how much of this the common laborer in Egypt knew and how much the Israelites in slavery knew. Most likely they knew little of it. The Israelites lived in the Nile delta in Goshen, which at that time was a center of Egyptian culture with temples and statuary. No doubt the Israelites saw the majesty of the Egyptian buildings and temples, but how much of the Egyptian religion they knew is, of course, another question.

On the other hand, Moses—prince of Egypt, heir to the throne, a man educated in "all the wisdom of the Egyptians"—would have been very familiar with the Egyptian view of the afterlife and with the ceremonies and preparations of the Egyptian religious ritual.

Moses Was Trained in Both Secular and Spiritual Things

We can be certain that Moses received considerable training and experience—in Egypt as a prince (the first forty-year period) and in Midian as son-in-law to Jethro (the second forty-year period)—that would prepare him for the great task of getting more than a million Israelites out of Egypt and leading them as a prophet. During that first forty-year period, no doubt he learned reading, writing, astronomy, architecture, leadership principles, and military strategy; moreover, as suggested earlier, he probably read the records of Abraham and Joseph in the sacred Egyptian archives. During the second period of forty years, he received the Melchizedek Priesthood, heard the counsel of his father-in-law, reared at least two sons, and no doubt had other revelations and spiritual tutoring.

Chapter 1 in the book of Moses shows Moses as a man of profound spiritual depth and intellectual curiosity—someone with a philosophic turn of mind. Clearly he was not an average man; he was one called of God, prepared not only in this life but in the premortal existence. Just as Joseph of Egypt prophesied, Moses was a man mighty in writing and in judgment but not so much in speaking (see JST, Genesis 50:35). Paul and Stephen also spoke of these particular accomplishments of Moses.

Following the description of Moses' life in Midian, the Old Testament relates the episode of the burning bush, during which God called Moses back to Egypt (see Exodus 3). Moses, being out with the sheep, saw that the bush was aflame and that it was not consumed, which attracted his attention. Seeing a piece of sagebrush burn would be nothing new to a shepherd; they cooked their food that way every day. But for a bush to burn and not be consumed—that was something new indeed.

The Exodus account states that God spoke to Moses out of the bush and told him that he must go back to Egypt and deliver the children of Israel by power and by wonders. Moses was naturally reluctant and said: "But, behold, they [the Israelites] will not believe me . . . for they will say, The Lord hath not appeared unto thee" (Exodus 4:1). There appear to be at least two reasons for Moses' reluctance. First, forty years earlier Moses had tried to help his countrymen, but they would not receive him. As Stephen said centuries later, "For he supposed his brethren would have understood how that God by his hand would deliver them: but they understood not" (Acts 7:25). Second, Moses must have been concerned about what Pharaoh's reaction would be. At this time Egypt was mighty and powerful—probably the most powerful nation on the earth, with armies and wealth and influence. Here was Moses with neither army, wealth, nor influence (maybe even without the support of his own people), and he was being asked to take on the whole Egyptian establishment. It is no wonder that Moses said, "Who am I, that I should go unto Pharaoh, and that I should bring forth the children of Israel out of Egypt?" (Exodus 3:11.)

This is an example of the way the Lord works—not by physical or worldly force but by divine power and miracles. The children of Israel would know that they were delivered out of the land of Egypt not by their own strength but by the power of God. Their faith was to be in God, not in their armaments or their own strength. The principle involved here is expressed in this New Testament scripture: "God hath chosen the weak things of the world to confound the things which are mighty" (1 Corinthians 1:27–29; see also D&C 1:19). We see the principle at work again in the episode of David and Goliath (1 Samuel 17) and in the account of Gideon's victory with his army of three hundred men, a number reduced from a larger one (Judges 7). The Israelites had to believe that God would deliver them, over and beyond what they could do themselves. They were not to trust in the arm of flesh. This is still the way the Lord works among the children of men today.

As the account in Exodus tells us, ten grievous plagues were brought upon Egypt before Pharaoh was willing to let the Israelites go (Exodus 7–12). The first was the turning of the waters into blood; then followed the plagues of frogs, lice, and flies. Next, sickness came upon the Egyptian cattle and boils upon the people, which were followed by the plagues of hail, locusts, and three days' darkness. The tenth and final plague was the death of the firstborn in the house of any family that did not put the blood of the lamb on the door post (Exodus 12:12–13).

It was a mighty struggle, but Moses eventually got a large population—the record says six hundred thousand men, besides women and children (JST, Exodus 12:37)—out of Egypt and into the wilderness.

Soon they came to the Red Sea, where by command the prophet Moses stretched his hand over the waters and the Lord caused them to be parted; whereupon the Israelites passed through on dry ground. But while the pursuing Egyptians in their six hundred chariots were going through the newly made opening, the way became difficult, and they said, "Let us flee from the face of Israel; for the Lord fighteth for them against the Egyptians." And then the waters came in upon the Egyptians, and many of them drowned. (See Exodus 14.)

Spiritual Training of Moses

The biblical record contains little information about any spiritual preparation for Moses between the time of his call at the burning bush and his encounters with Pharaoh. It briefly tells of Moses' leaving Midian, meeting his brother Aaron, and then returning to Egypt. It is at this point that latter-day revelation gives us a huge boost in our understanding of Moses' spiritual preparation in his role as a prophet and a seer.

Before Moses embarked on his mission back to Egypt, the Lord gave him a series of visions to prepare him. We find a record of this in the book of Moses, chapter 1, which record was given by revelation to the Prophet Joseph Smith as he commenced his Bible translation. It provides us with a perspective on Moses unavailable in any other source, being a revelation containing knowledge entirely lost to all other records. We are fortunate and blessed to have it available to us in the Pearl of Great Price, where it is published as an extract from the Joseph Smith Translation of the Bible. In that revelation we read that Moses was shown the whole earth and all the inhabitants thereon; he talked with God face to face; he beheld the brightness and glory of God and discovered that he could not stand in His presence unless he was transfigured before God (Moses 1:1–11).

Even for a man who had been a prince of Egypt and a great military leader, one mighty as to the strength of men, the comparison of all these things with the works of God made him feel quite small —"which thing he never had supposed" (Moses 1:10).

Next Satan came to him. Moses could see distinctly the difference between the light of God and the darkness of Satan. The Lord had told Moses that he (Moses) was in the similitude of the Only Begotten, and Moses, taking strength in what the Lord had told him, referred to this several times in his encounter with Satan. When Satan demanded Moses' allegiance, Moses told Satan that he would not worship him, that he had better things to do—he wanted to commune again with the God of glory and of knowledge. (Moses 1:12–23.)

Then the Lord spoke to Moses again and told him that he (Moses) would command the waters, and they would obey him—

evidently an allusion to his future experience with the Red Sea (Moses 1:24–26).

The Lord then showed Moses a vision of many lands and many peoples, even all the people of this earth and of many earths. At this point in the record, we are given evidence of the great mind and spiritual capacity of Moses, for he asks the Lord two important and fundamental questions about life. There are many things a person might ask about the earth: How long did it take to create it? How long has it been since the Creation? But Moses asked two even more basic questions: Why, Lord, did you create worlds and people? and, How did you do it? (See Moses 1:30.) The answers to these two questions lead to some of the most fundamental concepts regarding man's existence, and we have the Lord's answers right here in the book of Moses. The Lord's response to the first question reads: "This is my work and my glory—to bring to pass the immortality and eternal life of man" (Moses 1:39). These are the things that gods do—they create worlds for their children and provide them with the opportunity to become gods themselves. The Lord answered the second question regarding *how* with the account of the six-day creation process.

All of these great revelatory, spiritual experiences occurred in Moses' life after the burning bush episode and before his parting of the Red Sea (see Moses 1:17, 26). The Bible is entirely silent regarding these important experiences recorded in Moses 1.

Is it not plain to see that God was turning this prince of Egypt, great as that designation was, into a prophet and a seer, a far greater calling? Moses would not have been able to endure the opposition and those forty years in the wilderness if he had not been prepared and mature spiritually. Presumably, somewhere along the line Moses received the endowment. It probably surprised him a little to see the similarity to the imitation Egyptian endowment.

When the Lord wants to change things on the earth, he has a baby born—a baby such as Noah, Enoch, Abraham, Joseph, Moses, Peter, Paul, Joseph Smith, Spencer W. Kimball, Ezra Taft Benson, or the greatest of all, Jesus Christ. As these babies grow to maturity the Lord trains and tutors them, and then commands them and helps them to bring about certain events that often change the destiny of nations. Such was the case with the prophet Moses.

Dramatic Events at Sinai

It was a struggle to get Israel out of Egypt, but it was an even greater struggle to get Egypt out of the Israelites. The geographical change was not as difficult as the cultural and personal changes needed in the people's thinking and habits.

Three months after crossing the Red Sea, the Israelites were camped in the approximate area of Mount Sinai (which is probably the same mountain on which Moses had seen the burning bush), and the Lord gave Moses instructions relative to receiving the Ten Commandments and giving the people the fulness of the gospel.

This has to be one of the most dramatic events in the scriptures and of all time. The people remained at the foot of the mount, a respectable distance back, while Moses ascended the mountain. The Lord then descended, met with Moses, and wrote upon the tablets of stone. The people could hear the loud trumpet, the thunder, and the voice of God; they could see the fire and smoke and feel the quaking of the earth. (See Exodus 19, 20.)

At this time the Lord gave to Moses and the people the Ten Commandments. The record says they actually heard God speak the words (see Deuteronomy 4:10–12). This occurred just three or four months out of Egypt, and so the memory of the great pyramids and of the stone statues of the pharaohs, the Egyptian gods, the falcons, and the crocodiles were fresh on the people's minds. Thus we can see that there was a clear context for the giving of the first two commandments: "Thou shalt have no other Gods before me" (Exodus 20:3); "Thou shalt not make unto thee any graven image" (Exodus 20:4). Even the altars were to be of unhewn stone (Exodus 20:25; Deuteronomy 27:5).

The Lord Gave the Law of Moses as a Lesser Law

We note also that the people were troubled at the thought of their coming into the presence of God, and they said to Moses, in effect, "You deal with God, we'll deal with you"—"but let not God speak with us, lest we die" (Exodus 20:19).

This last condition is a very telling commentary on the spiritual state of the Israelites. They did not want to come up to the presence of God. This was a symptom of a spiritual malady and deficiency that eventually led them to reject the gospel, and as a consequence the Lord gave them the law of Moses and a lesser priesthood instead of the gospel and the Melchizedek Priesthood. This whole concept has been greatly misunderstood by biblical scholars and even by some of our own Church members, because it is not clear in the Bible. However, it has been made clear in the Joseph Smith Translation and in the Doctrine and Covenants.

When Moses came down from the mount after forty days, he saw that the people had built a golden calf to worship. They said they were not even sure Moses was ever coming down from that awful, smoking mountain. When Moses saw the calf and the revelry, he threw down the tablets of stone and broke them. These contained the Ten Commandments and the fulness of the gospel, including the ordinances of the Melchizedek Priesthood.

Thereupon the Lord told Moses to make a new set of tablets and come up again to the mount. He did so and received the Ten Commandments again, but in place of the higher law the Lord gave him the law of carnal commandments, which functioned under the Aaronic, not the Melchizedek, Priesthood. One of the major differences in these two laws is that the gospel and the Melchizedek Priesthood will prepare a person to be brought into the presence of God, while the law of Moses and the Aaronic Priesthood, by themselves, will not. Furthermore the Melchizedek Priesthood is connected with the ministry of Jesus Christ and the beholding of the face of God; the Aaronic Priesthood is connected with the ministry of angels. The Joseph Smith Translation makes all the difference in our understanding what happened in the wilderness and what the difference was between the first and second set of tablets. No one can understand these things properly without the help of the revelations given to the Prophet Joseph Smith. (See JST, Exodus 34:1–2; JST, Deuteronomy 10:1–2; also D&C 84:19–27.)

Because of their lack of desire for righteousness and their cultural attachment to Egypt, the Lord kept the children of Israel in the wilderness forty years, until all who had come out of Egypt at the age of twenty or above had died and a new generation—born in the wilderness and therefore not personally acquainted with Egypt—was growing up. Of that older generation, only Joshua and Caleb were permitted to make the complete trip to the promised land. There is a symbolism attached to the journeyings of the Israelites: They came out of Egypt, were tested in the wilderness, and crossed over Jordan; similarly, in our spiritual journeyings we must come out of Egypt (or the world), endure the wilderness of mortality, and then we can eventually "cross over" into heaven, into the rest of the Lord.

Moses Was Blessed in Not Entering the Promised Land

This leads us to another question concerning the life of Moses: Why was he not permitted to enter the promised land? The scriptures suggest that the reason was the Lord's anger with Moses because the latter took credit for getting water from the rock and didn't follow the Lord's directions properly (Numbers 20).

However, I think there is a much better and more fundamental reason. I assume the event at the rock really happened, but that does not really seem to be the reason why Moses did not go into the "good land" (Exodus 3:8). After all, Moses represented the Melchizedek Priesthood and was a man who could stand in the presence of God. I gather from reading Doctrine and Covenants 84:20–24 that the Lord was angry not with Moses, but with the children of Israel. They did not deserve Moses any longer, so Moses was translated and taken to heaven. Now, I have been to Israel several times, and it is a remarkable place; but it seems to me that being translated would be even better than entering that ancient promised land. Besides, if the Lord was too angry with Moses to let him go into the promised land, it seems strange that he would yet be pleased enough with him to take him into heaven. Moses was given the greater blessing of being translated, and I suppose that under such circumstances he may have felt properly repaid for missing the Israel trip. Furthermore, we know that Moses needed to be translated so that he, with Elijah, could lay on hands to confer the keys of the priesthood on Peter, James, and John on the Mount of Transfiguration.

Moses, Israel's Great Prophet

The scripture says of Moses: "And there arose not a prophet since in Israel like unto Moses, whom the Lord knew face to face" (Deuteronomy 34:10). Moses was preeminent in leadership, prophecy, law giving, and—through several visions—personal acquaintance with God. He was a military man, a pioneer; and he was versed in moral, civil, ceremonial, and religious law. Through him the Lord accomplished one of the greatest migrations in history and established a written code that laid the foundation and pattern of living for many millions of people. He was a prophet, seer, and revelator.

Moses ministered not only to the people of his time, but also to Peter, James, and John in the meridian of time (see Matthew 17) and to Joseph Smith in our day at Kirtland, Ohio (see D&C 110). The Doctrine and Covenants often extols the greatness of Moses (see D&C 8:10; 28:2; 84:6, 17–25; 103:16–20; 107:91–92). Moreover, the scriptures describe the Prophet Joseph Smith as being a man "like unto" Moses, a compliment to both of these great leaders (Moses 1:40–41; D&C 28:2). Likewise, other scriptures speak of

Christ's being a prophet like unto Moses (Deuteronomy 18:18–19; Acts 3:22–23; Joseph Smith—History 1:40). Yet through it all, we find that Moses did not seek his own glory; he was a reluctant leader and was "very meek, above all the men which were upon the face of the earth" (Numbers 12:3).

Notes

1. See Josephus, *The Antiquities of the Jews,* trans. William Whiston, II, IX, 6.
2. See *Antiquities,* II, X, 1–2.
3. See Hugh Nibley, *The Message of the Joseph Smith Papyri: An Egyptian Endowment* (Salt Lake City: Deseret Book Co., 1975), pp. xii–xiii.

Chapter 6

WHY THE BOOK OF MORMON IS THE KEYSTONE OF OUR RELIGION

Most of us are familiar with the Prophet Joseph Smith's statement in which he identified the Book of Mormon as the "keystone of our religion." However, it may be that not all of us have actually read the entire statement, and perhaps some of us do not know to whom the Prophet made it, nor when or where it was recorded, nor why he considered the Book of Mormon to be the keystone.

Joseph Smith gave the "keystone" declaration on Sunday, 28 November 1841, at Nauvoo, Illinois, during a meeting with the Council of the Twelve Apostles. The account we have of it is not a verbatim report made on the spot, but a recollection written by the Prophet himself in his journal after the meeting.

Since the statement was written by Joseph Smith himself in reflection, we can have unshaken confidence that it conveys just what he wanted it to say and accurately reflects his feelings. It reads as follows: "I spent the day in the council with the Twelve Apostles at the house of President Young, conversing with them upon a variety of subjects. Brother Joseph Fielding was present, having been absent four years on a mission to England. I told the brethren that the Book of Mormon was the most correct of any book on earth, and the keystone of our religion, and a man would get nearer to God by abiding by its precepts, than by any other book."[1]

This is no doubt the shortest and probably the best-known evaluation of the Book of Mormon. If we examine it in its historical context, our understanding and appreciation of this declaration will increase, we will be more able to defend it against critics and nonbelievers, and we will be in a better position to explore the reasons why the Book of Mormon is indeed the "keystone of our religion."

Let us first consider the component parts of the Prophet's statement. He actually said three things about the Book of Mormon: (1)

it is the "most correct of any book on earth"; (2) it is the "keystone of our religion"; and (3) "a man would get nearer to God by abiding by its precepts, than by any other book."

"The Most Correct of Any Book on Earth"

The earliest edition of the Book of Mormon came from the press during the week of 18–25 March 1830, in Palmyra, New York. Readers familiar with this edition know that the punctuation is sparse and that paragraphs run to great length. The flow of thought is rather easy, but the sentences are often long and awkward.

The second edition came from the press in 1837 in Kirtland, Ohio. This edition, a revision of the first, contains thousands of punctuation changes as well as hundreds of word changes. Most of the corrections are grammatical and stylistic, although some involve changes in wording designed to clarify meaning. Many of the corrections, but not all, are based on a comparison with the handwritten Oliver Cowdery manuscript that was used as the source for the first printing. As with most first editions, the 1830 edition contained typographical errors that needed correcting, and the 1837 edition incorporates these corrections. The Prophet later used a printed copy of the 1837 edition as a basis for making some additional revisions and technical corrections. This edited copy partially formed the basis for the third edition of October 1840, printed in Cincinnati, Ohio. Thus when the Prophet said in November 1841 that the Book of Mormon was the most correct book on earth, we must keep in mind that he was speaking of the then current third edition. In any case, he no doubt had reference to the *contents*—the doctrines and teachings—of the Book of Mormon rather than to its grammatical construction, punctuation, and spelling.

Let us be quick to observe that these various editorial changes did not alter the central message of the book in any edition; they were minor, not major, revisions. However, from time to time critics have raised the question of the "perfection" of the Book of Mormon in light of the many editorial touches. In reply, it seems only reasonable that we at least point out that the Prophet was speaking from the context of 1841. The message of the Book of Mormon is the same no matter what edition one uses, but knowing the context of the Prophet's statement tends to blunt what might at first look like a sharp edge of the critics' attack.[2]

"The Keystone of Our Religion"

We are familiar with the concept of a keystone in a stone arch: without the wedge-shaped center stone the arch would tumble. Everything in the arch depends upon the keystone, and it locks all the other stones together. No doubt the Prophet had this in mind when he used the term *keystone,* applying it as a symbol for the Book of Mormon's crucial role in the latter days.

Indeed we could truthfully say that the Book of Mormon is at the center of this dispensation. Jesus Christ is the center point of our hope and the foundation of our faith, and the Book of Mormon is a sure witness of his existence, his divinity, his atonement, and his resurrection from the dead. These matters are evident to all who are familiar with the Book of Mormon.

Furthermore, no one can believe the Book of Mormon and disbelieve the Bible or the things the Bible stands for or teaches. If a person really accepts the Book of Mormon, he accepts the ancient as well as the current work of God on the earth—there can be no fragmentation, no partial or divided loyalty. He believes in God, in Christ, in the devil, in faith, in angels, in a judgment, in heaven, in hell, in prophets, in visions, and in miracles, ancient and modern. The Book of Mormon brings all of these things into perspective.

The Prophet Joseph said it this way:

> Take away the Book of Mormon and the revelations, and where is our religion? We have none; for without Zion, and a place of deliverance, we must fall; because the time is near when the sun will be darkened, and the moon turn to blood, and the stars fall from heaven, and the earth reel to and fro. Then, if this is the case, and if we are not sanctified and gathered to the places God has appointed, with all our former professions and our great love for the Bible, we must fall; we cannot stand; we cannot be saved; for God will gather out his Saints from the Gentiles, and then comes desolation and destruction, and none can escape except the pure in heart who are gathered.[3]

"A Man Would Get Nearer to God . . ."

We might ask, What does the Book of Mormon say that is so valuable and that causes it to exceed in greatness any other book, even the Bible? What *are* its precepts? The Prophet's statement was not a rejection of the Bible. It was, however, an implied comparison with the Bible and an acknowledgment that the Bible has not come to us in its original purity and completeness. Most Bible readers recognize that it mentions many things that were clear to the people of the Bible but are not clear to us. This is not an indictment against the Bible's authors but against its transmitters. If the Bible had been preserved in completeness and had been translated correctly in every instance, it would read in plainness as the Book of Mormon does, and there would then be no confusion or ambiguity about the ordinances of the gospel, or the plan of salvation, or the work of God in any age of the world.

The Prophet Joseph Smith said this about the Bible: "From sundry revelations which had been received, it was apparent that many important points touching the salvation of men, had been taken from the Bible, or lost before it was compiled." And at another time he said: "I believe the Bible as it read when it came from the pen of the original writers. Ignorant translators, careless transcribers, or designing and corrupt priests have committed many errors."[4]

From these statements of the Prophet we can ascertain more clearly the meaning of the eighth article of faith, part of which reads, "We believe the Bible to be the word of God as far as it is translated correctly" (Articles of Faith 1:8). Here the word *translated* appears to be used in a broader sense to mean *transmitted,* which would include not only translation of languages but also copying, editing, deleting from, and adding to documents. The Bible has undergone a much more serious change than merely translation from one language to another.

Let us take a moment to examine a bit of the Bible's textual history, since such an examination can help us better appreciate why "a man would get nearer to God by abiding by [the Book of Mormon's] precepts, than by any other book."

Textual Families and the Bible

One of the most prominent reasons for the variety of Bibles today is that the different versions are not translated from the same collection of manuscripts. No original manuscripts of any part of the Bible are extant. What is available are copies of copies of copies, all of them separated from the originals by centuries. Even when written in the same language, a handwritten copy of anything as extensive as the Bible is going to transmit a number of errors, and the most careful of scribes will make mistakes that will cause his copy to vary from the original. When an error goes undetected, it will be preserved in successive copies with the same care as the sacred text.

As early handwritten copies of the Bible were made from the original manuscripts, each would depart somewhat from the original, and each would depart differently. Second-generation copies may have had some mistakes in common, but in most they would have differed. As third-generation copies were made from these, they would preserve the peculiarities of each second-generation copy and omit other things, until there developed what has come to be known as "manuscript" or "textual families," manuscripts with common traits just as there are family traits in people who are genealogically related. One of the major reasons why various English editions of the Bible today differ from one another is that they represent different textual families. Consequently, learned translators today are capable of rendering into English the thoughts they find on the Greek and Hebrew manuscripts, but they cannot translate what is not written on the document they are translating from. Thus, depending on a person's preference, he chooses the King James Version, or the New English Bible, or the Catholic Douai Version, and so on.

How Variations Occurred in the Bible Manuscripts

Variants occur in many ways. There are planned and unplanned changes. The unplanned are the simplest to deal with, being innocent mistakes of the hand, the eye, the ear, or the mind, and will probably not occur in the same place in each copy. Such changes will be relatively few, generally quite harmless, and easily detected. A comparison with other copies can correct most of these mistakes.

It is the *planned* changes that are the most damaging. These are made when the copyist or the translator begins to think for himself and deliberately makes his copy differ from the written document. In this manner, substantial changes may occur in a very short time and can result in the addition or the loss of material. Even this kind of change could be corrected if one had the original to refer to for comparison, but if the master copy is unavailable the corrupted texts perpetuate the errors. Thus all subsequent copies made from the altered text will bear the same shortcomings because there is no master copy or archetype with which to correct it.

The Book of Mormon as a Witness for the Bible Text

Apparently the original manuscripts of the Bible disappeared very early. This seems particularly true of the New Testament. Sir Frederic Kenyon, one of the greatest textual scholars of the early twentieth century, commented thus: "The originals of the several books have long ago disappeared. They must have perished in the very infancy of the Church; for no allusion is ever made to them by any Christian writer."[5] Kenyon's statement is particularly important to us because it means that for centuries there has not been an original Bible manuscript to guide the reader. Even in the early decades of the original Christian church, the original texts seem to have been absent.

In the Book of Mormon we have an account of a vision and guided tour given to Nephi, during which he is accompanied by an angel and shown in advance much about the textual history of the Bible. The angel identifies the book as "a record of the Jews" that "containeth many of the prophecies of the holy prophets" and the testimony of the twelve Apostles of the Lamb (see 1 Nephi 13:23–24). This is without question the Old and the New Testaments. The angel tells Nephi that the book is similar to the record on the plates of brass, but not as extensive, and that it contains many covenants of the Lord (see 1 Nephi 13:20–23). The angel continues:

> When it proceeded forth from the mouth of a Jew it contained the fulness of the gospel of the Lord, of whom the twelve apostles bear record. . . .
>
> Wherefore, these things go forth from the Jews in purity unto the Gentiles. . . .
>
> And after they go forth by the hand of the twelve apostles of the Lamb, from the Jews unto the Gentiles, thou seest the formation of that great and abominable church, which is most abominable above all other churches; for behold, they have taken away from the gospel of the Lamb many parts which are plain and most precious; and also many covenants of the Lord have they taken away. (1 Nephi 13:24–26.)

The angel makes it clear that he is not talking about subtle accidents of hand and eye, resulting in a few misplaced letters or words —the unplanned errors of copyists. He pointedly ascribes these changes to the planned editorial work of designing men: "And all this have they done that they might pervert the right ways of the Lord, that they might blind the eyes and harden the hearts of the children of men. Wherefore, thou seest that after the book hath gone forth through the hands of the great and abominable church, that there are many plain and precious things taken away from the book, which is the book of the Lamb of God.'' (1 Nephi 13:27–28.)

The angel then declares that the textual corruption of which he spoke would not be a gradual, long-time process taking place over thousands of years, but something that would occur—at least for the New Testament—soon after the time of Jesus and *before* the distribution of the Bible among the nations of the Gentiles: ''And after these plain and precious things were taken away it [the Bible] goeth forth unto all the nations of the Gentiles; and after it goeth forth . . . because of the many plain and precious things which have been taken out of the book . . . because of these things which are taken away out of the gospel of the Lamb, an exceedingly great many do stumble, yea, insomuch that Satan hath great power over them'' (1 Nephi 13:29).

As we read the words of the angel, we discover that the world never has had a complete Bible, for it was massively—even cataclysmically—corrupted *before* it was distributed. Of course, in addition to the major willful corruption of the Bible in the early Christian era, the manuscripts have also continued to suffer the gradual and relatively mild changes, due to errors of hand and eye, that the scholars talk about. Thus there have been two processes at work: (1) a major, sudden, and deliberate editorial corruption of the text and (2) a gradual promulgation of variants that has occurred as a natural consequence of copying and translation.

The great scholars, employing the science of textual criticism, seem to be effectively correcting the errors made by the carelessness and weakness of man. As these scholars search the available manuscripts—such as the Vaticanus, Sinaiticus, Alexandrinus, and lesser fragments—the text of the Bible may yet be recovered to the condition it was in *after* it was cataclysmically corrupted, as described in 1 Nephi. However, the scholars have not been able to recover the critical missing parts mentioned by the angel because the texts they use are ''gentile'' texts of the fourth century. Hence the main issue with the text of the Bible today is not a matter of language and of words but the lack of an adequate manuscript.

It appears to me, then, that the world has mistakenly identified the text of the second or third generation as being the same as the original. But the angel in 1 Nephi indicated that the world of the

Gentiles has never known the complete Bible. Thus the great and highly regarded manuscripts are indeed precious for their antiquity and beauty, but they represent the depleted text, not the original.

The plain and most precious parts of the Bible are to be had not through secular scholars but through faith and testimony, not through an academician but through a prophet, not through the learning of man only but through the revelations of the Holy Spirit.

Therefore, because of the textual history of the Bible, we can confidently say that no one today, scholar or otherwise, really understands the doctrinal nature of the Bible without the help of latter-day revelation such as the Book of Mormon, the Doctrine and Covenants, the Pearl of Great Price, the Joseph Smith Translation, and the teachings of Joseph Smith. These are indispensable sources, along with the testimony of the Holy Ghost, for one to clearly grasp the doctrinal message of the Holy Bible. It is in that light that we begin to understand why, in 1841, the Prophet Joseph Smith placed such a high value on the clarity of the teachings of the Book of Mormon.

In comparing the Book of Mormon with the Bible, Elder Bruce R. McConkie stated:

> I have unbounded appreciation for both the King James Version and the Joseph Smith Translation. I stand in reverential awe as I read and ponder the wondrous words they contain. I do not believe there is a person on earth who has a greater respect for or appreciation of the Holy Bible than I do.
>
> Now, I say all this as a prelude to making these flat and unequivocal declarations:
>
> 1. Most of the doctrines of the gospel, as set forth in the Book of Mormon, far surpass their comparable recitation in the Bible.
>
> 2. This Nephite record bears a plainer and purer witness of the divine sonship of Christ and the salvation which comes in and through his holy name than do the Old World scriptures.
>
> 3. Men can get nearer to the Lord; can have more of the spirit of conversion and conformity in their hearts; can have stronger testimonies; and can gain a better understanding of the doctrines of salvation through the Book of Mormon than they can through the Bible.
>
> 4. More people will flock to the gospel standard; more

souls will be converted; more of scattered Israel will be gathered; and more people will migrate from one place to another because of the Book of Mormon than was or will be the case with the Bible (Ezek. 37:15–28).

5. There will be more people saved in the kingdom of God—ten thousand times over—because of the Book of Mormon than there will be because of the Bible.[6]

In other words, what the Bible does well, the Book of Mormon does better.

In the pages that follow, we will recount in detail some of the precepts of the Book of Mormon that make it such an outstanding book of religious knowledge and faith and the very "keystone of our religion."

The Book of Mormon Testifies of Jesus Christ

The Book of Mormon witnesses that the resurrected Jesus personally visited some ancient American people and showed himself to them in his immortal, glorified, celestial condition. He taught them, healed them, fed them, and let them touch his body (see 3 Nephi 11–27). There is no mistaking that the Book of Mormon says that Jesus is a real, living person, the Son of God, and that the biblical record of him is historically true. But it also clearly shows that the Bible is not the complete record of all that Jesus taught or did and that the Old World record does not contain all we need to know about him.

The Book of Mormon gives approximately one hundred different names for Jesus, each describing some phase or characteristic of his ministry (for example, Creator, Redeemer, Mediator, Judge, Shepherd), and this sacred record mentions the Savior at least 3,471 times in the course of the book. By using these many names for the Redeemer, the Book of Mormon gives a broad spectrum to his mission. By way of analogy we observe that there are eighty-eight sounds on a piano keyboard, and through the proper use and combination of these sounds, one can produce great melodious strains. Similarly the message about Jesus Christ given in the Book of Mormon is not monotone, not just a single note; rather, it is a symphony of delightful and essential information that harmoniously testifies of the Savior of the world. The Book of Mormon's role as a witness for Christ is demonstrated in the following chart:

Books	Number of Verses	Number of References to the Savior
1 Nephi	618	150
2 Nephi	779	576
Jacob	203	151
Enos	27	22
Jarom	15	8
Omni	30	20
Words of Mormon	18	13
Mosiah	785	484
Alma	1,975	917
Helaman	497	225
3 Nephi	785	290
4 Nephi	49	42
Mormon	227	189
Ether	433	218
Moroni	163	166
Total	6,604	3,471

The Book of Mormon not only attests to the reality of Jesus but also, more than any other book available to us, explains graphically why Jesus and his atonement are important. It is one thing to know that there is a Savior; it is another to realize why a Savior is so important, what the consequences would have been worldwide if there had been no Savior, and what the consequences will be individually—since there *is* a Savior—if any of us rejects him.

Since knowledge about Christ is the greatest knowledge mankind can possess, the book that most perfectly defines, supplies, and promotes that knowledge is the greatest of books. Our assertion is that the Book of Mormon gives a clearer exposition of the need for a divine Savior, the reality that Jesus of Nazareth is that Savior, and the process by which every individual man or woman can obtain the blessings of the atonement of Christ in his or her individual life than any other book known to and in circulation among the human family today.

The Book of Mormon teaches man's absolute dependence on the Savior. It leaves no doubt that Jesus Christ, born of Mary, is the one and only Redeemer of mankind, that he always was and always will be the only Savior of the world. We note this statement from Nephi, recorded around 559 B.C.: "Behold I say unto you, that as these things are true, and as the Lord God liveth, there is none other name given under heaven save it be this Jesus Christ, of which I have spoken, whereby man can be saved'' (2 Nephi 25:20). And about 500 years later Helaman testified to his sons: ''Remember that there is no other way nor means whereby man can be saved, only through the atoning blood of Jesus Christ, who shall come; yea, remember that he cometh to redeem the world'' (Helaman 5:9; see also 2 Nephi 31:20–21; Mosiah 3:17; 4:8; 5:8; Alma 38:9).

There is no book as effective as the Book of Mormon to teach plainly and directly the nature of the fall of Adam and the necessity of the atonement of Jesus Christ. It explains how the Atonement works, how a person must go about gaining a remission of sins, and then how he can ''retain a remission'' of his sins ''from day to day'' (see Mosiah 4:12, 26). That is the major message of the Book of Mormon. It offers comprehensive statements on the purposes of God in the fall of Adam and the atonement of Jesus Christ that are not found anywhere in the Bible. (See such major doctrinal chapters as 2 Nephi 2, 9; Mosiah 3; Alma 34, 42.)

In 2 Nephi we read a statement from Jacob which describes in greater clarity than perhaps any other reference what would be the consequence for all mankind if there had been no atonement of Jesus Christ:

> For as death hath passed upon all men, to fulfil the merciful plan of the great Creator, there must needs be a power of resurrection, and the resurrection must needs come unto man by reason of the fall; and the fall came by reason of transgression; and because man became fallen they were cut off from the presence of the Lord.
>
> Wherefore, it must needs be an infinite atonement—save it should be an infinite atonement this corruption could not put on incorruption. Wherefore, the first judgment which came upon man must needs have remained to an endless duration. And if so, this flesh must have laid down to rot and to crumble to its mother earth, to rise no more.
>
> O the wisdom of God, his mercy and grace! For behold, if the flesh should rise no more our spirits must become subject to that angel who fell from before the presence of the Eternal God, and became the devil, to rise no more.
>
> *And our spirits must have become like unto him, and we become devils, angels to a devil,* to be shut out from the presence of our God, and to remain with the father of lies, *in misery, like unto himself.* (2 Nephi 9:6–9, italics added.)

Here we see clearly what would have happened to the spirits and bodies of all mankind if there had been no atonement by the Savior. Do we realize what the consequences would have been? Do we fully appreciate Jesus' sacrifice? All mankind would have become devils, forever miserable, if there had been no atonement by Jesus Christ. If Jesus had not done what he did, nothing we could do would ever make up for the loss!

Thus, if we want to know the story of the Savior's life and death and resurrection, we turn to the four Gospels in the New Testament. If we wish to know why that life is so important, we turn to the Book of Mormon.

The Book of Mormon Testifies that Jesus Is God of the Whole World

The Book of Mormon testifies of the wide scope of the Lord's work among *all* peoples of the earth. He is the God of the whole world. He was born and grew up among the Jews, but he also went personally to the Nephites and to the lost tribes of Israel. The Savior has been no absentee landlord. He has been working among all peoples at all times—not always to the same extent perhaps, for all are not equally receptive or ready; but he has given them everything that they should have at any given time.

There are several references that deal with this subject. For example, Nephi records the Lord's words as follows: "For I command all men, both in the east and in the west, and in the north, and in the south, and in the islands of the sea, that they shall write the words which I speak unto them. . . . For behold, I shall speak unto the Jews and they shall write it; and I shall also speak unto the Nephites and they shall write it; and I shall also speak unto the other tribes of the house of Israel, which I have led away, and they shall write it; *and I shall also speak unto all nations of the earth and they shall write it.*" (2 Nephi 29:11–12, italics added.)

The title page of the Book of Mormon corroborates the information found in 2 Nephi, stating that "JESUS is the CHRIST, the ETERNAL GOD, manifesting himself unto all nations." Such statements give the broadest possible range to the mission of Jesus Christ.

We are familiar with the feelings expressed by Alma: he wished he were an angel so he could preach the gospel to all the world. Then he rescinded that wish because he knew the Lord had other people in the various nations to do the teaching there: "Why should I desire more than to perform the work to which I have been called?

. . . For behold, the Lord doth grant unto all nations, of their own nation and tongue, to teach his word, yea, in wisdom, all that he seeth fit that they should have." (Alma 29:6, 8.)

The world in general has come to an awareness that there is a record of the Jews—we call it the Bible. As Latter-day Saints we are also aware that there is a record of the Nephites—we call that the Book of Mormon. And the Book of Mormon tells us that there is a record of the ten tribes that will come forth someday. And the Book of Mormon also explains that there are many other records from other nations. (2 Nephi 29:11–13.) So in these days we are just beginning to get acquainted with what will someday be a long list of standard works and books from which we will be able to learn the history of God's dealings with many branches of the human family.

The Book of Mormon Touches on a Wide Range of Religious and Secular Topics

The Book of Mormon, in its terminology and its vocabulary, is plain and simple, with rather elementary use of the language and with words of few syllables. (That is generally true, although some of us probably first learned the word *ignominious* from the Book of Mormon.) Yet, in spite of its plainness and singleness of purpose, it is not an easy book to read or to master. It is heavy reading, serious and ponderous. No one will be justified in treating it lightly or casually. Elder James E. Faust explained: "The Book of Mormon did not yield its profound message to me as an unearned legacy. I question whether one can acquire an understanding of this great book except through singleness of mind and strong purpose of heart."[7]

This greatest of all books touches on many topics, but it deals primarily with spiritual things and confirms or verifies religious subjects. For example, the Book of Mormon speaks of angels, spirits, devils, and God, and it testifies most often and most powerfully of Jesus Christ and his mission. It speaks of God's intervention in human life and tells of visions, revelations, voices, healings, miracles, prophets, and prophecy. It plainly points out the exact fulfillment of prophecy and shows how civilization can be lost. It talks of the spirit world, death, hell, paradise, dreams, truth, and falsehood. It tells about seers and revelators, covenants, sacred writings, God's love, heavenly rewards, and divine punishments. It talks about the premortal existence, the purposes of God, the gospel's being preached from the beginning, the shallowness of man's wisdom, the judgments of God, and the purpose of man's existence. It teaches about prayer, repentance, obedience, faith, baptism, the Holy Ghost, man's accountability before God, and the inevitable and eternal judgment to come to each person for his or her deeds, desires, and thoughts. It speaks of sanctification, a change of heart, being born again, salvation, damnation, missionary work, apostasy, welfare work, tithing, capital punishment, secret combinations, priestcraft, pride, war, family, sin, and happiness. It relates important information regarding the law of Moses, the fall of Adam, the second coming of Jesus Christ, and the earth's being cleansed by fire. It talks about Elijah, temples, the scattering of Israel, the gathering of Israel, the New Jerusalem, the old Jerusalem, the ten tribes, Columbus, the American Revolutionary War, and (as we have seen) Bible manuscript history and biblical textual criticism.

In addition to all of these religious topics, the Book of Mormon touches on items such as political governments, legal systems, monetary systems, migration and formation of different groups and cultures, geography, astronomy, record keeping, ship building, shipping, exploration, architecture, horticulture, medicine, and so on.

The Book of Mormon Identifies the Enemies of Christ

In helping us to "get nearer to God," the Book of Mormon not only declares what the doctrine of Christ is but also tells what the doctrine of Christ is *not.*

In speaking about the Book of Mormon, President Ezra Taft Benson observed:

> The Book of Mormon exposes the enemies of Christ. It confounds false doctrines and lays down contention. (See 2 Nephi 3:12.) It fortifies the humble followers of Christ against the evil designs, strategies, and doctrines of the devil in our day. The type of apostates in the Book of Mormon are similar to the type we have today. God, with his infinite foreknowledge, so molded the Book of Mormon that we might see the error and know how to combat false educational, political, religious, and philosophical concepts of our time. . . .

> Now, we have not been using the Book of Mormon as we should. Our homes are not as strong unless we are using it to bring our children to Christ. Our families may be corrupted by worldly trends and teachings unless we know how to use the book to expose and combat the falsehoods in socialism, organic evolution, rationalism, humanism, etc. Our missionaries are not as effective unless they are "hissing forth" with it. Social, ethical, cultural, or educational converts will not survive under the heat of the day unless their taproots go down to the fulness of the gospel which the Book of Mormon contains. . . .
>
> Do eternal consequences rest upon our response to this book? Yes, either to our blessing or our condemnation.
>
> Every Latter-day Saint should make the study of this book a lifetime pursuit. Otherwise he is placing his soul in jeopardy and neglecting that which could give spiritual and intellectual unity to his whole life. There is a difference between a convert who is built on the rock of Christ through the Book of Mormon and stays hold of that iron rod, and one who is not.[8]

Because of the great mission and powerful effect of the Book of Mormon, and its centrality in this dispensation, we begin to see why the Lord is displeased when we do not use it more effectively. In the Doctrine and Covenants we read:

> And your minds in times past have been darkened because of unbelief, and because you have treated lightly the things you have received—
>
> Which vanity and unbelief have brought the whole church under condemnation.
>
> And this condemnation resteth upon the children of Zion, even all.
>
> And they shall remain under this condemnation until they repent and remember the new covenant, even the Book of Mormon and the former commandments which I have given them, not only to say, but to do according to that which I have written—
>
> That they may bring forth fruit meet for their Father's kingdom; otherwise there remaineth a scourge and judgment to be poured out upon the children of Zion. (D&C 84:54–58.)

Conclusion

The Book of Mormon, then, is the keystone: it testifies that the biblical record of Jesus is historically true, and it exceeds the present translations of the Bible in plainness about what a person must do to be saved. The Book of Mormon teaches the fulness of the gospel, which means it clearly explains the fundamentals of life. It testifies that there is a God, that mankind is God's offspring, that there is a divine law, that life has a purpose, and that there is a judgment and an endless existence after death. It tells why a Redeemer is needed as a result of the fall of Adam and man's own sins, and it explains that Jesus—being a God—is the only redeemer able to save mankind. It explains what a person must do to gain the maximum benefit of the Redeemer's atonement. Finally, it teaches that every person will die, be raised in a resurrection, and then be judged according to his or her works.

For these reasons and others, the Book of Mormon is of unique and unparalleled importance. Yet with all its greatness, there is still much we do not understand about it, and it demands our further study and research. There are elements of the translation process used in bringing it forth and items of culture, geography, and history in the book itself that we simply do not know. But we do know that it is a true and sacred record, a testament of Jesus Christ. There is a spirit about the Book of Mormon that whispers of its authenticity. No matter how many marvelous, delightful, and delicious things might be found in its pages, if they weren't true, they wouldn't be worth much. But because the Book of Mormon *is* true, no man or woman can be saved in the celestial kingdom and not be a believer in this scriptural witness for Christ.

Everything about the Book of Mormon—each item individually and all of them collectively—trumpets loudly the assertion that it is the "keystone of our religion."

Notes

1. *History of the Church* 4:461. The statement can also be found in *Teachings of the Prophet Joseph Smith,* comp. Joseph Fielding Smith (Salt Lake City: Deseret Book Co., 1976), p. 194; hereafter cited as *TPJS.*

2. Extensive studies on the editorial changes in various editions of the Book of Mormon can be found in Jeffrey R. Holland, "An Analysis of Selected Changes in Major Editions of the Book of Mormon, 1830–1920" (Master's thesis, Brigham Young University, 1966); Stanley R. Larson, "A Study of Some Textual Variations in the Book of Mormon, Comparing the Original and Printer's Manuscripts and the 1830, the 1837, and the 1840 Editions" (Master's thesis, Brigham Young University, 1974). See also the author's article, "The New Publications of the Standard Works—1979, 1981," *BYU Studies* 22 (Fall 1982): 387–423; Hugh G. Stocks, "The Book of Mormon, 1830–1879, a Publishing History" (Master's thesis, University of California, Los Angeles, 1979).

3. *TPJS*, p. 71.

4. *TPJS*, pp. 9–10, 327.

5. Frederic Kenyon, *Our Bible and the Ancient Manuscripts* (New York: Harper and Row, 1958), p. 155.

6. Bruce R. McConkie, *Doctrines of the Restoration: Sermons and Writings of Bruce R. McConkie*, ed. and arr. Mark L. McConkie (Salt Lake City: Bookcraft, 1989), pp. 267–68.

7. James E. Faust, "The Keystone of Our Religion," *Ensign* 13 (November 1983): 9.

8. Ezra Taft Benson, "The Book of Mormon Is the Word of God," *Ensign* 5 (May 1975): 64–65.

PART II

The Joseph Smith Translation

Chapter 7

THE JOSEPH SMITH TRANSLATION: WHAT, WHY, AND HOW

In this chapter we will discuss what the Joseph Smith Translation is, why such a translation was needed, how it adds to and clarifies the biblical record, and how it was accomplished. In discussing this last item—how the translation was accomplished—we will consider the kind of attitude about learning that rendered Joseph Smith capable of making the translation, an attitude that I feel each of us should have in order to benefit from the translation.

Each of us has a need to gain spiritual knowledge—the greatest amount possible—and I believe the Joseph Smith Translation can help us in more than one way as we seek this knowledge. That is, we can benefit not only by comparing verses and texts of this translation with those of the King James Bible, but also by listening to the louder message that is transmitted to us by the very fact that there is a Joseph Smith Translation. This translation is an illustration of true spiritual learning, of how the Lord teaches his children. The Lord simply could have handed Joseph Smith a better translation of the Bible, an English translation of the Book of Mormon, and so on; but he didn't. He required the Prophet to struggle and work out all of these things for himself. To be sure, without the Lord's help none of these things could have been done, but let's not overlook the part that Joseph Smith played as a man in the process of the translation. Can any of us gain spiritual growth without a struggle? There seems to be a law in the plan of salvation for mankind that a person must do everything for himself that he can do.

Some Historical Background

In June 1830, the Prophet Joseph Smith, assisted by Oliver Cowdery as his scribe, began what they called a "new translation" of the Bible. Joseph Smith was twenty-four years of age. Oliver was twenty-three. Their formal schooling was meager. They did not have a knowledge of Greek, Hebrew, or Aramaic, and they had no ancient manuscripts. However, they had had some excellent spiritual preparation and experience that qualified them for this kind of work.

After serving a few months as scribe for the new Bible translation, Oliver was called to other responsibilities and was succeeded as scribe by John Whitmer in October and Sidney Rigdon in December. Work on the new translation was pursued vigorously from June 1830 until July 1833, by which time the initial translation of the Old Testament and the New Testament had been accomplished. Thereafter, the Prophet and his scribes—usually Sidney Rigdon and Frederick G. Williams—that is, the First Presidency, reviewed and revised the manuscript, preparing it for the press. In the review process additional revelations were received on some points over and beyond what had been done the first time. This is significant, because it illustrates the principle of learning spiritual matters line upon line.

There were at least three major anticipations for publication of Joseph Smith's Bible translation. The first was in Missouri, but the press was destroyed by a mob before the project was even begun. The second attempt was at Kirtland, and the third at Nauvoo. These two latter ventures failed for want of money and time. Publication of the new Bible translation was a significant undertaking that the Prophet was seeking to accomplish in Nauvoo at the time of his death in 1844. (See the detailed discussion in chapter 10 of this book.)

At the death of Joseph Smith the manuscript of his Bible translation became the possession of his widow Emma Smith, and still later it became the property of the Reorganized Church of Jesus Christ of Latter Day Saints. Beginning in 1867 that organization published several editions of the Joseph Smith Translation and it currently holds the legal copyright. I have examined the original manuscript carefully, comparing every word with its published counterpart, and I feel that the printed editions by the RLDS church are correct and careful representations of the Prophet's work.

Now, it seems to me that the Church could have had the Joseph Smith Translation in published form as early as the 1830s or 1840s, but apparently the members didn't want it strongly enough to make the necessary sacrifices for its publication. I think they just didn't fully appreciate the value of this work. In our time, I have heard some Church members say, "If the Lord had wanted the Church to have the Inspired Version, he would have seen to it, and would not have let the Prophet die without publishing it." That is not sound reasoning. If that kind of thinking prevailed, we would also have to say that the Lord didn't really want the children of Israel to have the things on the first set of tablets; that he did not want us to have the date of the First Vision or of the restoration of the Melchizedek Priesthood; that he did not want us to have the 116 manuscript pages of the Book of Mormon translation; that he did not want the Saints to stay in Missouri; that he did not want the New Jerusalem to be built; and so on.

Principally because of the early Saints' neglect, then, we might say that the Church lost the new translation, but now part of it is available to us again in the 1979 LDS edition of the King James Version of the Bible; moreover, we have reasonable access to the original manuscript. We seem to have been given a second chance now. Paul Cheesman, a former colleague of mine, said to me one day, "I think the Lord has given us the Joseph Smith Translation to see what we will do with it." I agree with him. I think the Lord has given us the Book of Mormon, the Doctrine and Covenants, the priesthood, and everything else on the same basis. Spiritually we can't afford to neglect the Prophet's Bible translation again. Certain principles taught by Jesus, principles we will discuss again later in this chapter, seem to apply here: A candle is not brought forth to be put under a bushel; if we do not continue to receive the light and truth that the Lord offers us, we may lose what we have.

Many things are yet to be done in this dispensation—Zion is to be established, the New Jerusalem is to be built, Israel is to be gathered, and so forth. Many of these things were begun during the early days of the restored Church, but they suffered delays because the people were not ready. Today we seem to be getting ready in the Church for greater strides again. I think it is not by accident that we also now have some official access to the Joseph Smith Translation.

Why a New Translation Was Needed

A new translation of the Bible was needed because information necessary for the establishment and well-being of the restored Church was lacking in all the current translations of the Bible; the new translation was the Lord's way of revealing that information. All other translations of the Bible were insufficient, and no original manuscripts of that sacred record were available from which to make an adequate translation with all the necessary information in it. The basic problem with the Bible is not one of language; nor is it that we lack scholars who are capable of reading an ancient manuscript. The problem is the absence of an *adequate* manuscript. The knowledge that was needed just wasn't to be found in any known document.

In 1 Nephi 13 and 14 we read that many plain and precious things have been taken out of the Bible by persons who deliberately wished to weaken the message. Thus no amount of scholarship, without either an adequate manuscript or a new revelation, could produce the lost material. The Lord chose to restore the information through Joseph Smith, giving the latter-day prophet revelation upon revelation to bring again many of the things that were taken from the Bible or were lost before it was compiled.

The Prophet's Approach to the New Translation

The translation process was a learning experience for Joseph Smith. He learned new things by reading the Bible and by receiving the inspiration of the Lord in response to his study. It was a process of inquiry. It required effort, prayer, energy, desire, and serious contemplation. Had he not been willing to follow these requirements, he would not have gained the insight or received the revelation, and none of us would have had the benefit of a new translation.

In many places in the Doctrine and Covenants we read the Lord's counsel to ask, seek, and knock. Some of these instances pertain to the Prophet's work on the Bible translation, as the context of the passages makes clear; for example, Doctrine and Covenants 42:56 reads: "Thou shalt ask, and my scriptures shall be given as I have appointed." (On the principle of asking, see also D&C 4:7; 6:6; 29:33; 42:61; 132:1.)

One thing is clear: There is no revelation without a student. Unless a person is a seeker, he isn't likely to get a revelation, whether he is the President of the Church or anyone else. When the Lord told us to ask, seek, knock, he was inviting us to get busy and get ready, to compare and to think.

As members of the Church seek to gain more spiritual knowledge, they do not have to settle for the inherent limitations of a Protestant, Catholic, or Jewish translation of the Bible derived from an inadequate manuscript. They have access to the best Bible that is available—the Joseph Smith Translation.

A passage from the Joseph Smith Translation of the Gospel of Mark illustrates the process of spiritual learning we have been discussing. As this passage relates, the disciples asked Jesus concerning the parable of the sower; his answer included the concept that parables hide the truth from the unready, but he also emphasized the idea that knowledge begets *more* knowledge: "And he said unto them, Is a candle brought to be put under a bushel, or under a bed, and not to be set on a candlestick? I say unto you, Nay. . . . Take heed what ye hear; for with what measure ye mete, it shall be measured to you; and unto you that *continue to receive*, shall more be given; for he that *receiveth*, to him shall be given; but he that *continueth not to receive*, from him shall be taken even that which he hath." (JST, Mark 4:9–11, 18–20, italics added.) The spirit craves knowledge as the body craves food, and he who seeks sincerely to satisfy those spiritual cravings will find a bounteous feast at the Lord's table, all based on that person's willingness to receive.

We need to keep learning in order to maintain a spiritual uplift. What lifted us yesterday may not be sufficient tomorrow to help us retain the same level of spirituality; we will need more knowledge, new insights, new viewpoints, and new learning experiences.

Studying the Joseph Smith Translation

It seems to me that a person can approach his study of the Joseph Smith Translation on at least three different levels. The first and easiest level is to simply find the verses in the Joseph Smith Translation text that differ from those in the King James Version. The second is to discover the doctrinal or informational meaning of those passages. The third level of study is a little more subtle but often extremely informative: it is to note how the change in the text is accomplished—that is, the literary style. When examining a particular change, a person can ask himself the following: (1) Does the change appear as inspired commentary material interjected by Joseph Smith? (2) Is it given as part of the narrative of the biblical author? or (3) Is it given as a direct quotation, the kind for which there would be quotation marks if such were used in the Bible? Sometimes interesting implications arise as we consider not only the text of new material but also the literary form in which the new material appears and—in the case of a direct quotation—the speaker to whom the words are attributed. There is quite a difference, not only in style but also in meaning, between first and third person and between dialogue and simple narrative. Note, for example, that in the King James Version the account of the Creation is given in third person, with Moses telling the story of what the Lord accomplished: "In the beginning God created . . ." and so forth. On the other hand, the Joseph Smith Translation gives the account in first person, with the Lord telling the story himself: "I, God," did so and so. Many such changes occur throughout the Joseph Smith Translation which enhance the record and say something about the restorative nature of what Joseph Smith was doing.

Let us now take a specific look at some of the things the Joseph Smith Translation has to offer us as gospel students.

An Introduction to the Book of Genesis

In the new translation, there is a whole chapter of information prior to the beginning of the book of Genesis. We know it as Moses 1, but it is part of the Joseph Smith Translation. It tells of some visions that were given to Moses previous to his writing Genesis. Hence we might say that just as Genesis serves as an introduction to all that follows in the Bible, these visions recorded in the new translation serve as an introduction to Genesis.

This introductory material is critical to our understanding of Moses' mission and writings, of the biblical record as a whole, and of God's purposes relative to mankind and this earth. Of particular relevance here is the Lord's marvelous statement: "This is my work and my glory—to bring to pass the immortality and eternal life of man" (Moses 1:39). The Joseph Smith Translation thus provides us with a precious perspective on God's eternal plan. Other scriptures (D&C 88:17–23; 1 Nephi 17:36; Abraham 3:23) round out the concept that the earth is a home for mankind—that it is not only a mortal laboratory and training ground but also an eternal home. And all of this points back to the great introductory chapter in the Joseph Smith Translation of Genesis (see the more detailed discussion in chapter 8 of this book).

The Spirit, the Physical, and the Temporal Creations

We find in the Joseph Smith Translation an explanation of the creative process, showing that life as we now know it—mortality—is the culmination of a three-step process (see JST, Genesis 1–5; Moses 2–5). We learn that all things were created first as spirits, and that this was done in heaven. Then all things—men, animals, and plants—were created on earth as physical beings, with tangible bodies, but in a condition in which they were not yet subject to sin or death. As the third step in the process, these physical beings underwent another essential change and became mortal, a change which occurred when Adam and Eve, while in the Garden of Eden, ate of the tree of knowledge of good and evil. Adam and Eve were physical in their nature while they were in the garden, but they were not mortal until they partook of the forbidden fruit. This three-step process, outlined so well in the Joseph Smith Translation, is scarcely hinted at in any other version of the Bible.

Origin of Animal Sacrifice

The King James Version tells us that, after Adam and Eve were cast out of the garden, children were born to them and that their sons Cain and Abel offered sacrifices to God. The King James Version informs us what was done, but it does not tell us why. In the Joseph Smith Translation, however, we read that if they had not become mortal, Adam and Eve would not have had children (Moses 5:10–11). Also, the new translation tells us that animal sacrifice was revealed from heaven as a special ordinance—to be performed in a particular manner—as a similitude of the sacrifice of the Son of God (Moses 5:7–8). Hence the King James Version reports that there *was* sacrifice; the Joseph Smith Translation tells us *why*.

Further, we learn from the Joseph Smith Translation that, after Adam and Eve were cast out of the Garden of Eden and had become mortal, they were given revelation on how to live in order to receive a redemption from sin and death; they were taught concerning the mission of Jesus Christ. Other Bible versions hardly touch upon these matters. In cases such as this, the Joseph Smith Translation not only tells us why certain things occurred anciently but also serves as our best or our only source for what was done in that early day.

Enoch and Melchizedek

Two of the greatest among the early patriarchs were Enoch and Melchizedek. In our present Bible, Enoch and Melchizedek are almost totally neglected. Little is said about either one. In three minutes you could read all that the King James Version says about both of them.

Enoch and Melchizedek are important figures in Mormonism, and it is through the Joseph Smith Translation that most of what we know about these two patriarchs has been made available to us.

Credentials of the Patriarchs

The Joseph Smith Translation gives us the credentials of the ancient patriarchs; that is, it states that they were called of God, ordained to the priesthood, and engaged in preaching the gospel of Jesus Christ. In most cases the King James Version says nothing about such matters. By providing these details, the Joseph Smith Translation gives a continuity and a compactness to the Genesis account of these early patriarchs that is not available in any other Bible version.

The Covenant with Abraham

In the King James Version it is relatively clear that the Lord made a covenant with Abraham, giving him and his posterity certain responsibilities. The Joseph Smith Translation adds a dimension to all of this not found in any other version of the Bible. From the Prophet's translation we learn that a covenant was made with Enoch, which was then passed on to Noah, then to Melchizedek, and then to Abraham. In the case of each of these men, the Joseph Smith Translation mentions that the patriarch received the same covenant that God made with Enoch. (See JST, Genesis 9, 12, 14.) Of course, there were certain ramifications of the covenant that were particular to each man, but the general covenant was the same. Again, this gives a needed continuity to the book of Genesis.

Prominence of Joseph

The King James Version devotes considerable space and gives great prominence to the story of Joseph of Egypt (Genesis 37–50). The Joseph Smith Translation gives even more prominence to the account. Chapters 48 and 50 of Genesis provide particularly significant information about Joseph. Chapter 48 deals with the placement of Joseph's two sons, Ephraim and Manasseh, as regular, first-line tribes of Israel. The King James Version briefly mentions this, but the Joseph Smith Translation enlarges upon it, offering a lengthy addition in which Jacob praises Joseph and tells of Joseph's mission as the preserver and protector of the house of Israel. One important feature of Jacob's statement is the allusion to Joseph as a light bringing salvation to the house of Israel, a salvation from sin and spiritual bondage (JST, Genesis 48:11). This seems to point to the latter days, when the gospel is to be carried to the world through Joseph's seed.

The Jewish historian Josephus, in discussing Jacob's death, says that before Jacob died he "enlarged upon the praises of Joseph."[1] Josephus does little more than mention this; the Joseph Smith Translation, however, actually provides Jacob's words of praise (see JST, Genesis 48:3–11).

Genesis 50 contains an account of the prophecy of Joseph, of which a much more extensive account is found in the Joseph Smith Translation. This is the prophecy that Lehi discusses in 2 Nephi 2, but the Joseph Smith Translation contains even more information concerning the prophecy than the Book of Mormon account.

The Name Jehovah

In Exodus 6:2–3 of the King James Version we read that the Lord revealed himself to Moses by the name of Jehovah, but that Abraham, Isaac, and Jacob did *not* know the Lord by that name. This is corrected in the Joseph Smith Translation to convey the truth that not only Moses but also Abraham, Isaac, and Jacob knew the Lord by that name (see JST, Exodus 6:2–3).

"There Shall No Man See Me, and Live"

As recorded in the King James Version of Exodus 33:20, the Lord said to Moses, "Thou canst not see my face: for there shall no man see me, and live." Thereupon the Lord said he would arrange for Moses to hide in the cleft of a rock as He passed by; Moses would be able to see the back parts, but the Lord's face would not be seen. Without further explanation, these scriptures seem to contradict an earlier passage that reads: "The Lord spake unto Moses face to face, as a man speaketh unto his friend" (Exodus 33:11).

The Joseph Smith Translation confirms that Moses was not privileged to see the face of the Lord, but adds the significant qualifying information that the restriction was temporary and applied only "at this time" (see JST, Exodus 33:20–23).

The Law of Moses

The value of the Joseph Smith Translation can also be seen in the clarifications it makes concerning the law of Moses. Indeed, a person cannot come to a correct understanding of why the law of Moses was given without examining the relevant information in the Joseph Smith Translation. We know from the King James Version that Moses was given a second set of stone tablets after he destroyed the first set, the people having been denied the blessings of the gospel because of their wickedness. But the King James text gives the impression that this second set contained the same information as the first. The Joseph Smith Translation, on the other hand, explains that the information on the second set of tablets differed from that on the first, thus correcting the notion shared by many in the world that the law of Moses was on both sets of tablets. The Joseph Smith Translation informs us that the first contained the higher ordinances of the gospel, which had power to bring men into the presence of God. The second contained the law of Moses, which was a preparatory law that did not include the fulness of spiritual blessings—that blessing of being brought into the presence of God. (See JST, Exodus 34:1–2; JST, Deuteronomy 10:2.) However, certain gospel principles were retained on both sets of tablets, and thus one can discern many elements of the gospel in the law of Moses.

The Joseph Smith Translation and the Doctrine and Covenants

It is generally necessary to use the Joseph Smith Translation and the Doctrine and Covenants together in order to gain a broader understanding of what the Lord has revealed about biblical subjects. Many times in the Joseph Smith Translation the doctrinal information must be gleaned from the narrative into which it is woven. In the Doctrine and Covenants the doctrinal information is usually given in more direct, didactic form. These two sources complement one another, and when used together they greatly increase our understanding of both the Old Testament and the New Testament. (See the discussion in chapter 11 of this book.)

An Enlarged View

As many of the preceding examples illustrate, one of the main contributions of the Joseph Smith Translation is that it provides us with an opportunity to see a bigger picture, to gain a greater perspective. We might be exposed to a thousand religious facts, but only when we have this greater perspective can we really come to a deeper understanding of the gospel. Organization seems to be the important factor: a five-hundred-dollar watch lying in fifty scattered pieces doesn't say much about the time of day; the scattered pieces of a jigsaw puzzle do not present the best possible picture. In the book of 1 Nephi we learn that when designing and mischievous persons took from the Bible many plain and precious things, their motive was to confuse the people and keep them in spiritual darkness (see 1 Nephi 13:27). This they did very effectively by removing certain things so as to destroy the perspective, the purpose, and the continuity of the biblical narrative. They left many of the whats, but removed many of the whys and the hows.

We can't be content with only knowing *what* when we can also know *why* and *how*. Having the Joseph Smith Translation we can read a more complete biblical account and gain an improved perspective. The nature of salvation and the nature of revelation require that we constantly become better informed and more skillful in our gospel teaching. The fact that the Church saw fit to produce the 1979 LDS edition of the King James Version of the Bible, with its many excerpts from the Joseph Smith Translation, is indicative of the desire to do things better—to teach with precision, to be more accurate, to provide more information, to do a better job.

As members of the Church we are not merely invited to become acquainted with Joseph Smith's translation of the Bible; we are, I feel, expected to do so, if for no other reason (and there *are* plenty of reasons) than the fact that it exists and is available for study. If any member of the Church does not already have a testimony by the Spirit of the worth of the Joseph Smith Translation, then there is waiting for that member—through committed, prayerful study of the Prophet's translation—one of the most fruitful experiences of his or her life. I can bear testimony of this because I am familiar with the contents of the Joseph Smith Translation. I know a little of its worth. I have tasted of its spirit, and I know it serves as a great aid in teaching the gospel and as a tangible witness for the divine ministry of the Prophet Joseph Smith and for the mission of Jesus Christ. The Joseph Smith Translation represents a search for more light and knowledge; it exemplifies how revelation comes and how spiritual knowledge is obtained. It is a monument to the attitude about spiritual learning that characterized the Prophet Joseph Smith and which ought to characterize each of us.

Notes

1. Josephus, *The Antiquities of the Jews*, trans. William Whiston, II, VIII, 1.

Chapter 8

THE BOOK OF MOSES

What is the book of Moses? The most direct answer I can give to that question is that the book of Moses consists of the first eight chapters of Genesis from the Joseph Smith Translation of the Bible (JST). Since the book of Moses has been published separately in the Pearl of Great Price, and since the Church does not publish the JST as a separate, complete volume, the historical connection between the book of Moses and the translation of the Bible has eluded many Latter-day Saints. However, the original manuscript of the Prophet's translation leaves no doubt that the book of Moses is an extract from the JST.

The complete story of the book of Moses, however, is quite complex, and it is not sufficient for us simply to say that the book of Moses is part of the JST. We want to know a good many other things about it, such as the following:

1. How, when, where, why, and by whom was this part of the translation made?
2. By what means did the material get from the original handwritten manuscript into the printed Pearl of Great Price?
3. Of what specific historical value to the book of Moses are the original manuscripts of the JST?
4. Of what historical and doctrinal value is the material known as the book of Moses?

How the Book of Moses Was Obtained

The material that constitutes our present book of Moses was revealed to the Prophet Joseph Smith as part of his translation of the Bible. Originally this material consisted of three separate revelations. The first, dated June 1830 on the original manuscript, is titled, "A Revelation given to Joseph the Revelator," and is now published as Moses 1. This revelation, apparently recorded by

Oliver Cowdery at Harmony, Pennsylvania, must have been given just prior to or at the beginning of the Bible translation.

The second revelation is titled, "A Revelation given to the Elders of the Church of Christ on the first Book of Moses, Chapter First." This is also part of the JST manuscript, appearing in Oliver Cowdery's handwriting, and covers the material found in Moses 2, 3, and 4. No date is given on this part of the manuscript, but other evidences show that it was received and recorded in Harmony, Pennsylvania, between June and October 1830.

The third portion, also received in the process of making the new translation of the Bible, is titled, "A Revelation concerning Adam after he had been driven out of the Garden of Eden." The content of this revelation actually covers much more than what is suggested by the title, for it not only deals with Adam but also relates the biblical story from Adam down to Noah, with an especially long section about Enoch. This material can be found in Moses 5:1 to 8:12.

At this point in the JST manuscript several dates are given, and it is evident that several scribes were involved. The material comprising what we now call Moses 4:1 to 5:42 was recorded by Oliver Cowdery between June and 21 October 1830, at Fayette, New York, and at about this time Oliver Cowdery left New York on a mission to Ohio and Missouri (see D&C 32); consequently, at this point in the JST manuscript, the handwriting changes from that of Oliver Cowdery to that of John Whitmer. The latter recorded a few verses on 21 October 1830 (comprising what we now call Moses 5:43 to 5:51), and some additional material on 30 November 1830 (comprising what is now Moses 5:52 to 6:18). John Whitmer continued to write, and on 1 December 1830 he recorded what is now Moses 6:19 to 7:2. All of this took place at Fayette, New York. Then John Whitmer, having been called previously, left New York on a mission to the Kirtland, Ohio, area.

At this point Sidney Rigdon came into the picture. He had joined the Church in Ohio a few weeks earlier (on 14 or 15 November 1830), and had arrived in Fayette on or about 10 December 1830. Soon after his arrival, he was appointed by revelation to be a scribe for the Prophet Joseph (see D&C 35:19–20) and began to record what was revealed as the Prophet translated the Bible. Sometime after Sidney Rigdon's arrival (and before 30 December) the Prophet Joseph received, as part of the Bible translation, an extended revelation about Enoch. The manuscript shows that this revelation was originally recorded in the handwriting of Sidney

Rigdon. It is the material now printed as Moses 7, and was the first contact that Sidney Rigdon had with Joseph Smith's translation of the Bible.

Later during the same month of December (probably on 30 December), soon after the reception of the revelation about Enoch, the Lord directed Joseph Smith to cease translating the Bible until the Prophet had moved to Ohio (see D&C 37). The actual move from Fayette, New York, to Kirtland, Ohio, did not take place until late in January 1831, and the Prophet arrived in Kirtland on about 1 February 1831.[1] A few days later, after the Prophet and his company became settled in Kirtland, work on the translation resumed with Sidney Rigdon as scribe. During the month of February and continuing until 8 March 1831, the translation was carried through to Genesis 19:35.

I am grateful to the Reorganized Church of Jesus Christ of Latter Day Saints for making it possible for me to study carefully the original manuscripts. These manuscripts, when used in conjunction with the *History of the Church* and the Doctrine and Covenants, make it possible to reconstruct, almost on a day-to-day basis, the history of this important period of June 1830 to March 1831.[2] Among the important historical items that become very clear are the following:

1. The material we know as the book of Moses was revealed as part of Joseph Smith's translation of the Bible, but it was not at that time called the book of Moses.

2. The original manuscripts make it evident that most of the book of Moses material was revealed in the summer and early fall of 1830, some portions being revealed in November and December 1830 and some in February 1831.

3. Much of the material was already recorded before Sidney Rigdon entered the picture. He was neither the genius nor the recorder for the early part of the Bible translation.

4. The movements of the early brethren—such as Oliver Cowdery's call to Ohio and Missouri; John Whitmer's call to Ohio; Sidney Rigdon's entry into the Church and his arrival in Fayette, New York—are all reflected in the changes of handwriting and the dating found on the original manuscripts of Joseph Smith's translation of the Bible. This gives a certain historical importance as well as textual confirmation to these original manuscripts, and greatly facilitates our day-to-day reconstruction of those early events in Church history. This is illustrated in the accompanying chart, "Time Sequence of the New Translation."

5. In early editions of the Pearl of Great Price, the dates given at the beginning of each chapter in the book of Moses were partially

Time Sequence of the New Translation[1]

SCRIPTURE REFERENCE[2]	*DATE*	*PLACE*	*SCRIBE*	*MANUSCRIPT REFERENCE*
Visions of Moses (follows the preface in JST; Moses 1; RD&C 22)	June 1830	Harmony, Pa.	Oliver Cowdery	OT 2, p. 1 to p. 3, line 14
Genesis 1:1-5:28; (Moses 2:1-5:43a)	Between June and October 1830	Harmony, Pa., and Fayette, N.Y.	Oliver Cowdery	OT 2, p. 3, line 15, to p. 10, line 5
Genesis 5:29-5:37 (Moses 5:43b-5:51)	October 21, 1830	Fayette, N.Y.	John Whitmer	OT 2, p. 10, line 6, to p. 10, line 23
Genesis 5:38-6:16 (Moses 5:52-6:18)	November 30, 1830	Fayette, N.Y.	John Whitmer	OT 2, p. 10, line 24, to p. 11, line 39
Genesis 6:17-7:2a (Moses 6:19-7:2)	December 1, 1830	Fayette, N.Y.	John Whitmer	OT 2, p. 11, line 40, to p. 15, line 16
Genesis 7:2b-7:78b (Moses 7:2b-7:69; RD&C 36)	Between December 10 and 31, 1830	Fayette, N.Y.	Sidney Rigdon	OT 2, p. 15, line 17, to p. 19, line 34
Genesis 7:78b-19:35 (Moses 8:1-8:30)	Between February 1 and March 8, 1831	Kirtland, Ohio	Sidney Rigdon	OT 2, p. 19, line 35, to p. 49, line 5
Matthew 1:1-9:2	Between March 8 and April 7, 1831	Kirtland, Ohio	Sidney Rigdon	NT 1, p. 1, to p. 21, line 2
Genesis 19:36-24:42a	Between March 8 and April 5, 1831	Kirtland, Ohio	Sidney Rigdon	OT 2, p. 49, line 6, to p. 61, line 5
Matthew 9:2-26:71a	Between April 7 and June 19, 1831	Kirtland, Ohio	Sidney Rigdon	NT 1, p. 21, line 3, to p. 63, line 12
Matthew 26:71a-Mark 8:44	Between September 12 and early November 1831	Hiram, Ohio	John Whitmer	NT 2, folio 2, p. 4, line 16, to folio 2, p. 24, line 22
Mark 9:1-John 5:29	Between November 1831 and February 16, 1832	Hiram, Ohio	Sidney Rigdon	NT 2, folio 2, p. 24, line 23 to folio 4, p. 114, line 16
John 5:30-Revelation 22	Between February 16, 1832, and February 2, 1833	Hiram and Kirtland, Ohio	Sidney Rigdon and small amounts by others	NT 2, folio 4, p. 114, line 17, to p. 154
Genesis 24:42a-Malachi 4:6	Between February 2 and July 2, 1833	Kirtland, Ohio	Sidney Rigdon	OT 3, p. 59, line 2, to p. 119

1. This chart shows the time of original translation. Much of the text was revised afterward.
2. Biblical references are according to the printed JST.

This chart is taken from Robert J. Matthews, *"A Plainer Translation": Joseph Smith's Translation of the Bible, A History and Commentary*, p. 96.

incorrect. From 1920 until 1981, Moses 1 was properly dated June 1830; but chapters 2 through 8 of Moses were all dated December 1830. As explained earlier in this chapter, the material comprising Moses 2 through 6 was received actually during June to December 1830; the material in Moses 7, in December 1830; and the information now known as Moses 8, in February 1831. These dates were all corrected in the 1981 edition of the Pearl of Great Price. This may seem a small matter to some, but it is historically interesting and very important for a correct understanding of the content. Access to the original manuscript has given us this information.

6. The great doctrinal contributions of the book of Moses concerning Adam, Cain, Satan, Enoch, and Noah are of inestimable value to Church members. This material, especially that pertaining to Enoch, constitutes some of the most significant evidence of Joseph Smith's divine calling as a prophet and seer, and should be recognized for what it is—a part of his translation of the Bible. I emphasize the significance of the Enoch material because today apocryphal and archaeological evidences tend to corroborate what Joseph Smith gave us about Enoch. These evidences were not available in Joseph Smith's day.

How the Moses Material Became Part of the Pearl of Great Price

The initial draft of the translation of the early chapters of Genesis was written from June 1830 to March 1831. This is known as Old Testament manuscript #2 and extends to Genesis 24:42.[3] Beginning in 1831 the Prophet went over this material again, making additional revisions, and produced another manuscript separate and apart from the first. This later manuscript is now identified as Old Testament manuscript #3. It repeats the material of Old Testament #2 with additional revision but also extends to the end of the Old Testament. Subsequently the Prophet went over the same material (Old Testament #3) yet again, making many additional revisions by writing in the margins and between the lines, and also by pinning on scraps of paper containing notes and revisions. This means that these early chapters of Genesis were repeatedly revised and added to by the Prophet Joseph Smith.

Portions of the Genesis translation were printed in early Church publications, such as the *Evening and Morning Star* (1832–33) in Independence, Missouri, the *Lectures on Faith* (1835), and the *Times and Seasons* (1843) in Nauvoo. These excerpts were all taken from the early draft, containing the preliminary revision (Old Testament #2), and thus the early periodicals do not reflect the full revision and translation eventually effected by the Prophet. When Joseph Smith was killed in 1844, the Bible translation manuscripts were retained by his widow, Emma Smith, and were not made available to the LDS church. Thus the Church came to Utah without the new translation of the Bible.

In 1845 John Bernhisel made a partial copy of the original manuscripts, but as we will show later, his copy did not become a source for any of the materials in any edition of the Pearl of Great Price. In 1851 Elder Franklin D. Richards, president of the British mission, published certain excerpts of Joseph Smith's Bible translation, along with some other items, in a pamphlet which he titled the *Pearl of Great Price*. This was in Liverpool, England. Since President Richards did not have access to the original JST manuscripts, the Moses material he included consisted of excerpts from such sources as the *Evening and Morning Star* and the *Times and Seasons*. It appears that he also had access to a handwritten copy of some portions of the new Bible translation that had not been printed in the Church periodicals. By use of these sources, then, he was able to include the Moses material from the Prophet's translation of the Bible in this first edition of the Pearl of Great Price. He did not give this material a unifying title; he did not call it the book of Moses. It was printed only as excerpts—quite disjointed, separate, and incomplete. As noted earlier, these excerpts represented the text of the early draft, not the final, more complete revision. For example, consider the different rendering of Moses 1:39 in the two drafts:

OT #2	**OT #3**
this is my work to my glory to the immortality and eternal life of man	this is my work *and* my glory to *bring to pass* the immortality and eternal life of man

The 1851 Pearl of Great Price follows the first draft; current publications follow the later revision.

The book of Moses seems to end rather abruptly, and many have wondered why President Richards didn't include more, especially to round out the story of Noah and the Flood. The answer is simple: He published all that he had.

As mentioned previously, after Joseph Smith's death his widow retained the manuscripts of the new Bible translation until 1866, when she gave them to the RLDS church. Subsequently, in 1867 the RLDS church published its first edition of Joseph Smith's

Sources for the Book of Moses

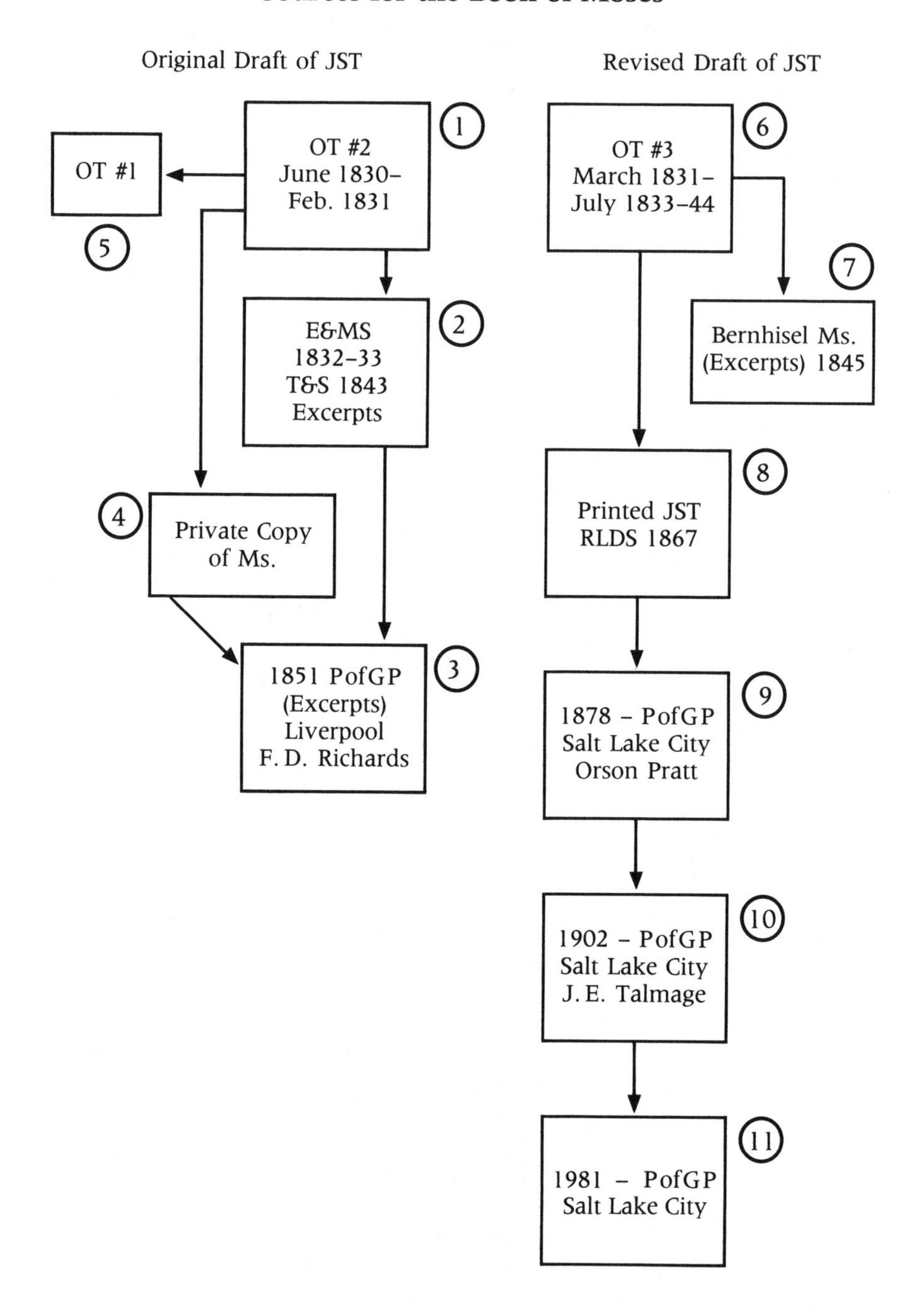

Explanation of Chart, "Sources for the Book of Moses"

1. The original draft of the Old Testament portion of the JST now contained in the book of Moses was made by Joseph Smith and his scribes from June 1830 until February 1831. It is identified as Old Testament #2. (See item 5 below and also note 3 at end of chapter for the identification of Old Testament #1.)
2. Excerpts of this material were published in the *Evening and Morning Star* from August 1832 to April 1833, and in the *Times and Seasons*, January 1843.
3. In 1851 the excerpts of the JST in the *Evening and Morning Star* and *Times and Seasons* were used by Elder Franklin D. Richards in publishing the Moses material in the first edition of the Pearl of Great Price.
4. Private copies of parts of the JST were made by early brethren. Elder Franklin D. Richards evidently had a personal manuscript of at least part of the early Genesis materials, which he used to supplement the materials from the *Evening and Morning Star* and the *Times and Seasons* in publishing the Moses material in the 1851 Pearl of Great Price. Even so, the 1851 Pearl of Great Price contained only about three-fourths of the present content of the book of Moses.
5. The manuscript which is here identified as Old Testament #1 is a lateral copy of Old Testament #2. It did not precede #2 but is a side copy consisting of the first seven chapters. It was made by John Whitmer, probably just before his departure from New York to Ohio in late December 1830. It has no direct connection with the book of Moses material. It is included here only to show its origin and existence. Actually it has been mislabeled and should not carry a manuscript number at all, since it is not a true manuscript in the genealogical line. But since it has been labeled Old Testament #1 by the RLDS historians, it is included here for clarity and to show why the *earliest* manuscript is incorrectly labeled Old Testament #2. (See note 3 at end of chapter.)

The editions of the Pearl of Great Price used from 1878 to the present are from a different line of manuscripts than the first edition and contain many passages that differ from the 1851 edition.

6. The final draft of the JST of the Old Testament is currently numbered Old Testament #3 and contains many revisions over the earlier Old Testament #2. This manuscript represents Joseph Smith's lattermost revisions of Genesis. The Prophet continued to labor with this manuscript of the translation until his death in 1844.
7. The Bernhisel manuscript does not represent the same text as the 1851 Pearl of Great Price because the former has the later revisions of Old Testament #3. Neither was the Bernhisel manuscript the source for the Moses material in any later edition of the Pearl of Great Price, for it does not have the Enoch material of Moses 7, nor the material of Matthew 24, and it contains only excerpts from the original JST manuscript.
8. The printed JST of 1867 published by the RLDS church represents the lattermost revisions by Joseph Smith and a few interesting modifications by the RLDS publishing committee. These modifications also appear in the 1878 LDS edition of the Pearl of Great Price, as prepared by Elder Orson Pratt.
9. In 1878 Elder Orson Pratt revised the Pearl of Great Price in Salt Lake City. He used the 1867 RLDS printed JST as the source for an updating and enlargement of the Moses material. This edition of the Pearl of Great Price became a standard work in 1880.
10. In 1902 another revised edition of the Pearl of Great Price was published in Salt Lake City. It was the work of Elder James E. Talmage, who was under the direction of the First Presidency. Although some parts of the Pearl of Great Price were greatly altered from earlier editions, it retained practically the same text of Moses as the 1878 edition. Chapters, verses, and cross-references were supplied. A later 1921 edition contained a change in format but not in text.
11. In 1981 an updated edition of the Pearl of Great Price was published by The Church of Jesus Christ of Latter-day Saints. It contains corrected dates for the Moses chapters and a few very minor changes in the Moses text. Access to the original JST manuscript made the correct dating possible. Chapter headings were also added, as well as a clear statement that the book of Moses is an excerpt from the JST. This last point is also affirmed in the preface to the 1981 edition.

Bible translation, using the manuscript that contained the Prophet's final and more complete revisions. Thus, this 1867 RLDS publication of the JST represented a better and more complete text than did the corresponding material in the 1851 Pearl of Great Price published by President Richards. The accompanying chart, "Sources for the Book of Moses," illustrates the textual genealogy of various items related to the JST and the book of Moses.

In 1878 Elder Orson Pratt, a member of the Council of the Twelve and Church historian, made a revision of the Pearl of Great Price. For the Moses material he simply extracted the corresponding chapters from the printed JST of 1867, as published by the RLDS church. This not only gave the 1878 Pearl of Great Price a text differing in some places from the 1851 edition, but also supplied many passages that were lacking in the first edition. Also, Elder Pratt was the first to label the material as the Visions of Moses (chapter 1) and the Writings of Moses (chapters 2–8).

This 1878 edition became the basis for another edition, prepared by Elder James E. Talmage under the direction of the First Presidency and published in 1902. Elder Talmage divided the material into chapters and verses and added cross-references. It was also Elder Talmage who finally gave this material its present title, "Book of Moses." With the exception of some minor alterations, the 1902 edition kept the same text as that of the 1878 edition.

Finally, the 1981 edition of the Pearl of Great Price contains, among other things, corrected dates for the Moses chapters and some minor textual changes.

Thus our present book of Moses represents the text of the early chapters of Genesis in Joseph Smith's translation of the Bible as published by the RLDS church in 1867, borrowed by Elder Orson Pratt in 1878, and retained in our present edition of the Pearl of Great Price.

Some may think it strange that Elder Orson Pratt would use the Moses material from the 1867 RLDS printing of the JST. However, that Elder Pratt did so can be confirmed by examining all the documents involved—namely, the original JST manuscripts, the 1867 RLDS publication of the JST, and the 1878 Pearl of Great Price. Such an examination shows that the RLDS publishing committee made some interesting minor modifications when printing the 1867 edition of the JST, and these modifications all appear in the 1878 Pearl of Great Price prepared by Elder Pratt. Nearly all of these are still found in our present text of the book of Moses. Following are a few samples of the modifications made by the RLDS publishing committee that have been carried over into our current book of Moses through the 1878 Pearl of Great Price.

Moses 7:29

OT #2	**OT #3**	**1867 RLDS edition of the JST**
And Enoch said unto the heavens how is it that thou canst weep	And Enoch said unto the heavens how is it that thou canst weep	And Enoch said unto the *Lord*, How is it that thou canst weep

In the above example, the original JST manuscripts use the word *heavens*. The RLDS publication committee substituted it with the word *Lord*. This has been carried over into our current book of Moses through the 1878 Pearl of Great Price.

Moses 1:21

OT #2	**OT #3**	**1867 RLDS edition of the JST**
And Moses receiving strength called upon God saying In the name of Jesus Christ depart hence Satan	And Moses receiv*ed* strength *and* called upon God in the name of *his Son*, saying *to* Satan depart hence	And Moses received strength and called upon God in the name of *the Only Begotten*, saying to Satan, Depart hence

The 1867 RLDS edition of the JST uses the term *Only Begotten* instead of *Son*, a change which has been carried over into our current book of Moses.

Moses 7:41

OT #2	**OT #3**	**1867 RLDS edition of the JST**
Enoch . . . wept and stretched forth his arms wide as eternity OT #2 was later revised by Joseph Smith to read: "Enoch . . . wept and stretched forth his arms *and his heart swelled* wide as eternity	Enoch . . . wept and stretched forth his arms *and he beheld* eternity	Enoch . . . wept and stretched forth his arms *and his heart swelled* wide as eternity

Note that Joseph Smith revised the above passage twice. However, in its 1867 edition of the JST, the RLDS church used the first revision instead of the later one and thus did not use the words *he beheld eternity*. Our present book of Moses follows the RLDS printing.[4]

It was the 1878 edition of the Pearl of Great Price, as edited and arranged by Elder Orson Pratt, that was canonized as a standard work of the Church in 1880. This was done by the voice of the members at general conference in Salt Lake City.

A View of Revelation and Translation

As noted earlier in this chapter, not all of the textual revisions made by Joseph Smith in his Bible translation were made at one time; later manuscripts of the new translation contain more revisions than do the earlier ones. This leads to the conclusion that the revisions were revealed to the mind of the Prophet somewhat gradually, not all at once in complete form. Thus we can gain an insight into what Joseph Smith meant by the term *translation* and what process was involved in his translating the Bible. Apparently, when the Prophet translated the Bible he was not limited to what was found on the working page in front of him, whether that page was a sheet from the King James Version or a handwritten draft of his own early revision. It seems that the text was a starting point but that the spirit of revelation was always an additional source of information. In the case of the Bible translation, the initial starting point was the King James Version; this source suggested certain ideas, but apparently the Spirit suggested many enlargements, backgrounds, and additional concepts not found on the page.

Thus the term *translation*, when used in reference to Joseph Smith's translation of the Bible, has a broader meaning than it normally does when one thinks of translating languages. To a prophet, a revelation is a more vital and dependable source than a written text. This progressive, open-ended revelatory process that apparently was used in translating the Bible may give us a most instructive clue toward understanding Joseph Smith's "translation" of the Egyptian papyri from whence came the book of Abraham. That is, this latter work may not have been a literal translation at all, and the book of Abraham may go far beyond what was actually written on the papyri.

Some Doctrinal Contributions of the Book of Moses

The book of Moses contributes much to our understanding of the gospel of Jesus Christ. Paramount among these contributions are the following:

1. The gospel of Jesus Christ, including baptism and other ordinances, was had from the beginning. The early patriarchs, beginning with Adam, worshipped Jesus and taught his gospel to their children and to the rest of mankind. (See Moses 6:22–23, 48–68.) This fact is almost entirely lacking in all other translations of the Bible available today.

2. The Holy Ghost was operative among men from the beginning. Some persons have thought that the declaration in the New Testament that the Holy Ghost had not yet come (see John 7:39) means that the Holy Ghost had never been enjoyed by mankind on this earth until the day of Pentecost, as recorded in Acts, chapter 2. However, the book of Moses makes it very clear that the Holy Ghost was operative among people who had the gospel from the very beginning of man on this earth (see Moses 6:52–68; 8:23–24). What, then, is the meaning of the statement in John 7:39 that the Holy Ghost had not yet come? Simply that the gift of the Holy Ghost had not yet been manifest in the New Testament dispensation.

3. There was a symbolic purpose to animal sacrifice. The symbolic nature of animal sacrifice is portrayed clearly in the book of Moses, wherein it is specified that the sacrifice had to be a firstling of the flock and that such a sacrifice was a similitude of the atoning sacrifice of Jesus Christ. All these things were revealed to Adam (see Moses 5:4–9), and *he* was the first man on this earth to offer animal sacrifice in the manner and for the purpose described above. Although blood sacrifices are repeatedly spoken of in the Old Testament, this record gives no explanation as to their specific purpose; nor is there anything in the Old Testament about Adam's having offered sacrifices. The book of Moses offers great clarity and explanatory information on this important subject.

4. Moses 1 has special doctrinal significance, and I will emphasize only a few very significant aspects of it. The events recorded in this chapter were originally experienced by Moses after the time of the burning bush but before he had parted the waters of the Red Sea and before he had written the book of Genesis (Moses 1:17, 25–26, 40–41).

Most students of the Bible recognize that the book of Genesis is a sort of introduction or preface to the Old Testament. *Genesis* means "the beginning," and in the book of Genesis we have an account of several beginnings. For instance, we find an account of the beginning or the creation of the physical earth, the beginning of man and animals on the earth, the beginning of sin upon the earth, the beginning of races and nations of men, the beginning of a covenant people, and the beginning of the house of Israel. All of these beginnings are introduced in the book of Genesis in order to establish a foundation and perspective for the remainder of the Old Testament.

In a similar manner, we can think of the first chapter of Moses as an introduction or preface to the book of Genesis. The experiences of Moses recorded in this chapter occurred prior to his writing of Genesis and seem to have been part of his preparation for writing Genesis. We read in this chapter that Moses saw that God had created worlds without number, "and there were inhabitants on the face thereof" (Moses 1:29). Furthermore, Moses was told that these creations were accomplished by the deliberate action of the Almighty (Moses 1:33). After Moses had viewed with great precision the lands and the inhabitants of this and other earths, he was greatly moved—almost overwhelmed. Impressed with the magnitude of it all, and with a somewhat philosophical turn of mind, Moses asked the Lord two searching questions: "Why did you do it?" and "How did you do it?"

In our current Pearl of Great Price, the exact quotation reads as follows: "Moses called upon God, saying: Tell me, I pray thee, why these things are so, and by what thou madest them?" (Moses 1:30.) Those are two of the most fundamental questions of existence, and we must be impressed with the depth of Moses' perception and presence of mind to think to ask such things. In answer to Moses' first question as to the *why* of things, the Lord replied that he had made all these things because "this is my work and my glory—to bring to pass the immortality and eternal life of man" (Moses 1:39). In other words, building worlds and populating them with people is the kind of work that God does. And why does he do it? For the salvation and exaltation of his children.

In answer to the second question as to the *how* of things, Moses was informed that all things were done by the power of the Only Begotten. "But," said the Lord to Moses, "only an account of this earth, and the inhabitants thereof, give I unto you." (Moses 1:32–33, 35.) In the subsequent explanation Moses was told of the six creative periods of the formation of the earth. Thus, the information contained in the early chapters of Genesis actually seems to have been given to Moses in answer to these two specific questions regarding why and how. Answers are always more meaningful to us if we know what the questions are.

These two basic questions asked of the Lord by Moses are not to be found today in our current text of Genesis, but fortunately they have been made available to us through the visions of Moses as revealed to Joseph Smith. We cannot overestimate the value of Moses 1 as an introduction to the book of Genesis. Nor should we forget that it was received by Joseph Smith as part of his translation of the Bible. Indeed, just as the visions recorded in chapter 1 of Moses were given to that prophet in preparation for his writing of Genesis, so it seems that in the last days an account of those same visions was revealed to the Prophet Joseph Smith in preparation for his translation and revision of Genesis.

Another striking topic in Moses 1 is the interesting record of a face-to-face encounter that Moses had with Satan (vv. 12–22). Satan challenged Moses; he advanced, ranted upon the ground, and cried with a loud voice. The record states that Moses feared and saw the bitterness of hell. Moses was able to overcome Satan only by the strength he received through his faith in Jesus Christ. This is a dramatic episode that is entirely lost to the Bible text.

Conclusion

In Moses 1:41 we read the following words of the Lord: "And in a day when the children of men shall esteem my words as naught and take many of them from the book which thou [Moses] shalt write, behold, I will raise up another like unto thee; and they shall be had again among the children of men—among as many as shall believe." We are fortunate that the Lord has given to us, to "as many as . . . believe," a knowledge of these things that happened so long ago.

The book of Moses, a revealed record of great interest and worth to us, bears a solemn witness that Joseph Smith was indeed a prophet of God and illustrates that the translation of the Bible is one of the greatest tangible evidences of that latter-day prophet's divine calling.

Notes

1. *History of the Church* 1:145.

2. For a detailed description and history of the manuscripts, see Robert J. Matthews, *"A Plainer Translation": Joseph Smith's Trans-*

lation of the Bible, A History and Commentary (Provo, Utah: Brigham Young University Press, 1975). Two LDS researchers and writers deserve special mention for their preliminary, pioneer work relative to the origin of the book of Moses. One of these, James R. Clark, published some interesting and informative information about the early history and printings of the book of Moses in his book, *The Story of the Pearl of Great Price* (Salt Lake City: Bookcraft, 1955). The other, James R. Harris, wrote a master's thesis (Brigham Young University, 1958) on the text of the book of Moses. He correctly postulated the existence of multiple copies of the early manuscripts made at various stages of the translation. Unfortunately neither of these brethren had access to the original manuscripts.

3. The original Old Testament manuscripts, now in the possession of the RLDS church, were not numbered by the Prophet or his scribes but have been labeled #s 1, 2, and 3 by RLDS scholars. One would naturally expect the earliest draft to be numbered Old Testament #1. However, through a mistake in identity, the earliest manuscript has since been labeled Old Testament #2. Consequently, for purposes of discussion in this chapter, the earliest draft of the Old Testament revision is identified by the label given it by the RLDS historians. The document labeled Old Testament #1 appears to be simply a private copy made by John Whitmer of part of Old Testament #2 and as such is not crucial to our present discussion.

4. For an extensive discussion of the 1866–67 RLDS publication committee and the modifications made in the 1867 edition of the JST, see chapter 7 in Matthews, "*A Plainer Translation.*"

Chapter 9

MAJOR DOCTRINAL CONTRIBUTIONS OF THE JOSEPH SMITH TRANSLATION

President Brigham Young, speaking of his high regard for the Prophet Joseph Smith, said: "Would he not take the Scriptures and make them so plain and simple that everybody could understand?"[1] President Young was never too busy to stop whatever he was doing and listen to the Prophet Joseph. He considered the Prophet's words and opinions to be of unequaled worth. Said he on various occasions: "An angel never watched him closer than I did, and that is what has given me the knowledge I have today. I treasure it up, and ask the Father, in the name of Jesus, to help my memory when information is wanted."[2] In 1868 President Young declared: "I never did let an opportunity pass of getting with the Prophet Joseph and of hearing him speak in public or private, so that I might draw understanding from the fountain from which he spoke."[3] And in 1877: "From the first time I saw the Prophet Joseph I never lost a word that came from him concerning the kingdom. And this is the key of knowledge that I have today, that I did hearken to the words of Joseph, and treasured them up in my heart, laid them away, asking my Father in the name of his Son Jesus to bring them to my mind when needed. . . . I was anxious to learn from Joseph and the spirit of God."[4]

The reason why President Young was so willing to listen was that he knew Joseph Smith offered something no one else could. As Church members we feel the same way about the Prophet, and we honor his blessed name and memory. We know what Joseph Smith can tell us about the Bible is very significant. Hence it is my conviction that Joseph Smith's translation of the Bible is a unique production, divinely inspired, worthy of study, and of importance to every soul who wants to understand the gospel of Jesus Christ.

Advantages of the Joseph Smith Translation

The reader of the Joseph Smith Translation of the Bible (JST) will be thrice blessed. First, he will gain an insight into the Prophet's understanding of various scriptures; second, he will learn many things about the gospel not found in other sources; and third, he will obtain a clue as to the content and meaning of the Old and the New Testaments in their original form.

As a person takes in his hands a printed copy of the JST, he has to wonder what it is, how it came to be, and what it has to offer that other Bibles do not have. It has been my experience that while other editions of the Bible contain much of the historical part of the ancient record, they are often flat or weak on doctrinal matters. My intention in this chapter is to highlight some of the doctrinal contributions of the JST and to demonstrate how this Bible translation not only often adds new historical information and perspectives, but also tells *why* certain things are so; that is, the JST gives the doctrinal substance or foundation of biblical events and teachings.

History of the Biblical Text

First, let us consider the Book of Mormon explanation about the history of the Bible text:

> And I, Nephi, beheld that the Gentiles that had gone out of captivity were delivered by the power of God out of the hands of all other nations. [These were the early colonists of America.]
>
> And it came to pass that I, Nephi, beheld that they did prosper in the land; and I beheld a *book*, and it was carried forth among them.
>
> And the angel said unto me: *Knowest thou the meaning of the book?*
>
> And I said unto him: I know not.
>
> And he said: Behold it proceedeth out of the mouth of a Jew. And I, Nephi, beheld it; and he said unto me: *The book that thou beholdest is a record of the Jews*, which contains the covenants of the Lord, which he hath made unto the house of Israel; and it also containeth many of the prophecies of the holy prophets; and it is a record like unto the engravings which are upon the plates of brass, save there are not so

many; nevertheless, they contain the covenants of the Lord, which he hath made unto the house of Israel; wherefore, they are of great worth unto the Gentiles.

And the angel of the Lord said unto me: Thou hast beheld that the book proceeded forth from the mouth of a Jew; and when it proceeded forth from the mouth of a Jew it contained the fulness of the gospel of the Lord, of whom the twelve apostles bear record; and they bear record according to the truth which is in the Lamb of God.

Wherefore, these things go forth from the Jews in purity unto the Gentiles, according to the truth which is in God.

And after they go forth by the hand of the twelve apostles of the Lamb, from the Jews unto the Gentiles, thou seest the formation of that great and abominable church, which is most abominable above all other churches; for behold, they have taken away from the gospel of the Lamb many parts which are plain and most precious; and also many covenants of the Lord have they taken away.

And all this have they done that they might pervert the right ways of the Lord, that they might blind the eyes and harden the hearts of the children of men.

Wherefore, thou seest that after the book hath gone forth through the hands of the great and abominable church, that there are many plain and precious things taken away from the book, which is the book of the Lamb of God.

And after these plain and precious things were taken away it goeth forth unto all the nations of the Gentiles; and after it goeth forth unto all the nations of the Gentiles, yea, even across the many waters which thou hast seen with the Gentiles which have gone forth out of captivity, thou seest—because of the many plain and precious things which have been taken *out of the book*, which were plain unto the understanding of the children of men, according to the plainness which is in the Lamb of God—because of these things which are taken away out of the gospel of the Lamb, an exceedingly great many do stumble, yea, insomuch that Satan hath great power over them. . . .

. . . The Lord God [will not] suffer that the Gentiles shall forever remain in that awful state of blindness, which thou beholdest they are in, because of the plain and most precious parts of the gospel of the Lamb which have been kept back by that abominable church, whose formation thou hast seen. . . .

> And it came to pass that I beheld the remnant of the seed of my brethren, *and also the book of the Lamb of God, which had proceeded forth from the mouth of the Jew*, that it came forth from the Gentiles unto the remnant of the seed of my brethren.
>
> And after it had come forth unto them I beheld *other books*, which came forth by the power of the Lamb, from the Gentiles unto them, unto the convincing of the Gentiles and the remnant of the seed of my brethren, and also the Jews who were scattered upon all the face of the earth, that the records of the prophets and of the twelve apostles of the Lamb are true.
>
> And the angel spake unto me, saying: These *last records*, which thou hast seen among the Gentiles, *shall establish the truth of the first, which are of the twelve apostles of the Lamb*, and shall make known the plain and precious things which have been taken away from them; and shall make known to all kindreds, tongues, and people, that the Lamb of God is the Son of the Eternal Father, and the Savior of the world; and that all men must come unto him, or they cannot be saved. (1 Nephi 13:19–29, 32, 38–40, italics added.)

To the above we could add the words of the Lord to Moses: "And now, Moses, my son, I will speak unto thee concerning this earth upon which thou standest; and thou shalt write the things which I shall speak. And in a day when the children of men shall esteem my words as naught and take many of them from the book which thou shalt write, behold, I will raise up another like unto thee; and they shall be had again among the children of men—among as many as shall believe." (Moses 1:40–41.)

As Latter-day Saints we reverence the Bible. Note that the angel asked Nephi if he knew the meaning of the book. When he said he did not, the angel explained that it was a record of the Jews—the Jewish prophets and the Twelve Apostles (Old and New Testaments)—that it contained the covenants of the Lord to the house of Israel, and that it was of great worth to both Israel and the Gentiles. This Jewish record in its original purity "contained the fulness of the gospel of the Lord, of whom the twelve apostles bear record." Hence we revere the Bible as a sacred record, not only for its history but also for its witness of Jesus Christ; it contains many parts of his gospel and the plan of salvation. But we also recognize, as the angel pointed out to Nephi, that the Bible has not come to us in its original completeness, for some things have been lost from it. We should take special note, however, that the scriptures speak of not only a loss but also a return, a restoration of the lost material so vital to salvation.

The doctrinal contributions of the JST are many, but we will cover only a few basic and representative examples. Our doing so might be compared to our standing on a mountain peak on a clear day—where we can see almost forever—and the grand view before us kindles in us an intense desire to explore not only all of the other peaks but also the valleys. Each of us, with his own scriptures, will have to explore and discover for himself the many great spiritual insights offered in the JST. When we make our own discoveries we are thrilled, our interest grows, and we are fed spiritually.

The Gospel Taught to Adam

We learn from the JST that the gospel, with its ordinances and the holy priesthood, was taught to Adam and was had among all the early patriarchs from Adam to Abraham. This concept is only hinted at in the King James Version and other translations, and not being taught convincingly or forthrightly stated as the crux of the message, it is at best something that an alert student of the Bible might arrive at only circumstantially or by inference. By contrast, in the JST, the central message is that Adam personally asked the Lord why repentance and baptism in water were necessary. The record goes on to show that, subsequently, Adam himself was baptized in water and received the Holy Ghost. This is an unmistakable message, and the JST is more clear upon this subject than anything that can be found in any other source. In the following excerpt from the Prophet's translation, Enoch explains Adam's experience:

> But God hath made known unto our fathers, that all men must repent.
>
> And he called upon our father Adam, by his own voice, saying, I am God; I made the world, and men before they were in the flesh.
>
> And he also said unto him, If thou wilt, turn unto me and hearken unto my voice, and believe, and repent of all thy transgressions, and be baptized, even in water, in the name of mine Only Begotten Son, who is full of grace and truth, which is Jesus Christ, the only name which shall be given under heaven, whereby salvation shall come unto the children of men; and ye shall receive the gift of the Holy

Ghost, asking all things in his name, and whatsoever ye shall ask it shall be given you.

And our father Adam spake unto the Lord, and said, *Why is it that men must repent, and be baptized in water?*

And the Lord said unto Adam, Behold, I have forgiven thee thy *transgression* in the garden of Eden.

Hence came the saying abroad, among the people, that the Son of God hath atoned for original guilt, wherein the sins of the parents cannot be answered upon the heads of the children, for they are whole from the foundation of the world. . . .

And I have given unto you another law and commandment; wherefore teach it unto your children, that all men, everywhere, must repent, or they can in no wise inherit the kingdom of God.

For no unclean thing can dwell there, or dwell in his presence; for, in the language of Adam, Man of Holiness is his name; and the name of his Only Begotten is the Son of Man, even Jesus Christ, a righteous judge, who shall come in the meridian of time.

Therefore I give unto you a commandment, to teach these things freely unto your children, saying, that by reason of transgression cometh the fall, which fall bringeth death; and inasmuch as ye were born into the world by water and blood, and the spirit, which I have made, and so become of dust a living soul;

Even so ye must be born again, into the kingdom of heaven, of water, and of the Spirit, and be cleansed by blood, even the blood of mine Only Begotten; that ye may be sanctified from all sin; and enjoy the words of eternal life in this world, and eternal life in the world to come; even immortal glory.

For, by the water ye keep the commandment; by the Spirit ye are justified; and by the blood ye are sanctified. . . .

And now, behold, I say unto you, This is the plan of salvation unto all men, through the blood of mine Only Begotten, who shall come in the meridian of time. . . .

And it came to pass, when the Lord had spoken with Adam our father, that Adam cried unto the Lord, and he was caught away by the Spirit of the Lord, and was carried down into the water, and was laid under the water, and was brought forth out of the water; and thus he was baptized.

> And the Spirit of God descended upon him, and thus he was born of the Spirit, and became quickened in the inner man.
>
> And he heard a voice out of heaven, saying, Thou art baptized with fire and with the Holy Ghost; this is the record of the Father and the Son, from henceforth and for ever;
>
> And thou art after the order of him who was without beginning of days or end of years, from all eternity to all eternity.
>
> Behold, thou art one in me, a son of God; and thus may all become my sons. Amen. (JST, Genesis 6:51–56, 59–63, 65, 67–71, italics added.)

We recognize the above passage as part of the book of Moses in the Pearl of Great Price (see Moses 6:50–54, 56–60, 62, 64–68). That book, of course, is an extract from Genesis in the JST. The material on Adam found in the book of Moses was revealed to Joseph Smith in 1830 and therefore predates by years the publication called the Pearl of Great Price.

The Book of Mormon and the Doctrine and Covenants inform us that all the prophets from the beginning knew of Christ (see Jacob 4:4; 7:11; D&C 20:25–28), but the unique contribution of the JST is that it actually presents the details and shows the gospel at work in the Old Testament setting. The passage from JST Genesis quoted above is part of a discourse by Enoch, seven generations after Adam, which shows that this clear exposition of the Fall, the Atonement, the mission of the Savior, and the very gospel of Jesus Christ was had among the early patriarchs not only through word of mouth but also through the written word.

Continuity in the Old Testament

As an extension and corollary to the antiquity of the gospel and its presence from the very beginning of this earth, we learn from the JST that all of the ancient dispensations were connected and associated through the gospel and its covenants; there is continuity and order in the kingdom of God. That the entire plan of salvation was revealed from the very beginning of man on earth is not a difficult concept to accept, because the plan is older than the earth. In fact, the earth was created in accordance with the provisions of the plan of salvation.

If one had only the Bible translations known throughout the world, one would not be aware that the ancient patriarchs had the fulness of the gospel and that there was a continuity in the way the gospel was handed down and communicated from one generation to another. Consider, for example, the concept of gospel covenants. In other Bibles, the first time the word *covenant* appears is in connection with Noah: "But with thee [Noah] will I establish my covenant; and thou shalt come into the ark, thou, and thy sons, and thy wife, and thy sons' wives with thee" (Genesis 6:18). In the King James Version there is no hint of any covenant between God and Adam or any of the patriarchs between Adam and Noah, a space of time covering some fifteen hundred years. And even the covenant that is mentioned in connection with Noah is not spoken of as a gospel or a priesthood covenant. Thus the King James Bible leaves the impression that there was no visible connection between Adam, Enoch, Noah, Melchizedek, and Abraham.

By contrast, the JST speaks of Adam's having had the priesthood and the gospel, and it shows that these were given also to Enoch, and then to Noah, and then to Melchizedek, and then to Abraham—the same covenant, the same priesthood, the same gospel. Here are a few of the relevant passages from the JST:

> And thus the gospel began to be preached from the beginning, being declared by holy angels, sent forth from the presence of God; and by his own voice, and by the gift of the Holy Ghost.
>
> And thus all things were confirmed unto Adam by an holy ordinance; and the gospel preached; and a decree sent forth that it should be in the world until the end thereof; and thus it was. Amen. (JST, Genesis 5:44–45.)

> And then began these men to call upon the name of the Lord; and the Lord blessed them; and a book of remembrance was kept in the which was recorded in the language of Adam, for it was given unto as many as called upon God, to write by the Spirit of inspiration;
>
> And by them their children were taught to read and write, having a language which was pure and undefiled.
>
> Now this same priesthood which was in the beginning, shall be in the end of the world also.
>
> Now this prophecy Adam spake, as he was moved upon by the Holy Ghost. (JST, Genesis 6:5–8.)

Next, in the JST we have the following from Enoch:

> And death hath come upon our fathers; nevertheless, we know them, and cannot deny, and even the first of all we know, even Adam; for a book of remembrance we have written among us, according to the pattern given by the finger of God; and it is given in our own language.
>
> And as Enoch spake forth the words of God, the people trembled and could not stand in his presence.
>
> And he said unto them, Because that Adam fell, we are; and by his fall came death, and we are made partakers of misery and woe. (JST, Genesis 6:47–49.)

Now note the JST rendering of the previously quoted passage concerning Noah: "But with thee will I establish my covenant, even as I have sworn unto thy father, Enoch, that of thy posterity shall come all nations. And thou shalt come into the ark, thou and thy sons, and thy wife, and thy sons' wives with them." (JST, Genesis 8:23–24.) The King James Version mentions a covenant with Noah, but it does not say what the covenant was. In the JST the statement is clarified to show that it was the same covenant that was given to Enoch, which was the same given to Adam, and so forth. The Lord's further instructions to Noah, as recorded in the JST, shed even more light on this subject:

> And God spake unto Noah, and to his sons with him, saying, And I, behold, I will establish my covenant with you, *which I made unto your father Enoch, concerning your seed after you. . . .*
>
> *And I will establish my covenant with you, which I made unto Enoch, concerning the remnants of your posterity. . . .*
>
> And the bow shall be in the cloud; and I will look upon it, that I may remember the everlasting covenant, *which I made unto thy father Enoch; that, when men should keep all my commandments, Zion should again come on the earth*, the city of Enoch which I have caught up unto myself.
>
> And this is mine everlasting covenant, that when thy posterity shall embrace the truth, and look upward, then shall Zion look downward, and all the heavens shall shake with gladness, and the earth shall tremble with joy;
>
> And the general assembly of the church of the firstborn shall come down out of heaven, and possess the earth, and

> shall have place until the end come. *And this is mine everlasting covenant, which I made with thy father Enoch.* (JST, Genesis 9:15, 17, 21–23, italics added.)

The following instruction, as we learn from the JST, was given to Abraham: "And remember the covenant which I make with thee; for it shall be an everlasting covenant; and thou shalt remember the days of Enoch thy father" (JST, Genesis 13:13). Then, regarding Melchizedek, the JST informs us:

> Now Melchizedek was a man of faith, who wrought righteousness; and when a child he feared God, and stopped the mouths of lions, and quenched the violence of fire.
>
> And thus, having been approved of God, he was ordained an high priest after the order of the covenant which God made with Enoch,
>
> It being after the order of the Son of God; which order came, not by man, nor the will of man; neither by father nor mother; neither by beginning of days nor end of years; but of God. (JST, Genesis 14:26–28.)

And later in JST Genesis we read:

> And it came to pass, that Abram fell on his face, and called upon the name of the Lord.
>
> And God talked with him, saying, My people have gone astray from my precepts, and have not kept mine ordinances, which I gave unto their fathers;
>
> And they have not observed mine anointing, and the burial, or baptism wherewith I commanded them;
>
> But have turned from the commandment, and taken unto themselves the washing of children, and the blood of sprinkling;
>
> And have said that the blood of the righteous Abel was shed for sins; and have not known wherein they are accountable before me.
>
> But as for thee, behold, I will make my covenant with thee, and thou shalt be a father of many nations. . . .
>
> And I will establish a covenant of circumcision with thee, and it shall be my covenant between me and thee, and thy seed after thee, in their generations; that thou mayest know forever that children are not accountable before me until they are eight years old.

> And thou shalt observe to keep all my covenants wherein I covenanted with thy fathers; and thou shalt keep the commandments which I have given thee with mine own mouth, and I will be a God unto thee and thy seed after thee. (JST, Genesis 17:3–8, 11–12.)

All of the above passages from the JST are available either in the book of Moses or in the footnotes and the appendix of the 1979 LDS edition of the King James Version. As these passages clearly illustrate, there is a continuity in the Genesis account as given in the JST that is not found in any other Bible. The JST gives an account of the early patriarchs in gospel context and setting, a setting which included the fulness of the gospel, the priesthood, faith in Jesus Christ, and the same covenant. These ancient patriarchs knew of each other and had a common bond, a common faith—a oneness that we never would have suspected or known about or understood without the Joseph Smith Translation of the Bible. This continuity in the Lord's work among the ancients is the same concept taught so clearly in the first and second of the lectures on faith given in the School of the Elders during the Kirtland period, and the JST is no doubt the source for the doctrine in those lectures.

The JST and the Plates of Brass

As shown earlier, 1 Nephi 13 states that many plain and precious things were taken away out of the record of the Jews (the Bible) and that many covenants of the Lord were lost in that process. In the last few passages of the JST quoted above, we see some of what Nephi was referring to, and we can see that the covenant is being restored. The angel told Nephi that the Jewish Bible, before it was altered, was like unto the record on the plates of brass (see 1 Nephi 13:23). We read further in 1 Nephi 13 that the Lord would bring forth "other books" to make known the plain and precious things that were lost from the Bible. Surely the JST is one of those "other books," along with the Book of Mormon, the Doctrine and Covenants, and the Pearl of Great Price. It would follow, therefore, that the JST—restoring, as it does, material lost from the Bible—reads more like the plates of brass than does any other Bible we know about (compare, for example, 2 Nephi 2:17 with JST, Genesis 3:1–5; 2 Nephi 2:22–25 with JST, Genesis 5:11).

Joseph Smith could not have restored these things without the spirit of revelation. He had that spirit. He held the keys of salvation.

Note what the Lord said about the Prophet and his work in an 1830 revelation directed to Sidney Rigdon:

> And I have sent forth the fulness of my gospel by the hand of my servant Joseph; and in weakness have I blessed him;
>
> And I have given unto him the keys of the mystery of those things which have been sealed, even things which were from the foundation of the world, and the things which shall come from this time until the time of my coming, if he abide in me, and if not, another will I plant in his stead.
>
> Wherefore, watch over him that his faith fail not, and it shall be given by the Comforter, the Holy Ghost, that knoweth all things.
>
> And a commandment I give unto thee [Sidney Rigdon] —that thou shalt write for him [Joseph Smith]; and the scriptures shall be given, even as they are in mine own bosom, to the salvation of mine own elect. (D&C 35:17–20.)

Fundamental Doctrines

There are some very basic doctrines that are prominent in the JST that are not presented so clearly in other Bible translations. In some cases the JST material is completely new, as in the early chapters of Genesis that detail the secret oaths of Cain (see JST, Genesis 5) and the ministry of Enoch (see JST, Genesis 6–7). In most instances, however, the JST consists of enlargement or clarification of existing material, as in the case of the New Testament Epistles or the Sermon on the Mount.

Often there is another type of benefit that comes as a result of the JST enlargements and additions. This arises because of the fact that the more we know, the more we are *able* to know. Thus, many of the clarifications in the JST are valuable not only in their own right, but also in that they supply key information that enables us to understand and see new significance in other passages not textually changed in the JST. This is the case with John 8:1–11, which speaks of the Pharisees' bringing before the Savior a woman taken in adultery. The JST rendering of this passage contains no clarifications regarding the Pharisees. But substantial clarification in JST Luke 16:13–22 sets a pattern for the hypocritical life of the Pharisees, a pattern that sheds much light on the Savior's statement: "He that is without sin among you, let him first cast a stone at her" (John 8:7).

The JST has everything any other Bible has; but the JST also supplies additional information about God's nature, man's nature, the origin of Satan, the premortal existence, the Grand Council and the War in Heaven (see JST, Genesis 3:1–5; JST, Revelation 12:6–10), and the gospel's having been taught to Adam and the early patriarchs.

Furthermore, in the JST God does not need to repent (compare Genesis 6:6 with JST, Genesis 8:15; Jonah 3:10 with JST, Jonah 3:10), nor does he harden men's hearts (compare Exodus 7:3, 13 with JST, Exodus 7:3, 13; Isaiah 63:17 with JST, Isaiah 63:17). Little children, we learn in the Prophet's translation, are saved by the atonement of Jesus Christ (JST, Genesis 6:56; JST, Matthew 18:10–11; 19:13).

Little information is given in any Bible about the ministry of Enoch, and there is no mention of his people or of a city called Zion; but in the JST eighteen times more column space is given to Enoch and his preaching than is given in the King James Bible, and the JST says much about his city Zion. This marvelous information about Enoch was revealed to Joseph Smith in November and December 1830 and forms an example and pattern for the building of Zion in our dispensation (see JST, Genesis 6–7). In like manner, little is given of Melchizedek in any other Bible; however, much is given of him in the JST (see JST, Genesis 14:16–40; JST, Hebrews 7:13).

One of the major contributions of the JST is the insight it gives about the personality and ministry of Jesus Christ. In the four Gospels of the JST, Jesus is more animated, more compassionate with sinners, more stern with the perfidious Jewish rulers, and more clearly shown to be the greatest person who has ever lived on earth than he is in any other Bible translation.

On 7 March 1831 the Prophet received a revelation now identified as Doctrine and Covenants 45, a major topic of which is the second coming of the Lord. In this divine communication the promise was given that through the Prophet's translation of the New Testament the Lord would yet reveal to the Prophet (and thus to the Church) much more about the Second Coming: "And now, behold, I say unto you, it shall not be given unto you to know any further concerning this chapter, until the New Testament shall be translated, and in it all these things shall be made known; wherefore I give unto you that ye may now translate it, that ye may be prepared for the things to come. For verily I say unto you, that great things await you." (D&C 45:60–62.) Just what "chapter" is meant we do not know, but given the subject matter of Doctrine and Covenants 45, this passage clearly indicates that the JST contains considerable information relative to the Lord's second advent.

Another major contribution of the JST is its emphasis on the first principles of the gospel. Many of the clarifications and additions in Genesis 5, 6, and 7 and in the four Gospels emphasize the messiahship of Jesus, faith, repentance, baptism in water, and the need all people have for the influence and power of the Holy Ghost. (See the Genesis passages quoted earlier in this chapter; see also JST, John 1; JST, Mark 1:1–6; JST, Matthew 3; JST, Luke 3.)

A Problem of Transmission

Now, why are these concepts and clarifications not in the Bibles the world uses? Were not the ancient biblical writers, Apostles, and prophets able to express themselves more clearly than the present Bible record shows? If the current Hebrew and Greek manuscripts of the Bible are anywhere near being correctly recorded, then we have to conclude that either those ancient writers did not have a clear knowledge of the gospel of Jesus Christ or, if they did have such a knowledge, they did not tell it.

I cannot believe that they did not know it, nor can I believe that they did not tell it or write it. What I do believe is that their writings as found in all known ancient manuscripts have been altered and diluted, so that what presently is regarded as their writing no longer contains many of the "most plain and precious parts of the gospel" that it once did (1 Nephi 13:34).

The major problem, it appears, is not one of translation but of transmission. Today there are able scholars who know well the ancient languages and who have the ability to translate clearly what is on the manuscripts. They do a great service in observing many technical points, updating changes in language, and clarifying different words and passages. But that is not the heart of the problem.

The pivot on which the whole subject turns is the absence of an adequate manuscript. There is no way that a translator using existing biblical manuscripts can get out of them the fulness of the gospel, with plain and extensive statements about the nature of God and about man, the devil, premortal existence, the Second Coming, the resurrection, and so forth. There simply is no way that a translator can make the currently available biblical manuscripts read the same way that the Book of Mormon, the Doctrine and Covenants, and the Pearl of Great Price do concerning these same doctrines.

What is it then? Did the Bible prophets—Moses, Enoch, Abraham, Paul, Matthew, John, and others—not know the gospel as clearly as the Book of Mormon prophets? Or is it that the records of the Bible prophets have not been preserved in complete clarity and accuracy?

If the currently available biblical manuscripts were correct, then, logically we would be forced to conclude that either the ancient biblical writers did not know the gospel in its clarity or, if they knew it, they did not write it. The testimony of the Book of Mormon, however, is that they *did* write about the gospel, but that much of what they wrote was lost through faulty transmission, both wilful and accidental, and that much of it would be restored in the latter days through the "other books" (the Joseph Smith Translation, the Book of Mormon, and the other revelations).

Frequently people ask me if the corrections made by the JST are supported in the Hebrew and Greek manuscripts. An answer to that seems to be that if the JST offered no more than the available biblical manuscripts do or if it were completely supported by them, there would have been no need for a new Bible translation from the Prophet. Of course it is *not* always supported by the manuscripts; present Bible manuscripts simply do not have the luxuriant supply of doctrine that the originals had. It is too late for them to do so. The plain and precious things were lost centuries ago.

This situation reminds me of an experience I have every now and again when I go for a haircut. Often preceding me in the barber's chair is some unappreciative young man who has more hair than three men ought to have. Generally some comment is made about my own contrasting lack of hair, and I say to the barber, "Make me look like him." The barber laughs, and the answer is always the same. He looks at me and says, "It is too late for that." Similarly, it is too late for the existing Hebrew and Greek manuscripts: they cannot provide the light and truth that once were there. That is why there had to be a restoration of the biblical text and those doctrines known anciently.

Joseph Smith a Restorer

Since all the other events, revelations, and restorations of this dispensation are true—the First Vision, the Book of Mormon, the restoration of the Aaronic and Melchizedek priesthoods, the temple endowment, and so forth (the whole package of the Restoration)—it is inevitable that the Prophet would also make a divinely inspired correction and supplemental edition of the ancient Bible. For him *not* to have done so would have been the surprising thing. If Joseph Smith had not corrected and restored the biblical text, his mission would have been left incomplete.

Revelation is progressive, and one revelation builds upon another. For example, as part of his Bible translation the Prophet produced a manuscript correcting certain passages in the book of Revelation. More information about the book of Revelation, given in connection with the Bible translation, can be found in Doctrine and Covenants 77, and still more relevant information can be found in Doctrine and Covenants 88. This reflects a very real relationship between the JST and the Doctrine and Covenants, for much of the doctrine of this dispensation came to Joseph Smith while he was translating the Bible.

The "Apollos Principle"

The need for using latter-day scriptures, including the JST, when interpreting the Bible is illustrated in what I am pleased to call the "Apollos Principle." Apollos was a bright and capable man from Alexandria. He was a believer and was very gifted in speech. The following is recorded of him in the book of Acts:

> And a certain Jew named Apollos, born at Alexandria, an eloquent man, and mighty in the scriptures, came to Ephesus.
>
> This man was instructed in the way of the Lord; and being fervent in the spirit, he spake and taught diligently the things of the Lord, knowing only the baptism of John.
>
> And he began to speak boldly in the synagogue: whom when Aquila and Priscilla had heard, they took him unto them, and expounded unto him the way of God more perfectly. . . .
>
> For he mightily convinced the Jews, and that publickly, shewing by the scriptures that Jesus was Christ. (Acts 18:24–26, 28.)

I will paraphrase the passage so as to illustrate the point:

> And a certain *teacher*, named Apollos, born in *Salt Lake City* [or anywhere], an eloquent man, and mighty in the scriptures, came to *the Church Educational System*.

> This man was instructed in the way of the Lord; and being fervent in the spirit, he spake and taught diligently the things of the Lord, knowing only the *King James Version*.
>
> And he began to speak boldly in the *classrooms and in firesides:* whom when *his supervisors and teacher trainers* had heard, they took him unto them, and expounded unto him the way of God more perfectly, *using the Book of Mormon, the Doctrine and Covenants, the Pearl of Great Price, the JST, and the teachings of Joseph Smith and of the living prophets.*
>
> *And afterwards* he mightily convinced the *students*, and that publickly, shewing by the scriptures that Jesus was Christ.

We see that the Apollos of the book of Acts had many of the valuable tools and skills helpful to be a great teacher. He was fervent, dedicated, eloquent, and had a knowledge of the scriptures. But as long as he was acquainted with only a portion of the scriptures or of the "way of God," he could not employ his great skills to fully benefit the work of the Lord. Similarly, today we need not only eloquence, skill, and dedication; we need the sources, the facts, and the substance of latter-day revelation if we wish to properly teach and interpet the Bible.

As regards the JST, we as members of the Church now have a second chance. The JST was offered in its entirety to the Saints in the early days of the Church. They did not reject it; they just *neglected* it. Therefore, the Church essentially lost it for about a century. We now have it again in the 1979 LDS edition of the Bible. We should be careful to not neglect and lose it again.

Testimony

The JST is a witness for Jesus Christ. It is a witness for the divine calling of Joseph Smith as a prophet and Apostle of Jesus Christ. Many people seem to go about it backwards. They want to test Joseph Smith by the content of the inadequate manuscripts. Actually the restoration of the gospel in this dispensation is as great as any other dispensation and can stand on its own record. Joseph Smith had an independent revelation of his own. The Book of Mormon and the JST are the proper standards by which to measure the accuracy of the ancient Bible. We are not measuring the prophets but the quality of the ancient record that tells about them. I think we should be more like President Brigham Young and not ignore the Prophet's teachings.

I have a testimony that what has been discussed in this chapter is true. Given all that the JST has to offer, our diligent study of it cannot help but yield great spiritual benefits. Studying the scriptures will not always answer all our personal problems, but it will increase our spirituality, and with that increased spirituality we can then see our way more clearly to gain the inspiration from the Lord for our immediate problems. I am grateful for the opportunity to have all the books—all of the standard works—and a testimony of the Spirit.

Notes

1. Brigham Young, *Discourses of Brigham Young*, sel. John A. Widtsoe (Salt Lake City: Deseret Book Co., 1941), p. 459.
2. 8 October 1866 sermon, Brigham Young Papers, Church Archives, The Church of Jesus Christ of Latter-day Saints, Salt Lake City, Utah.
3. Brigham Young, in *Journal of Discourses* 12:269–70.
4. 25 May 1877 discourse, *Deseret News*, 6 June 1877, p. 274.

Chapter 10

JOSEPH SMITH'S EFFORTS TO PUBLISH HIS BIBLE TRANSLATION

Joseph Smith's translation of the Bible (JST) has received increased attention in the Church since it became an important part of the 1979 LDS edition of the King James Version of the Bible, which presents hundreds of JST passages in the footnotes, includes lengthier JST passages in a seventeen-page appendix, and contains an explanatory entry in the dictionary.

Similarly, the 1981 edition of the Doctrine and Covenants contains many references to the JST in the footnotes (see, for example, D&C 9:2; 35:20; 37:1; 45:60; 124:89) and also in the historical headnotes and content outlines of numerous sections (for example, sections 35, 45, 73, 74, 76, 86, and 91).

Because of the increased use now given to the JST, it seems appropriate to present this special work of the Prophet in its historical perspective, to show his high regard for it and its use by early members of the Church. The Saints of that day were aware that the Prophet had made a new translation of the Bible, and many were eager to obtain the increased information it would afford. But since it was not published, access to it was limited. Eventually, excerpts from the JST were published in early Church periodicals, and selections were also used in the *Lectures on Faith*. There are, however, several instances recorded in the revelations in which the Lord directed that the entire translation be printed; and, accordingly, Joseph Smith made extensive plans to publish the translation in book form.

The Doctrine and Covenants, as well as the Prophet's journal, letters, Church periodicals, the JST manuscript, and other documentary sources, demonstrate that the translation was frequently discussed in the early Church and that several attempts were made by the Prophet to publish his work in its entirety, although such a publication was never realized in his lifetime. The historical records show that failure to publish the new translation was not due to any negligence or lack of interest on Joseph Smith's part, but rather to a neglect on the part of the Saints to provide the temporal necessities by which the Prophet could attend to the work. The story is fascinating and meaningful, with important lessons to be learned, not the least of which is that when an opportunity presents itself to render service to a prophet doing the Lord's work, we should act without delay or the opportunity may pass unfulfilled.

The translation was begun in June 1830, commencing with Genesis. The Prophet had just previously brought the Book of Mormon from the press (18–25 March) and organized the Church (6 April 1830). At this early time there was still much to be revealed to the Prophet about the doctrines of the gospel and the management of the young Church. As the facts are assembled, it becomes clear that one of the benefits of the Bible translation is that it provided the Prophet with the spiritual involvement necessary for the revelation of many important doctrines.

That these revelations came as a result of intense study of the holy scriptures is a lesson in itself. Answers are found while searching the scriptures because inspiration comes from studying the Lord's own words. They are an unfailing source of light and inspiration.

With his many responsibilities in guiding the Church and rearing a family, it was difficult for the Prophet to find the time required to make a Bible translation; yet the importance of the work did not allow for unwarranted delays. No one else could make the translation, but there were others who could help him with his temporal needs. Consequently, in February 1831 the Lord said to the members of the Church: "And if ye desire the glories of the kingdom, appoint ye my servant Joseph Smith, Jun., and uphold him before me by the prayer of faith. And again, I say unto you, that if ye desire the mysteries of the kingdom, provide for him food and raiment, and whatsoever thing he needeth to accomplish the work wherewith I have commanded him." (D&C 43:12–13.)

At the time this revelation was received, the Prophet was pursuing daily the translation of the Bible. The revelation is more meaningful when read with that understanding. Thus the message is that the "glories" and "mysteries of the kingdom" would be forthcoming if the members would provide food, clothing, and "whatsoever thing" the Prophet needed to accomplish the work to which he had been called—namely, at that time, the translation of the Bible.

A few months later, on 11 October 1831, the Prophet recorded in his journal: "A conference was held at Brother [John] Johnson's where I was living [Hiram, Ohio]. . . . A committee of six was appointed to instruct the several branches of the Church. Elders David Whitmer and Reynolds Cahoon were appointed as two of the said committee; with the further duty on their mission of setting forth the condition of Brothers Joseph Smith, Jun., and Sidney Rigdon, that they might obtain means to continue the translation."[1]

In plainer terms, this meant that the Prophet and his scribe were without means and would have to lay aside the translation in order to labor for the necessities of life. The journal of Reynolds Cahoon mentions this appointment under the date of 9 November 1831 in these words: "Started for hiram to fulfill my mission to the churches which was given to Br. David and myself to obtain mony or property for Brs Joseph and others to finish the translation."[2]

Two weeks later, on 25 October 1831, at another conference of the Church in Hiram, the Prophet again dwelt upon the need for temporal aid to enable him to do his work, specifically mentioning the translation of the scriptures. The minutes of the meeting include the following: "Brother Joseph Smith, Jr., said. . . . that the promise of God was that the greatest blessings which God had to bestow should be given to those who contributed to the support of his family while he was translating the fulness of the Scriptures. . . . that God had often sealed up the heavens because of covetousness in the Church. . . . and except the Church receive the fulness of the Scriptures that they would yet fail."[3]

These sources say at least this much: (1) the Lord was interested in the translation; (2) through it, information of significance to the Church would be obtained; (3) Joseph Smith and his scribes would need temporal aid to sustain their families during the time needed to complete the translation; (4) efforts to obtain help had begun; and (5) glorious spiritual rewards would be given to those who assisted.

The translation began with the Old Testament. About ten months later the Lord instructed Joseph Smith to make a translation of the New Testament also, and promised him that in doing so he would learn many great things (see D&C 45:60–62). Until this time the Prophet had translated from Genesis only, but the manuscript of the JST shows that in obedience to this command he began translating the New Testament on 8 March 1831, just one day after being instructed to do so. The promptness of the Prophet in responding to the commandment to translate the New Testament manifests his regard for the work he was engaged in and his desire to do what the Lord expected of him. Through this work great things would be revealed to him and through him be made known to the Church.

From March 1831 until February 1833, the Prophet and his scribes continued to work through the New Testament, making hundreds of corrections and additions, and a few deletions. On 10 January 1832 the Lord encouraged the Brethren to continue the translation "until it be finished" (D&C 73:3–4).

Although there were many interruptions, the work progressed, and on 2 February 1833, in Kirtland, Ohio, the Prophet recorded in his journal: "I completed the translation and review of the New Testament, on the 2nd of February, 1833 and sealed it up, no more to be opened till it arrived in Zion."[4] "Zion" meant Independence, Missouri, where William W. Phelps had established the Church printing press. In April 1833 an inquiry was received from Brother Phelps as to whether he should print the new translation in the monthly issues of *The Evening and the Morning Star*. The Prophet's reply, dated 21 April 1833, reads: "It is not the will of the Lord to print any of the New Translation in the *Star*; but when it is published, it will all go to the world together, in a volume by itself; and the New Testament and the Book of Mormon will be printed together."[5]

Having completed the New Testament, the Brethren then returned to the book of Genesis and continued with the translation of the Old Testament. On 8 March 1833, the Lord spoke to them about other duties that needed to be taken care of, but not until after they had "finished the translation of the prophets" (D&C 90:13).

Then on 6 May 1833, at Kirtland, Ohio, the Lord counseled the Prophet, "It is my will that you should hasten to translate my scriptures" (D&C 93:53). On the same day another revelation was received in which the Lord gave instruction concerning a printing house to be built: "And again, verily I say unto you, the second lot on the south shall be dedicated unto me for the building of a house unto me, for the work of the printing of the translation of my scriptures" (D&C 94:10).

These revelations suggest some urgency about completing the work and getting it printed.

On 25 June 1833 the Prophet wrote again to Brother Phelps in Missouri: "In regard to the printing of the New Translation: It cannot be done until we can attend to it ourselves, and this we will do as soon as the Lord permits."[6]

A week later, on 2 July 1833, in a letter to the brethren in Zion, the Prophet wrote that "we are exceedingly fatigued, owing to a great press of business. We this day finished the translating of the Scriptures, for which we returned gratitude to our Heavenly Father."[7] The words "Finished on the 2nd day of July 1833" also occur in bold handwriting on the JST manuscript at the conclusion of the book of Malachi.

Although the Prophet states that the translation activity was "finished" on 2 July 1833, the manuscript was not ready to be given to a printer. During the remaining eleven years of his life he continued to revise and add to the text and to make other editorial refinements to prepare the document for printing.

In August 1833 the First Presidency in Kirtland, Ohio, sent copies of three revelations (including Doctrine and Covenants 94, referred to above) to Bishop Edward Partridge in Independence, Missouri, with the following note: "You will see by these revelations that we have to print the new translation here at kirtland for which we will prepare as soon as possible."[8]

As a new year dawned in January 1834, the Church was beset by persecution and violence, both in Ohio and Missouri. On the evening of January 11, a group of brethren met in a prayer meeting with the Prophet to ask the Lord for help and protection. Their requests were itemized, and the fifth request read: "That the Lord would protect our printing press from the hands of evil men, . . . that we may print His Scriptures."[9] Such a plea had special meaning relative to the press in Ohio, for the W. W. Phelps printing press in Independence had been destroyed by a mob just six months earlier, on 20 July 1833.

On 23 April 1834 the Lord again spoke to the Prophet about printing the new translation: "And for this purpose I have commanded you to organize yourselves, even to print my words, the fulness of my scriptures, the revelations which I have given unto you" (D&C 104:58). Although more than the new Bible translation is involved in the scope of this revelation, the new translation is included.

Earlier plans did not permit the JST to be published piecemeal, yet portions of the translation of Genesis had already been published in *The Evening and the Morning Star* in August 1832 and in March and April 1833. Then, in July 1833, the *Star* announced: "At no very distant period, we shall print the book of Mormon and the [New] Testament, and bind them in one volume." However, hopes for this were postponed when the printing press in Independence was destroyed the same month.

As the years passed, the Prophet did not lose interest in publishing the JST, although he was greatly hampered by persecution, the administrative duties of the Church, the lack of financial and material means, and the burden of moving the Church from Ohio to Missouri and then to Illinois. During this time he also came into possession of some Egyptian papyri containing the writings of Abraham, and he was anxious to translate that record.

On 18 June 1840 in Nauvoo, Illinois, the Prophet presented the high council with a lengthy memorial. He lamented that he had to be concerned so much with the "temporalities" of the Church and explained that it was a duty that he owed to God and to the Church to give his attention more particularly to spiritual things. He requested that the Church build him an office in which he could "attend to the affairs of the Church without distraction, . . . [for] the time has now come, when he should devote himself exclusively to those things which relate to the spiritualities of the Church, and commence the work of translating the Egyptian records, [and] the Bible." The Prophet reminded the high council that he had "no means of support whatever" and requested that "some one might be appointed to see that all his necessary wants may be provided for."[10]

The plea fell on receptive ears, and in July of that year the First Presidency and high council appointed two brethren to go throughout the Church to obtain money for the publication of various books, including the JST, or as they called it, the "new translation of the scriptures." An extract from an epistle by the First Presidency, July 1840, states: "To all whom it may concern:—This is to certify that Elders Samuel Bent and George W. Harris are authorized agents of the Church of Jesus Christ of Latter-day Saints, being appointed by the First Presidency and High Council of said Church to visit the branches of the Church . . . to obtain donations and subscriptions for the purpose of printing the Book of Mormon, Doctrine and Covenants, hymn-books, the new translation of the Scriptures. . . . We do hope the Saints will do all in their power to effect the object proposed."[11]

A few days later in Nauvoo an editorial appeared in the *Times and Seasons*, the official Church periodical, bearing the headline "BOOKS!!!" The editorial reiterated the call of Elders Bent and Harris and stated, among other things, that "the authorities of the church" were taking definite steps to make the scriptures available to the members of the Church, including "also the necessity of Publishing the new translation of the scriptures, which has so long been desired by the Saints."[12]

The labors of Elders Bent and Harris are illustrated in several pages they prepared showing a record of money collected in their assignment. The document, located in the archives of the Harold B. Lee Library at Brigham Young University, is prefaced with these words: "An account of money received (of subscribers for the Book of Mormon, Doctrine and Covenants, Hymn Books, & the new Translation of the scriptures)—by Sam'l Bent & G. W. Harris agents for the Church of Jesus Christ of Latter Day Saints to aid in printing the above named Books."[13]

Then follows a list of fifty names, places, dates, and amounts donated. The total recorded on this list is $207.25, the largest single entry being twenty-five dollars and the smallest, twenty-five cents. Most donations were for three to five dollars. The dates are all in July and August 1840, and the major areas where collections were made were Illinois, Ohio, Pennsylvania, New Jersey, and Massachusetts. One receipt reads: "Brown Co., Ill., August 14, 1840. Received of Stephen Lity, & Samuel Bickmore and Wm Bickmore nine dollars by note as a subscription to aid in printing the Book of Mormon and new translation and hymn Book. Wm Bosley, agent for Geo. W. Harris of the Church of Latter day Saints."

Another epistle of the First Presidency to the "Saints Scattered Abroad" was sent out on or about 1 September 1840, and contained an appeal to the members to contribute financially to the building up of the kingdom. Particularly mentioned was "the printing and circulation of the Book of Mormon, Doctrine and Covenants, hymn-book, and the new translation of the Scriptures."[14]

These epistles make it clear that the Church leaders intended to publish the JST along with the other scriptures and a hymnbook, but in order for it to happen the Saints would have to make a financial contribution.

On 19 January 1841, in counsel to William Law, the Lord spoke again about publishing the JST: "If he will do my will let him from henceforth hearken to the counsel of my servant Joseph, . . . and publish the new translation of my holy word unto the inhabitants of the earth" (D&C 124:89). That William Law did not "hearken to the counsel" is shown in the following excerpt from the minutes of a meeting of the Nauvoo City Council, a meeting held to consider matters in which Law was involved: "*Daniel Carn was sworn:* Said, 'I told Brother Norton that certain men had been counseled by the Prophet to invest their means in publishing the new translation of the Bible; and they instead of obeying that counsel, had used their property for the purpose of building a steam-mill and raising a hundred acres of hemp; and the Lord had not blessed them in the business, but sunk their hemp in the Mississippi river.' "[15]

On 15 January 1842 the *Times and Seasons* contained a notice that the "Trustee" [Joseph Smith] needed time to arrange the scriptures, including the "New Translation of the Bible . . . for the press." Therefore, the recorder's office would be open only one day a week.[16]

In February 1842 the Council of the Twelve placed a notice in the *Times and Seasons* over the signature of President Brigham Young. The entire document dwelt upon the financial straits of the Church and the need for assistance from the Saints, especially in the building of a temple and loosing the Prophet's hands from temporal bondage so that various works could be done, "such as the new translation of the bible, and the record of Father Abraham [can be] published to the world."[17]

Eight months later an announcement was made in the *Times and Seasons* that the Book of Mormon and the hymnbook had been republished, but "the new translation of the bible, and the book of Doctrine and Covenants are entirely dependent on the liberality of the well-disposed for the cause of our Redeemer."[18] The Brethren had been successful in reprinting the Book of Mormon and the hymnbook, but more time and money were needed before the Doctrine and Covenants and the JST could go to press. Since all except the JST had been published before, less time would be required to arrange them for republication than to prepare the JST for its first appearance in print. That may be the reason why the other books were ready first.

On 1 March 1843 at Nauvoo, the Council of the Twelve issued another epistle to the Saints requesting financial and material aid for the Prophet and his family to enable him to find the time to bring forth the spiritual things of the Church. Particularly mentioned are the "revelations, translation, and history." Although the "translation" is not identified, it is quickly discernible that this has reference to the Bible, since the record of Abraham had already been published a year earlier in 1842 in the *Times and Seasons.* The epistle is extremely interesting and illustrates not only the meager financial situation of the Prophet, but also the determination of the leading Brethren to put the scriptures, including the JST, into the hands of the membership of the Church. The entire epistle follows:

> BELOVED BRETHREN:—As our beloved President Joseph Smith is now relieved from his bondage and his business, temporarily, and his property, too, he has but one thing to hinder his devoting his time to the spiritual interests of the Church, to the bringing forth of the revelations, translation, and history. And what is that? He has not provision for himself and family, and is obliged to spend his time in providing

therefor. His family is large and his company great, and it requires much to furnish his table. And now, brethren, we call on you for immediate relief in this matter; and we invite you to bring our President as many loads of wheat, corn, beef, pork, lard, tallow, eggs, poultry, venison, and everything eatable at your command, (not excepting unfrozen potatoes and vegetables, as soon as the weather will admit,) flour, etc., and thus give him the privilege of attending to your spiritual interest.

The measure you mete shall be measured to you again. If you give liberally to your President in temporal things, God will return to you liberally in spiritual and temporal things too. One or two good new milch cows are much needed also.

Brethren, will you do your work, and let the President do his for you before God? We wish an immediate answer by loaded teams or letter.

Your brethren in Christ, in behalf of the quorum,

BRIGHAM YOUNG, President.

WILLARD RICHARDS, Clerk.

P.S. Brethren, we are not unmindful of the favors our President has received from you in former days. But a man will not cease to be hungry this year because he ate last year.[19]

The epistle says nothing about the Book of Mormon or the hymnbook, since these had recently been republished. Attention was now centered on the "revelations" (Doctrine and Covenants) and the JST.

A year later in June 1844, the Prophet lay dead, felled by assassins' bullets, and the JST was not yet published. The Doctrine and Covenants was nearly ready for a republication at the time of his death and came forth from the press in September 1844. The JST would probably have been next, but the Prophet had been unable to get it published. He worked diligently on it during the closing years of his life when time would permit. Perhaps if he had not been forced to leave the "spiritualities" of the Church so often to attend to the "temporalities," he would have been able to see the translation of the Bible through to publication as he had hoped to do.

There has been an assumption that the JST was deliberately not published because it was grossly unfinished. That assumption is not based on all of the facts. The epistles of the First Presidency and of the Twelve as published in the *History of the Church* and the *Times and Seasons*, some of which are cited in this chapter, lead to the unmistakable conclusion that the intention was to publish. The major reason for failure to publish appears to have been an inadequate response from the Saints in providing temporal assistance. The basic conclusion seems to be that the *work* of translation was acceptable as far as the Lord required it of the Prophet at that time, but the *manuscript* was not fully prepared for the press.

Perhaps one reason for the feeling about the "unfinished" nature of the JST has been a statement by President George Q. Cannon in his *Life of Joseph Smith the Prophet:* "We have heard President Brigham Young state that the Prophet before his death had spoken to him about going through the translation of the scriptures again and perfecting it upon points of doctrine which the Lord had restrained him from giving in plainness and fulness at the time of which we write [2 February 1833]."[20]

We note, however, that what is referred to in the above quotation is the nature of the translation as it existed in 1833. During the eleven years of his life after that time, the Prophet apparently did much of what he desired to do with the JST. The original manuscript tends to bear this out, since it shows an original draft and a later more complete revision, clarified in language and thought, and versed and punctuated. That the work was not perfected is clear. But it is equally clear that it was nearer the stage necessary for publication than casual observers have realized. We must also recognize that although the manuscript was ready for publication, this does not prevent more information from being added when the Lord desires to reveal it.

Those familiar with the JST know that it contains important truths not available elsewhere. The desire of the early Brethren was to make these truths available by publication, but they were not able to accomplish it during the Prophet's lifetime. After Joseph Smith's death, the manuscript was retained by his widow, Emma Smith, and later given to their son Joseph Smith III. He published the JST in book form and copyrighted it through the RLDS church. However, because of this, many in the LDS church have been reluctant to use it.

Church leaders have expended much effort to make the translation available to the members. The 1979 LDS edition of the Bible contains hundreds of doctrinally significant passages from the JST in the footnotes and reference section. How beneficial it would have been to the Church and to the world through the intervening years if the Prophet Joseph Smith had been able to provide an official publication of his Bible translation in his day! How we might wish that those early Saints had been able to respond fully to the opportunity that was theirs to provide the needed financial assistance! They would have brought blessings not only to themselves but also to millions of lives for generations. After all these years, the time is right and the official scriptures of The Church of Jesus Christ of Latter-day Saints now offer much light and truth from the Joseph Smith Translation.

Notes

1. *History of the Church* 1:219. Hereafter cited as *HC.*
2. Journal of Reynolds Cahoon, Historical Department, The Church of Jesus Christ of Latter-day Saints.
3. See *Teachings of the Prophet Joseph Smith,* comp. Joseph Fielding Smith (Salt Lake City: Deseret Book Co., 1976), p. 9.
4. *HC* 1:324.
5. *HC* 1:341.
6. *HC* 1:365.
7. *HC* 1:368.
8. Joseph Smith, Jr., Sidney Rigdon, and F. G. Williams to Edward Partridge, Historical Department, The Church of Jesus Christ of Latter-day Saints.
9. *HC* 2:3.
10. *HC* 4:137.
11. *HC* 4:164.
12. *Times and Seasons* 1 (July 1840): 139–40. Hereafter cited as *TS.*
13. Whitney Collection, box 3, folder 7.
14. *HC* 4:187; also *TS* 1 (October 1840): 179.
15. *HC* 6:164–65.
16. *TS* 3 (15 January 1842): 667.
17. *TS* 3 (1 March 1842): 715.
18. *TS* 3 (15 October 1842): 958.
19. *HC* 5:293.
20. George Q. Cannon, *Life of Joseph Smith the Prophet* (Salt Lake City: Deseret Book Co., 1986), p. 148.

Chapter 11

THE JOSEPH SMITH TRANSLATION AND THE REVELATORY PROCESS

For years I have enjoyed the simple testimony of the gospel unmixed with sophisticated words and multisyllabic explanations. I know in my heart that Jesus Christ is the Savior and the Redeemer of mankind and that Joseph Smith is his prophet. Sometimes I come in contact with intellectual and high-sounding explanations and proposals that do not set right. I can't always detect what it is that is out of order, but a monitor within me says that there is something not right in the particular proposal or program. I have learned to trust my feelings in these matters, for nearly always time has borne my impressions out. My chief sorrow in many of these instances has been that I haven't said anything about my feelings until afterwards, because I thought no one would listen.

I am often made uneasy by the tendency among educators to complexify and sophisticate things so that simple matters become hard to understand. Sometimes we almost become smothered in oratory. Often when I dwell on problems that arise I begin to feel ill at ease, and I have a sense of helplessness and discouragement. But then when I go to the scriptures and read them I get new courage, and hope springs up again; I feel edified because I begin to think in terms of fundamentals. When that happens I feel reassured and faith grows and happiness returns. It is as the scriptures tell us: "Faith cometh by hearing, and hearing by the word of God"; and this faith, or hope, "maketh an anchor to the souls of men" (Romans 10:17; Ether 12:4).

I have also discovered it is impossible to prove by tangible evidence any doctrine as being absolutely true. You can marshal all the scriptures, all the evidences, all the logic and reason—all the ingredients you want; yet ultimately on every spiritual principle, on every doctrine, there is the unavoidable leap of faith. There is always at least a small gap, and a person needs that spark of faith to get across it. I think that is the test of mortality. That may be why the Lord said we must "seek learning, even by study and also by faith" (D&C 88:118). There is no other way to learn spiritual things.

Because this is true, we need to be very careful about whom and what we choose as our standards. I have come to distrust much of the conjecture and learning of the world and worldly men and women, no matter how wise, intellectual, educated, and well-mannered they appear to be. I trust the Book of Mormon, the Doctrine and Covenants, and the Pearl of Great Price more than I do the Bible. I trust prophets more than politicians, and prophets more than scholars for basic understanding. Many biblical scholars, for example, have given much valuable information about the Bible and about history and culture, but they generally do not understand the eternal things and the purposes of God upon the earth in the last days. They do not understand doctrine because they do not know that every dispensation has been a gospel dispensation with Melchizedek Priesthood, and they do not accept the Restoration. It seems as though scholars have assembled the most extensive and detailed information sometimes, but prophets have the better perception.

The New Testament Church encountered the learning of the world among the Jews and the Greeks. Paul said, "The Jews require a sign, and the Greeks seek after wisdom" (1 Corinthians 1:22). The New Testament Church was finally done in by the worldly-wise because it sought to accommodate their learning. As a result there developed a popular and learned philosophy containing the philosophies of men mingled with scriptures.

Revelation Provides Needed Answers

When a prophet comes with a new revelation, all is clear, faith abounds, and the truth is known. As time puts distance between the prophet and later generations, invariably the wise and the learned and the intellectually minded comment upon every phrase and word of the revelation until they read into each point so many variations and meanings that eventually no one reading the commentaries knows for sure what is right. The Jews did this with the great revelation at Mount Sinai. Others have done it with the New Testament. Some writers have tried to do it with the first vision of Joseph Smith and with the Book of Mormon. Jacob warns us about looking beyond the mark and despising words of plainness and seeking for things we cannot understand (Jacob 4:14). I think we have to be careful about getting in a mode in which we are "ever learning, and never able to come to the knowledge of the truth" (2 Timothy 3:7). The Book of Mormon is especially strong in its opposition to worldly knowledge as a substitute for revelation.

It almost seems that the literary people do not really want answers; they only want information. Answers have become a contradiction of their goal. It is a paradox that the philosopher and the worldly-wise place great emphasis on the proliferation of words and ideas but object to coming to final answers. Knowledge is what they set out to learn, but the more they learn the less willing they are to accept or arrive at answers. I think that may be why many of the learned have not accepted the Restoration more readily: clear, simple answers are repugnant to their network of suppositions; they do not like absolutes. Since possession of the truth makes much of man's philosophy invalid, could it be that philosophy makes absolute truth unwelcome?

We have to be careful as students of the gospel that we do not get so caught up with the pursuit of learning that we find no room for, and become suspect of, direct answers and testimony. We are not going to be able to learn everything; we are not going to be able to prove everything. If we don't have an unshakable testimony and the current guidance of the Spirit in making decisions, we will get so confused and mixed up that we might make serious mistakes in our own lives and cause others to stumble through the influence we have on them. We would do well to stay close to the President of the Church and the Twelve and to the standard works.

It has been my experience that the discovery of facts is only a minor part of learning. The real challenge and accomplishment is not in the discovery but in the *interpretation* of those facts. This is where inspiration and revelation are so important to us.

The Role of the Joseph Smith Translation in the Restoration

Having said that, I would now like to turn to a discussion of the process of revelation and what the Joseph Smith Translation of the Bible can teach us about that process. It has been customary through the years to deal with the Joseph Smith Translation only on a textual basis, comparing some of its passages with the corresponding passages in the King James Version. However, I would like to discuss some other aspects of the Joseph Smith Translation of which I feel we as Latter-day Saints ought to become aware.

The Joseph Smith Translation is not just another Bible. It is inseparably connected with the Doctrine and Covenants and the Pearl of Great Price—chronologically, historically, textually, and doctrinally. It is because of these ties and connections between the standard works that we cannot do justice in teaching the restoration of the gospel in this dispensation without an understanding of the history and the doctrinal content of the Joseph Smith Translation. A person gains additional insights into the unfolding of our dispensation when he understands the role of the Joseph Smith Translation. He begins to comprehend how revelation comes, and he also sees a background behind many of the revelations in the Doctrine and Covenants that he would otherwise miss.

There are several reasons why each of us should have this wider understanding of the role of the Joseph Smith Translation. As we study Church history, for instance, we will come to realize that the Joseph Smith Translation is an important ingredient in the life of Joseph Smith and that it is an impressive and profound work from his hands. In our study of the Bible the Joseph Smith Translation will further our understanding of that ancient record, and we will come to view the Prophet's translation not as an attempt to "Mormonize" the Bible but as one of his major revelatory products. With the Joseph Smith Translation we see the Prophet in his role as a restorer of lost material. Thus we will find that the Joseph Smith Translation was not an experiment by the Prophet; rather, it was a day-by-day unfolding of the ancient gospel by revelation. If Joseph Smith is a true prophet, then his translation of the Bible is a book of true scripture, and a person ignores it at his own peril.

Likewise, a broader understanding of the Joseph Smith Translation will aid us in our study of the Doctrine and Covenants, the Pearl of Great Price, and Latter-day Saint theology. We will see that there is a close doctrinal and informational connection between the Joseph Smith Translation and the development of Church doctrine. In numerous instances the Prophet's Bible translation is a forerunner or preliminary revelation to some of the other doctrinal revelations. I would invite you to observe that the Doctrine and Covenants and the Joseph Smith Translation do not just have *similar* roots entwined with each other, but rather they have the *same* root—the root of revelation—and there is no difference, in terms of their nature and source, between the revelations in the Joseph Smith Translation and those in the Doctrine and Covenants and the Pearl of Great Price. Hence we have not really done our homework unless and until we examine the textual and doctrinal relationship of the Joseph Smith Translation, as well as its revelatory and historical association, with all the elements of the latter-day restoration of the gospel.

The Joseph Smith Translation, then, is not an expendable work, nor is it of private interest only. It is as central to the development of the doctrine of this dispensation as any book we have. It is a tangible evidence of the prophetic calling of the Prophet Joseph Smith, and it is a testament of the Lord Jesus Christ. It is important that we not judge the Joseph Smith Translation merely by textual criticism or by the wisdom of man or of scholars. This work and its history should have a permanent place in the curriculum of every gospel student because of its pivotal position in relation to the doctrinal restoration as a whole.

Original Manuscripts Provide Valuable Historical Framework

One situation that has blurred our vision is that the Joseph Smith Translation is published as one book, the Doctrine and Covenants as another, and the Pearl of Great Price as still another. Having these revelations, most of which were given during the formative years of the Church, printed in separate books obscures the context and thus the historical and doctrinal relationships between these early revelations. The books have become compartmentalized, whereas in reality the revelations in these books were revealed on a day-to-day basis in the same real-life situations.

Every revelation that has been received was given at some specific place and time and in some specific situation. But the past becomes blurred by time and tradition. Time passes, leaders pass on, and new personalities come into prominence. As a consequence, a vacuum of understanding often forms; false concepts gradually develop and incorrect impressions form. To correct this situation we often have to become literary archaeologists and dig down to the original sources so as to view them as they really are. When we do this we will see things we had not noticed before, no matter how many times we have trodden the path.

No matter how well a person knows the surface of the ground, he can never know what lies even just under the surface—what forms of architecture, what relics of art, or what message the past can convey—until he or someone else removes the surface accumulation and examines the facts of an earlier day. It is the same way with books such as the Doctrine and Covenants and the Joseph

Smith Translation. If a person reads only the surface of the printed page, he misses the significance of some of the plainest messages of these scriptural works. Sometimes it is only by going to sources earlier than the printed page, to the original or at least prepublication manuscripts, that one can recreate enough historical framework to see the various historical and doctrinal relationships. When we see the development that has taken place, we gain a more accurate perception and appreciation for the printed page. Until we know the background of our latter-day revelations, our understanding is apt to be superficial and fragmented.

In looking at the Joseph Smith Translation and the revelatory process within the context of the Restoration, we need to begin with a few basic dates and concepts. The Prophet Joseph Smith said, "Could you gaze into heaven five minutes, you would know more than you would by reading all that ever was written on the subject."[1] In like manner, if we could go back in time and talk with the Prophet or walk about and observe conditions generally, we would no doubt learn new things about how and why some revelations were received. But as we cannot go back in time, we are obliged to reconstruct the history as best we can with the facts that are available. This can be pleasantly rewarding because by excavation we can discover things we had not seen before.

A Chronological Approach

When we sort them out chronologically, we will not have difficulty in seeing the connections between the Joseph Smith Translation and the revelations recorded in other latter-day scriptures. We are not accustomed to doing that because we tend to think in terms of books rather than in terms of history. Without an awareness of the context, we sometimes do not see the connections and do not perceive that the gospel was revealed line upon line, precept upon precept, here a little and there a little.

Consider what the Church was like in June 1830. What were the offices, the doctrines, and the practices of the Church in that day? It would be easier to describe what was *not* yet a part of the Church. In June 1830 there were no wards, no stakes, no First Presidency, no Council of the Twelve, no patriarchs, no Seventies, no bishops, no Word of Wisdom, no revelation on the degrees of glory, no tithing, no welfare program, no law of consecration, no priesthood quorums of any kind, no temples, no endowments, no sealings, no marriages for eternity, no real understanding of the

New Jerusalem, no baptisms for the dead, no Doctrine and Covenants, no Pearl of Great Price, and no Joseph Smith Translation. How did these things, which today we recognize as vital to our spiritual life and as basic to the Church, come to be? They came when the time was right and in answer to prayer—the result of earnest search. Each of these things was revealed at some particular time and place and in some particular situation; and each became, one by one, part of the doctrine and the structure of the Church. Many of the fundamental doctrines of the gospel which are contained in the Doctrine and Covenants were first made known to the Prophet Joseph Smith as he worked through the pages of the Bible while making his inspired translation.

The Book of Mormon came from the press during the week of 18–25 March 1830. In a few more days, on 6 April, the Church was organized. A few weeks later, in June 1830, came the earliest revelation associated with the Joseph Smith Translation. We are most familiar with it as the book of Moses, chapter 1, in the Pearl of Great Price. We do not know the exact day in June on which the material was written, but it was in Harmony, Pennsylvania, and chronologically would be just before Doctrine and Covenants 25.

Fortunately the prepublication manuscripts of the Joseph Smith Translation have been preserved. They are very informative as to the history of the translation because they contain dates showing when certain portions of the Bible translation were in process. These dates, along with the varying styles of known handwriting that reflect the services of different scribes, have enabled us to identify certain relationships with the Doctrine and Covenants that otherwise would have escaped us.

The pages of the manuscript that follow the material that we know as Moses 1 contain Joseph Smith's translation of Genesis 1–5 (Moses 2–5), which should be placed chronologically in proximity to Doctrine and Covenants 29. Since exact dates are not given in the manuscripts of either Genesis 1–5 or Doctrine and Covenants 29, the placing of these dates has to be approximate. The chapters from Genesis were received and recorded sometime between June 1830 and October 1830, and thus very likely were given previous to the reception of the revelation known as section 29.

The subjects of these chapters of Genesis translated by the Prophet have to do with the spiritual and temporal creations, agency, the rebellion of Lucifer, the fall of Adam, and the introduction of the gospel to Adam and his posterity. The doctrinal emphasis is clear and prominent in the Joseph Smith Translation but is almost totally lacking in any other Bible.

In the Prophet's translation of Genesis 1–5, principles are woven into a story line relating the events of the Garden of Eden, Satan's rebellion, his temptation of Adam and Eve, their eating the forbidden fruit, and their being ushered out of the garden. In contrast, the material in Doctrine and Covenants 29:30–45 is a brief statement of doctrinal principles—without the story—actually a summary of the doctrine found in the longer narrative of Joseph Smith's translation of Genesis 1–5. Thus, for maximum comprehension, the Prophet's translation of Genesis 1–5 (Moses 2–5) should be read just prior to a study of Doctrine and Covenants 29, since that appears to be the order in which they were received.

The historical relationship between these two revelations begins a pattern repeated in later revelations, a pattern which shows that many of the concepts contained in the Doctrine and Covenants were first presented to the mind of the Prophet during his translation of the Bible and actually were recorded first in that translation. Later many of these subjects were enlarged upon and appeared as parts of various sections of the Doctrine and Covenants. We will now proceed to examine other examples.

The Joseph Smith Translation and the Concept of Zion

Both the Old Testament and the New Testament tell about Zion and a New Jerusalem to be built in the last days. The Book of Mormon specifies more particularly that this New Jerusalem will be built on the American continent. The Joseph Smith Translation also makes a special contribution to our understanding of Zion and the New Jerusalem.

In December 1830 the translation had reached Genesis, chapter 5, of the King James Version, where the great patriarch Enoch is mentioned. The Prophet Joseph Smith and Sidney Rigdon were living in Fayette, New York. The fifth chapter of Genesis in the King James Version contains only a few skinny comments about Enoch, saying that he was the son of Jared and was a good man, and implying that he was translated. But it says nothing about Enoch's having a city or a people, nothing about Enoch's Zion. You can read everything the Bible has to offer about Enoch in less than thirty seconds. While the Prophet Joseph was translating these passages about Enoch in Genesis 5, he received an extensive revelation about Enoch and his ministry; his teachings; his prophetic call; and his city and their laws, happiness, unity, and harmony. He learned that they were of one heart and one mind and that there were no poor among them. The length of the material about Enoch in the Joseph Smith Translation is eighteen times as long as that in any other Bible.

This new information about Enoch and his people includes a statement that Enoch's city will come down from heaven and be joined with the city of New Jerusalem that is to be built on the earth by the Saints in the last days (see JST, Genesis 7:70–72, or Moses 7:62–64). The information about Enoch and his city is one of the most extensive and valuable contributions of the Joseph Smith Translation. Enoch is a big man in Mormonism, but he is almost obliterated from the Bible and nearly forgotten in present-day Judaism, Catholicism, and Protestantism. Almost everything we know about Enoch we learn from the Joseph Smith Translation. The same is true about Melchizedek. He has been nearly lost to the Bible, yet he is large on the horizon of this dispensation. Almost all we know about Melchizedek we learn from the Joseph Smith Translation.

Soon after the revelation about Enoch was received and recorded, the Lord instructed Joseph Smith to cease translating temporarily and to move the headquarters of the Church to Ohio; there they would receive the "law" (see D&C 42) by which they would be governed. Let us look at the sequence: the Enoch material was received in December 1830; the command to cease translating and move, recorded in Doctrine and Covenants 37, was also received in December; the promise of the "law," recorded in Doctrine and Covenants 38, was received in January 1831; and the reception of the law, recorded in Doctrine and Covenants 42, came in February. The revelations recorded in the next twenty sections or so of the Doctrine and Covenants, from 42–64, were all received in the next ten months, and they dealt with the law of consecration, the founding of the New Jerusalem and Zion, and the economic system sometimes called the united order.

The revelation about Enoch given in the Joseph Smith Translation was a pattern or a backdrop which introduced the idea of Enoch's Zion to the young Church. Then the Lord poured forth many specific revelations to the Prophet, showing him how to build a similar society, or Zion, or New Jerusalem, preparatory to the Second Coming and the return of Enoch's city.

It would be helpful to us, when studying the Doctrine and Covenants, if we would read the Enoch material just before reading sections 37–64. This sequence is chronologically accurate, and following it helps recreate the setting in which the sections of the Doctrine and Covenants were received.

The revelation about Enoch was received in December 1830, just before section 37 was received. Therefore it is not surprising that Enoch is mentioned again in sections 38 and 45. The whole concept of a latter-day Zion, of which Enoch's city was the prototype, was the principal topic of divine revelation at that period of time.

The Joseph Smith Translation and the Brass Plates

As we have seen, close connections exist between the Joseph Smith Translation and the Doctrine and Covenants. The Book of Mormon is also related to the Prophet's Bible translation in an interesting way: the Nephite scripture serves as evidence that the Joseph Smith Translation is indeed a work of restoration—the revealing anew of plain and precious truths once enjoyed anciently.

By way of illustration, let us consider the second chapter of 2 Nephi, in which Lehi gives a remarkable discourse. He tells how Satan came to be the devil in the premortal world; that Adam and Eve would have had no children and all things would have remained in their original state if there had been no Fall; and that the Messiah was necessary by reason of the Fall. Lehi seems to have learned all this from reading the plates of brass. Absolutely none of these things is contained in the King James Version nor in any other Bible known to the modern world; however, all of these things—Satan's history; Adam's transgression; the fact that man, the animals, and the earth would all have remained in their original state; the fact that there would have been no children without the Fall; and the role of the Messiah—are found in the third, fourth, fifth, and sixth chapters of Joseph Smith's translation of Genesis. What is the point? Simply this: it is very clear that the contents of the Joseph Smith Translation, having received the touch of restoration through the hand of the prophet of God, resemble the doctrinal content of the brass plates more fully than do those of any other Bible.

This is demonstrated further in connection with the Book of Mormon's description of the secret combination entered into by Cain (see Helaman 6:22–30; Ether 8:14–19). From the Joseph Smith Translation it seems clear that this was mentioned originally in the Genesis record of Cain as well as on the brass plates, but is not in our current Bible (see JST, Genesis 5:14–16, 35–37, or Moses

5:29–31, 49–51). Moreover, the prophecies of Joseph of Egypt, as recounted in 2 Nephi 3, are also missing from our King James Version but are presented in the Prophet's translation of Genesis 50. Likewise, the emphasis on Melchizedek given in Alma 13 is borne out—not in the same words but in principle—in Joseph Smith's translation of Genesis 14. Thus, in making his Bible translation the Prophet Joseph Smith was instrumental in restoring many concepts with which the ancient Nephites were acquainted through their having the plates of brass.

It seems to me that we have not begun to appreciate the value of the Joseph Smith Translation, nor have we used it as a textual source as we could. We seem to be too timid, perhaps a little too reluctant, maybe even a little embarrassed when we confront the academic world with a Bible based on revelation from God through a prophet and not certified by a manuscript already accepted by the world. It is as though Joseph Smith, in confronting a monolithic, traditional, learned Goliath, were saying, "You have come armed with ancient manuscript and language and tradition, but I come to you in the name of Israel's God and new revelation."

If the Prophet Joseph Smith were a famous athlete, actor, or race car driver, his opinions would be sought regarding all kinds of things not even close to his expertise—what breakfast cereal would he prefer? which shampoo or shaving cream? and which mouthwash is most effective? When it comes to gospel truth, revelation, and scripture, Joseph Smith is the greatest prophet in twenty centuries or more, yet we seem to ignore his contributions in the subject of his greatest expertise.

Of course I recognize that the Prophet could have gone through the Book of Mormon and gotten his ideas and then simply inserted them in the Bible without the idea of restoration, but why would any of us want to deny him of his calling as a seer? Why should he not restore, by revelation, the ancient text? In a revelation directed to Sidney Rigdon, the Lord emphasized Joseph Smith's role as revealer and restorer:

> And I have sent forth the fulness of my gospel by the hand of my servant Joseph; and in weakness have I blessed him;
>
> And I have given unto him the keys of the mystery of those things which have been sealed, even things which were from the foundation of the world, and the things which shall come from this time until the time of my coming, if he abide in me, and if not, another will I plant in his stead.

> Wherefore, watch over him that his faith fail not, and it shall be given by the Comforter, the Holy Ghost, that knoweth all things.
>
> And a commandment I give unto thee—that thou shalt write for him; and the scriptures shall be given, even as they are in mine own bosom, to the salvation of mine own elect. (D&C 35:17–20.)

And Moses 1:40–41 affirms that Joseph Smith was to actually restore lost information, even lost text: "And now, Moses, my son, I will speak unto thee concerning this earth upon which thou standest; and thou shalt write the things which I shall speak. And in a day when the children of men shall esteem my words as naught and take many of them from the book which thou shalt write, behold, I will raise up another like unto thee; and they shall be had again among the children of men—among as many as shall believe."

It Starts with the Joseph Smith Translation

The train of thought we have been pursuing is also demonstrated on other doctrinal topics. Several major doctrines of the Church were revealed during the process of the Bible translation, such as the age of accountability of children, the new and everlasting covenant of marriage, the role of priesthood quorums and councils, the history of Adam, and so on. It is advantageous to study the chronological sequence in which a particular doctrine was revealed, because then the progressive information unfolds naturally, and the doctrine is easier to understand, since that is the way it was revealed in the first place.

Consider, for example, the book of Revelation. We start with the King James Version. Then we compare the corrections, clarifications, and additions given in the Joseph Smith Translation. That helps considerably. Then we read Doctrine and Covenants 77, which was revealed in connection with the Joseph Smith Translation. This section carries the doctrinal enlargement even further. Lastly, we read Doctrine and Covenants 88, which is a still further extension.

Another example of this type of relationship concerns the degrees of glory. We begin first with the Bible and the Book of Mormon, both of which make it unmistakably clear that all persons will be resurrected with a physical body (see 1 Corinthians 15:21–22;

Alma 40:21, 23), never to die again. The Prophet was translating John 5:29 when he received the vision of the three degrees of glory, Doctrine and Covenants 76. Later he received Doctrine and Covenants 88. Each revelation in its sequence is built upon knowledge given earlier; each has given some new and additional concept not contained in the earlier. Can you see? Revelation is received line upon line—here a little and there a little. Looking at the Joseph Smith Translation in its historical context thus gives us a more comprehensive view of the revelatory process involved in the Restoration.

Specific Ties Between the Joseph Smith Translation and the Doctrine and Covenants

Since the relationship between the Doctrine and Covenants and the Joseph Smith Translation, as shown throughout this chapter, highlights better than anything else this revelatory process, let us more specifically identify those areas in which these two works of scripture are related. First, the Doctrine and Covenants contains specific instructions regarding the Bible translation. It records divine directions about when to start the translation, the appointment of scribes, encouragement to continue until completion, and several reminders to publish the translation and use it in teaching. Second, the Doctrine and Covenants presents doctrinal material revealed as a direct result of the Bible translation. Third, the Doctrine and Covenants presents doctrinal material which was obtained first through Joseph Smith's translation of the Bible and was then enlarged upon in the Doctrine and Covenants.

At this stage of my study, I feel I can identify at least 26 verses of the Doctrine and Covenants that are directly associated with the Joseph Smith Translation as regulatory instruction. These are as follows: Doctrine and Covenants 9:2; 35:20; 37:1; 41:7; 42:56–58; 43:12–13; 45:60–62; 47:1; 73:3–4; 90:13; 91:1–6; 93:53; 94:10; 104:58; and 124:89.

In the second category—doctrinal material revealed as a direct result of the Bible translation—I would list at least the following 141 verses: Doctrine and Covenants 76:1–119; 77:1–15; and 86:1–7.

In the third category, that of material originally revealed in the Joseph Smith Translation and enlarged upon when presented in the

Doctrine and Covenants (and this is the more difficult to identify, but is without question a legitimate area), I would list at least the following 200 verses: Doctrine and Covenants 45:11–12; 49:21; 68:15–21; 74:1–7; 84:6–28; 88:3–32, 92–116; 93:1–18; 107:59–100; 132:1–45; and probably many more. I cannot take the time at this writing to relate all the details that point to these conclusions, but in making this assertion I assure you that there is reasonable evidence and that it is not reckless speculation.

Because of our increasing awareness of the role of the Joseph Smith Translation in the development of the Doctrine and Covenants, the 1981 edition of the latter has some mention of the former. For example, the Prophet's work with the Bible translation is mentioned in the historical headnotes to sections 35, 71, 74, 76, 77, 86, and 91. There are seventeen footnote references at the following verses: Doctrine and Covenants 9:2; 35:20; 37:1; 41:7; 42:56; 45:12, 60; 49:21; 73:3; 76:17; 84:14, 24; 93:53; 94:10; 104:58; 107:2; and 124:89. In addition to this material in the Doctrine and Covenants, there are, as you know, 411 verses of the Pearl of Great Price that are excerpts from the Joseph Smith Translation.

We now see these connections more clearly, thanks to our being able to examine the dates recorded on the original Joseph Smith Translation manuscript and to the discovery by Robert J. Woodford and others that parts of many of the sections of the Doctrine and Covenants were written at earlier dates than the final drafts.

Conclusion

The background of the Joseph Smith Translation is discussed in other chapters of this book as well as in other published sources; therefore, for the purposes of this chapter it has not seemed necessary to recount those preliminary historical details. The focus here has been on relationships, applications, causes, and consequences —what all this means to you and me and to our families and our fellow Latter-day Saints. I have tried to show that the translation of the Bible was a major, mainstream activity in the prophetic life of Joseph Smith, and that the Joseph Smith Translation is a major document not only for biblical study but also for the study of the Doctrine and Covenants, the Pearl of Great Price, Church history and doctrine, and the revelatory process inherent in the events of the Restoration.

Notes

1. *Teachings of the Prophet Joseph Smith*, comp. Joseph Fielding Smith (Salt Lake City: Deseret Book Co., 1976), p. 324.

PART III

Spiritual Truths

Chapter 12

THE KNOWLEDGE THAT SAVES

The scriptures place a high premium on the acquisition of truth, but they also show that certain kinds of learning matter more than other kinds. In one sense all truth is of the same nature, for "truth is knowledge of things as they are, and as they were, and as they are to come" (D&C 93:24). Jacob, as recorded in the Book of Mormon, declared that "the Spirit speaketh truth" and that, therefore, "it speaketh of things as they really are, and of things as they really will be" (Jacob 4:13). However, not all truths are of the same worth. For instance, if a person happens to be standing six inches from a bare wire carrying two hundred thousand volts of electricity, knowing that truth is far more important to that person at that moment than knowing that Australian white rabbits have pink eyes. By extension we can say that truths that cause persons to change their life-styles are more significant to society than truths that are mere facts.

Those truths of greatest worth are the truths that lead to salvation; and in order for them to be efficacious in our lives, we must view them as eternal realities. We accept Adam and Eve, for example, as real persons who lived, transgressed, and brought about their own fall and the consequent fall of all mankind. If we had a complete record we could mark on the calendar the actual time that the Fall occurred. Likewise, if we had an adequate map, and I expect we will someday, we could mark the exact spot where the Fall occurred. The Fall is just that real and absolute: a real man and a real woman did, at a specific time and location, bring about the Fall, which has affected all of mankind.

In like manner, the birth of Jesus Christ, his miracles, the shedding of his blood in Gethsemane, his death on the cross, and his resurrection from the tomb could be, each one, marked on a calendar and also on a map with perfect accuracy if we but had the detailed information. These are historical facts—absolute truths—not simply philosophical, moral, or so-called "religious" truths; and a knowledge of these and other precious truths is essential to salvation.

However, it seems that the worldly wise, with their systems of philosophy and learning, are always clamoring for our attention. Jacob stoutly denounces trusting in the wisdom and the learning of the world, especially if these prevent a person from coming to a knowledge and acceptance of the gospel, or distract those who already have the gospel. A frequent topic in the Book of Mormon is the antagonism between the learning of the world and the things of God (see, for example, 2 Nephi 26–29; Jacob 4:14). Jacob is not shy in perpetuating the distinction between the two. It is not the worldly learning alone that places a barrier between man and his God; it is also man's pride in his learning—his trusting "in the arm of flesh"—that leaves him ignorant of spiritual things. A specific contribution of the Book of Mormon is that it explains not only what the gospel of Christ is but also what it is *not*. Hence the Book of Mormon draws a wide distinction between the secular and the spiritual, and it exposes the false concepts so prevalent in the world in the forms of secularism, humanism, materialism, organic evolution, and the like.

Obtaining Truth

But an even more pronounced and significant difference exists between various types or levels of truth than simply their relative importance: Different truths are comprehended by the mind of man in different ways. We perceive most truths that we deal with in mortality through our natural senses, but certain truths necessary to the redemption of our souls we perceive only by revelation through the Holy Ghost. We comprehend these truths not by intellectual activity alone but through spiritual discernment. Such truths are, in the language of the Lord, "great treasures of knowledge, even hidden treasures" (D&C 89:19). It is as Paul said, "If our gospel be hid, it is hid to them that are lost," that is, hidden to those without the Spirit (2 Corinthians 4:3).

And again, speaking of spiritual truths, Paul said: "God hath revealed them unto us by his Spirit; for the Spirit searcheth all things, yea, the deep things of God. . . . Even so the things of God knoweth no man, except he has the Spirit of God. . . . But the natural man receiveth not the things of the Spirit of God; for they are foolishness unto him; neither can he know them, because they are spiritually discerned." (JST, 1 Corinthians 2:10, 11, 14.)

Note that Paul does not say that the natural man simply *does not* know the things of God; he says the natural man *cannot* know them. The things of the Spirit are just as real as the things of the earth, but they are in a different sphere, and fallen man's ability to perceive and understand them is so limited that he can comprehend them only by the inspiration of the Holy Ghost.

This same principle is taught in Doctrine and Covenants 76:115–117, wherein is recorded Joseph Smith and Sidney Rigdon's explanation as to why they did not write more about the things they saw in the vision of the three degrees of glory. First, they said, they were forbidden to do so; and second, they explained, "man [is not] capable to make them known, for they are only to be seen and understood by the power of the Holy Spirit, which God bestows on those who love him, and purify themselves before him; to whom he grants this privilege of seeing and knowing for themselves."

This principle is also illustrated in the Savior's words to Peter. When Jesus asked the Twelve, "Whom do men say that I the Son of man am?" they replied, "Some say that thou art John the Baptist: some, Elias; and others, Jeremias, or one of the prophets." But when he asked, "Whom say ye that I am?" Peter said, "Thou art the Christ, the Son of the living God." Jesus' subsequent response suggests a difference between mortal and divine—secular and spiritual—truth: "Flesh and blood hath not revealed it unto thee, but my Father which is in heaven." (Matthew 16:13–17.)

These passages of scripture seem to indicate the existence of a hierarchy of truths and to say that not all truth is available to all persons just for the asking. This stratification of truth may be what the Lord refers to in the following statement: "All truth is independent in that sphere in which God has placed it, to act for itself" (D&C 93:30). This passage suggests that there are different categories (spheres) of truth and that each is independent of the other. In other words, apparently there are truths common to our mortal, fallen world and other truths peculiar to spiritual things. As we have already seen, there are some areas of truth that the natural man cannot know because he does not have the medium for acquiring them. Spiritual truth is made known only by the Spirit and only to those who believe, repent, and prepare themselves to obtain it.

Gaining the particular knowledge that saves is so important that "it is impossible for a man to be saved in ignorance" (D&C 131:6). Consequently, as the Prophet Joseph Smith stated, "a man is saved no faster than he gets knowledge" of these special truths.[1] The knowledge that a person possesses is fundamental to his thinking and his state of mind. What he doesn't know can't help him. And, contrary to a popular saying, what he doesn't know *can* hurt him. Even the approach of great danger, if not perceived by an individual, has no effect on the consciousness or emotion of that individual.

Without a knowledge of spiritual things, a person lacks the conviction, the determination, and the direction that this knowledge could give him. We see millions of people in the world today who are unaware and unconcerned about their relationship to God. We read in the third lecture in the *Lectures on Faith* that without a correct knowledge of God and his attributes, one cannot exercise the degree of faith necessary for life and salvation.[2] A person cannot have perfect faith in something he knows nothing about. Since this is true, and the scriptures say it is true, all of us are obliged to learn some spiritual truths if we want to be saved in the celestial kingdom. We cannot even have a testimony that Jesus is the Christ except by the revelation of the Holy Ghost. Saving truths are divine, not natural, knowledge.

Since not all truths are of equal value, and since those truths most necessary to salvation are gained only through the Holy Spirit of God, obviously a person stands in jeopardy if he is not gaining those particular truths through that particular Spirit while in this particular life. Job said that the things of God are "past finding out" (Job 9:10), and his "friend" Zophar asked, "Canst thou by searching find out God?" (Job 11:7.) It seems to me the correct answer to Zophar's question is no. The things of God do not yield themselves to searching alone. No one can obtain the things of God except by revelation, and God must reveal himself or remain forever unknown. Jacob wrote: "How unsearchable are the depths of the mysteries of him. . . . And no man knoweth of his ways save it be revealed unto him; wherefore, brethren, despise not the revelations of God." (Jacob 4:8.)

Borrowing the language of Paul from his writings about the different kinds of resurrected bodies and the different degrees of glory (1 Corinthians 15:39–44), we could give the following description of the different kinds of truth: All truth is not the same truth, for there is one kind of truth common among men, and another kind that pertains to God. There is also a truth that is gained through the mortal senses, and another that is gained only through the Spirit. There is one kind of truth that comes from God, and another kind that comes from men, for one truth differs from another truth in glory. So also is the truth that is had in the earth. There is a natural truth, and there is a spiritual truth.

But truth of a spiritual nature is different in yet another way. Spiritual truth is not simply bare fact or mere information. The scriptures speak of light *and* truth as companions. The glory of God, which is his intelligence, is both light *and* truth, not just truth alone (D&C 93:36). The presence of light in company with knowledge seems to be an essential quality that distinguishes God's truth—the knowledge that saves—from the type of truth that is mere intellectual fact and that even a natural or a wicked man can gain by research and study.

The Miraculous Is Essential to the Gospel

In addition, there has to be a miraculous character to the gospel, or it would be only an earthly philosophy. The ideas, the concepts, the doctrines, the truths thereof must come from a source beyond mortality, or the gospel would be earthbound; it cannot rise above the power and capability of its source. Divine truth comes from the other side of the veil; if this were not so, the gospel could not exceed the knowledge and powers that exist on this side of the veil.

In short, basing our conclusions on the scriptures, we see at least five distinctions between what we call natural, or secular, truth and spiritual truth: (1) spiritual truth is essential for redemption of the soul, but secular truth is only an aid, not a necessity; (2) spiritual truth is perceived only by revelation through the Holy Ghost, Spirit to spirit, whereas natural truth is learned through the five senses; (3) spiritual truth is revealed only to those who seek to obey the commandments of God, whereas secular truth can be gained by anyone, without regard to his or her moral status; (4) spiritual truth does not consist of fact alone but is accompanied by light, whereas secular truth may lack such light; (5) spiritual truth is ultimately more important than any other truth.

Spiritual Learning Should Have Primacy in Mortality

Given the preceding conclusions, we begin to see why it is so important that we stress spiritual learning in our lives. This is not to say that we should oppose secular learning; rather, we should set appropriate priorities. Let us not use up our time on the peripheral concepts; let us focus instead on the unique and basic message of the plan of salvation and the restoration of the gospel through the Prophet Joseph Smith. Those with teaching assignments in the Church have a particular responsibility to ensure that these gospel fundamentals are central to the spiritual learning of those they teach. A statement by President J. Reuben Clark, Jr., given on 21 June 1954 at a gathering of seminary and institute faculty, is applicable to all of us at any time:

> Only the prophet, seer, and revelator of the Church, the Presiding High Priest, the President of the Church, has the right to receive revelations for the Church or to declare the doctrines of the Church. No other member of the Church has any such right or authority. It is well that we all remember this. It is particularly important that you teachers instructing our youth should keep this constantly in mind. In matters of gospel doctrine there is no such thing as academic freedom in your teaching of youth. You declare the Word of God as written in the scriptures, and as interpreted by his prophet, seer, and revelator. Otherwise there is chaos and apostasy, and we shall follow the route of the primitive, post-Apostolic Church.[3]

As we consider the high priority that spiritual learning should have in our lives, we would do well to contemplate these words from President Spencer W. Kimball:

> The secular knowledge is to be *desired*; the spiritual knowledge is a *necessity*. We shall need all of the accumulated secular knowledge in order to create worlds and furnish them, but only through the mysteries of God and these hidden treasures of knowledge may we arrive at the place and condition where we may use that knowledge in creation and exaltation.[4]
>
> We understand, as few people do, that education is a part of being about our Father's business and that the scriptures contain the master concepts for mankind.[5]
>
> Peter was said to be ignorant and unlearned, while Nicodemus was, as the Savior said, a master, a trained one, an educated man. And while Nicodemus would in his aging process gradually lose his prestige, his strength, and go to the grave a

man of letters without eternal knowledge, Peter would go to his reputed crucifixion the greatest man in all the world, perhaps still lacking considerably in secular knowledge (which he would later acquire), but being preeminent in the greater, more important knowledge of the eternities and God and his creations and their destinies.[6]

Even in the spirit world after death our spirits can go on learning the more secular things to help us create worlds and become their masters. . . .

Secular knowledge, important as it may be, can never save a soul nor open the celestial kingdom nor create a world nor make a man a god, but it can be most helpful to that man who, placing first things first, has found the way to eternal life and who can now bring into play all knowledge to be his tool and servant.[7]

Peter and John had little secular learning, being termed ignorant. But Peter and John knew the vital things of life; that God lives and that the crucified, resurrected Lord is the Son of God. They knew the path to eternal life. This they learned in the few decades of their mortal life. This exaltation meant Godhood for them and creation of worlds with eternal increase for which they would probably need, eventually, a total knowledge of the sciences. But this fact escapes many: Peter and John had only decades to learn and do the spiritual but have had already about nineteen centuries in which to learn the secular or the geology of the earth, the zoology and physiology and psychology of the creatures of the earth. But mortality is the time to learn of God and the gospel first and to perform the ordinances, then to learn what can be secured of the secular things. Here are the so-called ignorant Peter and John heirs to exaltation. Accordingly the ignorance the Lord speaks of when he says "One cannot be saved in ignorance" is the lack of knowledge of the really first things—the kingdom of God and his righteousness.[8]

Thus, the words of the scriptures and of our latter-day prophets indicate that the knowledge of greatest worth to us, and that which we should most earnestly seek to obtain and apply, is the knowledge that saves. The great importance of gaining this knowledge is affirmed in another statement from President J. Reuben Clark, Jr., in which he emphasizes that, although all knowledge is useful, highest priority should be given to learning spiritual truths while in mortality: "There is spiritual learning just as there is material learning, and the one without the other is not complete; yet, speaking for myself, if I could have only one sort of learning, that which I would take would be the learning of the spirit, because in the hereafter I shall have opportunity in the eternities which are to come to get the other, and without spiritual learning here my handicaps in the hereafter would be all but overwhelming."[9]

Since, from an eternal perspective, we have such little time here in mortality, let us heed the counsel of Presidents Clark and Kimball and focus our time and attention on those matters of primary and sacred importance.

Notes

1. *Teachings of the Prophet Joseph Smith*, comp. Joseph Fielding Smith (Salt Lake City: Deseret Book Co., 1976), p. 217; see also pp. 301, 304, 331, 332.
2. *Lectures on Faith* 3:1–4, 19.
3. J. Reuben Clark, Jr., *Man—God's Greatest Miracle* [pamphlet] (Salt Lake City: Deseret News Press, 1971), pp. 5–6.
4. Spencer W. Kimball, *Faith Precedes the Miracle* (Salt Lake City: Deseret Book Co., 1972), p. 280, italics in original.
5. Spencer W. Kimball, *The Teachings of Spencer W. Kimball*, ed. Edward L. Kimball (Salt Lake City: Bookcraft, 1982), p. 387. Hereafter cited as *TSWK*.
6. *TSWK*, p. 389.
7. *TSWK*, pp. 390–91.
8. Spencer W. Kimball, "Beloved Youth, Study and Learn," in *Life's Directions* (Salt Lake City: Deseret Book Co., 1962), pp. 179–80.
9. J. Reuben Clark, Jr., in Conference Report, April 1934, p. 94.

Chapter 13

ORIGIN OF MAN: THE DOCTRINAL FRAMEWORK

Throughout my life I have read far more from the scriptures and the words of the Brethren than I have from the writings of the non-LDS theologians and philosophers of the world. I am only moderately acquainted with the teachings of the various branches of philosophy, language, and science. However, I have been exposed to them, and I am not a complete stranger to their theories.

I am much more familiar with the authors and the content of the standard works, particularly the latter-day scriptures, and with the history of the Church in this dispensation. I have been tutored and influenced by the writings and viewpoints of such prophets as Joseph Smith, Brigham Young, Hyrum Smith, Joseph F. Smith, Joseph Fielding Smith, J. Reuben Clark, Jr., Harold B. Lee, Marion G. Romney, and Ezra Taft Benson, as well as those of Elders Orson Pratt, Bruce R. McConkie, and Boyd K. Packer. I have especially tried to become thoroughly conversant with the doctrinal teachings of the Prophet Joseph Smith.

I know there is a kind of monitor in a person's soul that gives him direction and feeling. This monitor often exceeds human judgment and knowledge, and sometimes it is the source for viewpoints or feelings that a person cannot articulate and prove by the facts and logic in his immediate possession; yet these feelings are true. Regarding most matters I expect adequate tangible proof will come later. However, we generally need the guidance of this monitor now, since in many cases we cannot wait for the proof before we act. This monitor is the working of the Holy Ghost. It is the companion to research but is not dependent on it. It provides conviction and testimony and inspiration to the soul, whereas mere facts, however brilliantly displayed and stimulating to the intellect, sometimes leave the soul unconvinced or even troubled.

I am converted to the story of the gospel—the knowledge we have of the plan of salvation as taught in the scriptures and by the prophets of this dispensation. I believe that our spirits are literally the sons and daughters of heavenly parents and that we lived as intelligent individuals in a premortal sphere, where both sin and righteousness existed. I believe that a grand council was held, Lucifer rebelled, and there was war in heaven. I believe also that there were premortal foreordinations and appointments, that the world was created as a place where spirits could obtain bodies of flesh and bones, and that earth life was designed as a probationary state. Further, it is my conviction that there was a fall of Adam, that an atonement was made by Jesus Christ, and that after mortal life we all enter the spirit world to await the resurrection. A judgment will follow, and each person will be assigned to a kingdom to which he is best suited—some to become gods and goddesses, others to become angels, and some to become sons of perdition. I know there is a God, who has a body of flesh and bones, and I know there is a devil. I know there is a heaven, and I know there is a hell.

The entire plan as taught in the scriptures indicates that God is in charge and that there is order in his designs. God has a plan, and he has every necessary power and ability to carry out that plan to the fullest extent and to the minutest detail. Given these scriptural witnesses, our concept of God must be that he is perfect and has all power and knowledge, that he does not lack in any particular, and that no being can prevent, alter, or overturn his desires. This is the God of the scriptures and of the prophets. This is the message of the first three of the lectures on faith taught in the School of the Elders during the Kirtland period. There is order and unity in the plan that God has revealed. Thus, as we study the scriptures and read of the premortal existence, of mortality, and of the life beyond, we discover that there is security and wholeness in the way the gospel is unfolded in these sacred records.

In this chapter I wish to focus on three aspects of the plan of God and how they relate to an understanding of the origin of man. These three aspects are the Creation, the fall of man, and the atonement of Jesus Christ. Each of these is an item of history that actually took place in time and space, but all of them are beyond our immediate conscious frame of personal experience and remembrance; thus we have to depend on what we can learn of them from other sources, preferably from the revelations of God. The revelations are the only source from which we can obtain accurate information on these three subjects. Furthermore, if we accept the idea that God is perfect, we automatically come to the conclusion not only that God has a plan but also that this plan is the only right plan. Moreover, we can see that each part of the plan is essential to the function of every other part of the plan.

The Creation of the Earth and of Man

By the term *creation* I mean the creation of the world, man, animals, and so on. I don't know how long it took to create the earth or how it was done. Two of the informational contributions given by the scriptures and the prophets are that the Creation was accomplished by the Father through his Only Begotten Son and that the Creation was done for a specific purpose. Latter-day revelation shows that the purpose of the earth is (1) to provide a place for our spirits to get a body of flesh and bones, (2) to provide a place for embodied spirits to live in a probationary state, and (3) to provide eventually an eternal celestial sphere upon which those beings who lived on this earth may dwell—a sanctified place which even God the Father will visit. The scriptures explain that the earth was deliberately formed or organized for these very definite purposes. (See Moses 2–3; 1 Nephi 17:36; D&C 49:15–17; Abraham 3:24–25; Alma 12:24; 42:4, 10, 13; D&C 88:17–20, 25.)

The Fall of Man

We will next consider the fall of man. In doing so, it must be emphasized that mankind's fallen condition, the condition brought about by the fall of Adam, is a step beyond that state in which the world and man were found when first created. That is to say, the conditions that characterize the mortal world and with which you and I are acquainted are not the same conditions that characterized the world at its creation, as described in the early chapters of Genesis, Moses, and Abraham. New conditions were introduced, and the scriptures say this change was the result of the Fall.

More specifically, the world as we know it is really the result of a three-step process, and it is necessary that we view each step in its proper sequence and that we use the proper terminology to describe all three. We should speak of the "spirit creation," the "physical-spiritual creation," and the "mortal, or temporal, creation." Thus the full process of creation as we know it was not complete until there had been a fall. Creation was a joint venture: we know that God created the world, but it was Adam and Eve who brought about the Fall.

The scriptural account of the Creation tells us that there was a spirit creation, but it does not give us a detailed record of it. All we know is that there was such a creation. All things—people, animals, plants—existed as spirits before anything existed physically on the earth. (See step 1 on the accompanying chart.)

As created physically during the six periods of creation, the earth and everything in it were physical, or tangible, in their nature, but *spiritual* in their condition (see 2 Nephi 2:22; Moses 3:9). That is, there was no blood in the veins, no death, no children, and no sin. In this step, the plants and animals were placed upon the earth on the third, fifth, and sixth days; Adam and Eve were placed here on the sixth day, *after* the animals. (See step 2 on the accompanying chart.)

When Adam and Eve partook of the tree of knowledge of good and evil, a change came over them—they became mortal. This brought upon them, first, the spiritual death, which means separation from the presence of God, or alienation from the things of God—to die as to things of righteousness. This death came upon Adam and Eve as a result of, and soon after, the transgression. The Fall also introduced physical death, although Adam did not die that death for nearly a thousand years; yet as Abraham points out, Adam experienced the physical death within a "day" of the Lord's time, since the earth was on the Lord's time when the promise was made that man would die within a day. Our present form of reckoning was not given to man until after the Fall. (See Abraham 5:13.)

As a result of the transgression of Adam and Eve, blood, death, reproduction, and sin entered the world. This change came upon not only Adam but also the whole creation, and so the earth and all life became part of the mortal, fallen world we now know. Although in sequence Adam was placed upon the earth after the animals, he was the first to become mortal—the "first flesh" (Moses 3:7). (See step 3 on the accompanying chart.)

At this point we should note that each of us, since the Fall, has come directly from the premortal spirit world into mortality, whereas Adam and Eve—and whatever animals, birds, and plants were placed upon the earth at the physical-spiritual creation—went through the in-between stage (step 2 on the chart).

This in-between stage—that is, the physical-spiritual creation described in Genesis 1 and Moses 2—was a necessary stage to set up the program and enable man to bring about the conditions of

Creation, Fall, and Atonement

Our present mortal world is the result of a three-step process:

1. Spirit Creation

- No detailed account given; we only know it occurred.
- Earth, plants, animals, and mankind all created as spirits—"In heaven created I them" (Moses 3:5).

2. Physical-Spiritual Creation

- Accounts given in Genesis 1; Moses 2–3; Abraham 4–5.
- Consisted of six creative periods.
- A physical, tangible creation, but no blood, no death, no reproduction, and no sin.
- Animals and plants created and placed on earth *prior* to man.

3. The Mortal, Temporal, Fallen World

- Accounts of Fall given in Genesis 3; Moses 4–5.
- The physical, tangible world with blood, death, reproduction, and sin.
- Man the first to fall, become mortal; other forms of life became mortal *after* man.

The Fall brought two kinds of death:

1. Temporal—physical death.
2. Spiritual—separation or alienation from things of God.

The Atonement rescues man from these two deaths.

mortality. In the garden Adam and Eve had physical bodies to house their eternal spirits, but those physical bodies were living subject to spiritual conditions. They were real bodies with tangible muscle and bone, but they did not contain blood. This was a physical creation under spiritual conditions. It was deathless. Doctrine and Covenants 88:27 describes resurrected beings as spiritual. They are physical but also spiritual. Saying they are ''spiritual'' bodies is different than saying they are ''spirit'' bodies. This is the same sense in which Paul uses the term *spiritual bodies* in 1 Corinthians 15:44–46.

The Importance of a Divine Plan

Before going further and discussing specific items relative to the Atonement, let us look first at some other pertinent issues. In considering the doctrines of the Creation, the Fall, and the Atonement and how they relate to a correct understanding of man's origin, it is absolutely essential that we acknowledge and remember that there is a perfect, eternal plan and that it existed in the mind of God before the foundation of the world. The end was known ever since the beginning. And everything in between was also known to God. The whole plan is one eternal ''now'' in the mind and vision of God. Every day is a clear day with the Lord, and he can see forever. It is as Nephi stated: ''The Lord knoweth all things from the beginning; wherefore, he prepareth a way to accomplish all his works among the children of men; for behold, he hath all power unto the fulfilling of all his words'' (1 Nephi 9:6).

That God has a plan for mankind is mentioned at least twenty-eight times in latter-day scripture. These scriptures give various names for the divine plan, such as the following:

''Great and eternal plan'' (Alma 34:16)
''Great plan of happiness'' (Alma 42:8)
''Great plan of redemption'' (Jacob 6:8; Alma 34:31)
''Plan of deliverance'' (2 Nephi 11:5)
''Plan of mercy'' (Alma 42:15, 31)
''Plan of our God'' (2 Nephi 9:13)
''Plan of redemption'' (Alma 12:25, 26, 30, 32, 33; 17:16; 18:39; 22:13–14; 29:2; 39:18; 42:11, 13)
''Plan of restoration'' (Alma 41:2)
''Plan of salvation'' (Jarom 1:2; Alma 24:14; 42:5; Moses 6:62)

"Plan of the Eternal God" (Alma 34:9)
"Plan of the great Creator" (2 Nephi 9:6)
"Their [the Gods'] plan" (Abraham 4:21)

In contrast, the Bible does not speak specifically of a divine plan. However, the Joseph Smith Translation of the Bible restores to the biblical record at least one direct reference to God's plan (see Moses 6:62). Evidently this concept is one of the plain and precious things taken away from the Bible (see 1 Nephi 13).

The plan of God calls for a creation, a fall that brings two kinds of death, a probationary period, a set of commandments and ordinances, an infinite atonement by a God, a resurrection, a judgment, and an assignment to one's everlasting destiny. It would destroy the plan if any part or any step were changed or omitted (see Alma 42:8). The plan is a package—none of it is superfluous, none is optional. The whole of it is "fitly joined together" by that which "every joint supplieth" (Ephesians 4:16).

Organic Evolution Not Part of Plan

Clearly, the items we have so far discussed (as well as the accompanying chart) do not provide for organic evolution. Nor do they need to. It is not my intention to attack the evolutionist, but I will point out what I see in the theory of evolution that is inconsistent with the revelations. While I do not agree with the concept of organic evolution for the origin of man, that does not mean I have ill will toward the evolutionist. This is not an indictment against anyone's goodness but rather a statement about what I believe the scriptures say.

There are particular things in the revealed accounts of the Creation and of the fall of man that, in my mind, preclude organic evolution from being the process by which man's body was created on this earth. To accept organic evolution as the process by which man came upon the earth is to say that the processes of birth and death, including the element of blood, existed upon the earth before the fall of Adam. This seems contrary to the teachings of the scriptures, for in several instances the scriptures say that it was Adam who introduced death and also reproduction. If those scriptural teachings are correct, I do not see how there could have been death or reproduction before Adam or how Adam's body could have been the offspring of animal life on this earth. It simply is not theologically sound for Adam's pedigree chart and family group sheet to show him at the bottom of a list of animal ancestors. Thus, it seems to me that to accept the concept of organic evolution as the origin of man's physical body would be to negate and deny the doctrine of the fall of Adam; to do so would be to seriously alter the plan of salvation as it has been revealed to us.

The Idea of Theistic Evolution

Some have developed a hypothesis asserting that God created Adam by the evolutionary process. This is sometimes labeled "theistic evolution" and is an attempt to harmonize what is perceived as scientific evidence for organic evolution on the one hand with faith in God and the divine origin of man on the other. The theistic evolutionist often speaks of a guided evolution, in which God intervenes in the process. There are those in and out of the Church who, because they believe in a divine being, sincerely attempt to hold to both the theory of evolution and their faith in God as creator. It is my opinion that in the eternal plan of God these two positions are incompatible, and that a person cannot ascribe to both if he understands what the issues are. I am not qualified to discuss the scientific issues, but I am somewhat acquainted with the doctrinal and theological issues. I am aware that there are varieties of theistic evolution and that not all its advocates see it in precisely the same way. But it appears to me that there is a fundamental sameness among all brands of evolution that makes them discordant with the revelations recorded in the scriptures.

The Fixed Principles of the Plan of God

Let us examine some statements from the scriptures and from the Prophet Joseph Smith that provide guidelines for understanding any gospel subject and that can also assist us in evaluating the theory of organic evolution. Undergirding these statements are the concepts that a plan existed in the mind of God before the world was created, that the earth and all things in the earth were created as part of that plan, and that the plan is based on certain fixed principles.

Consider the following from Joseph Smith the Prophet:

> All men know that they must die. . . . What is the object of our coming into existence, then dying and falling away, to

be here no more? It is but reasonable to suppose that God would reveal something in reference to the matter, and it is a subject we ought to study more than any other. We ought to study it day and night, for the world is ignorant in reference to their true condition and relation. If we have any claim on our Heavenly Father for anything, it is for knowledge on this important subject. . . . Could you gaze into heaven five minutes, you would know more than you would by reading all that ever was written on the subject.

We are only capable of comprehending that certain things exist, which we may acquire by certain *fixed principles.* If men would acquire salvation, they have got to be subject, before they leave this world, to certain rules and principles, which were *fixed by an unalterable decree* before the world was. . . .

The organization of the spiritual and heavenly worlds, and of spiritual and heavenly beings, was agreeable to the *most perfect order and harmony:* their *limits and bounds were fixed irrevocably,* and voluntarily subscribed to in their heavenly estate by themselves, and were by our first parents subscribed to upon the earth. Hence the importance of embracing and subscribing to *principles of eternal truth* by all men upon the earth that expect eternal life.

I assure the Saints that truth, in reference to these matters, can and may be known through the revelations of God in the way of His ordinances, and in answer to prayer.[1]

And again from Joseph Smith:

God has made certain decrees which are fixed and immovable; for instance, God set the sun, the moon, and the stars in the heavens, and gave them their laws, conditions, and bounds, which they cannot pass, except by His commandments; they all move in perfect harmony in their sphere and order, and are as lights, wonders and signs unto us. The sea also has its bounds which it cannot pass. God has set many signs on the earth, as well as in the heavens; for instance, the oak of the forest, the fruit of the tree, the herb of the field, all bear a sign that seed hath been planted there; for it is a decree of the Lord that every tree, plant, and herb bearing seed should bring forth of its kind, and cannot come forth after any other law or principle.[2]

In the book *Teachings of the Prophet Joseph Smith*, a footnote, apparently written by Joseph Fielding Smith, makes the following comment about the Prophet's statement above: "This very positive statement by the Prophet, that every tree, plant, and herb, and evidently every other creature, cannot produce except after its kind, is in harmony not only with the scriptures, but also with all known facts in the world."[3]

Note that the Prophet is very definite in his pronouncements about "fixed principles" that are "unalterable" and that pertain to the earth and to man. He said these fixed principles were ordained and established before the earth came into existence. Continuing, the Prophet described gospel ordinances in the same terms as these fixed principles—they are all part of the plan of salvation:

> Upon the same principle do I contend that baptism is a sign ordained of God, for the believer in Christ to take upon himself in order to enter into the kingdom of God, "for except ye are born of water and of the Spirit ye cannot enter into the Kingdom of God," said the Savior. It is a sign and a commandment which God has set for man to enter into His kingdom. Those who seek to enter in any other way will seek in vain; for God will not receive them, neither will the angels acknowledge their works as accepted, for they have not obeyed the ordinances, nor attended to the signs which God ordained for the salvation of man, to prepare him for, and give him a title to, a celestial glory; and God had decreed that all who will not obey His voice shall not escape the damnation of hell.[4]

None of us will question what the Prophet said about the necessity of baptism. But do we catch the full force of his statement? He indicated that everything in the plan of salvation—which includes creation, reproduction, and baptism—is governed by the same set of fixed, unalterable principles. Each item is indispensable to the operation of the whole plan.

The Prophet further explained that baptism, the priesthood, and the gift of the Holy Ghost are all essential for salvation and are all governed by fixed principles that permit neither variation nor omission.[5] Since that is the case with the ordinances, can we not also see that such things as the creation of the earth and of men, the fall of Adam, and the introduction of death, sin, and reproduction were also accomplished on the basis of God's fixed principles? These are part of the same eternal plan of salvation, all aspects of which are essential and none of which can be rationalized away or omitted.

Notice the way Alma 42:6–8 is worded. This passage points out, as many others do, that death is an integral part of the plan of God. If death were omitted, "it would destroy the great plan of happiness" (Alma 42:8). Alma doesn't say that the omission of death would merely alter, affect, or inconvenience the plan; he says it would *destroy* it. There is at least a suggestion here that the plan of God isn't subject to change.

These statements from the Prophet Joseph and the scriptures are clearly an affirmation or declaration that everything is governed by the laws of God that were established before the world was formed. Similar affirmations are found in the Doctrine and Covenants. Note that all of the following passages emphasize that the law was established before the world was created:

> There is a law, irrevocably decreed in heaven before the foundations of this world, upon which all blessings are predicated—
>
> And when we obtain any blessing from God, it is by obedience to that law upon which it is predicated (D&C 130:20–21).

> For all who will have a blessing at my hands shall abide the law which was appointed for that blessing, and the conditions thereof, as were instituted from before the foundation of the world (D&C 132:5).

> Behold, mine house is a house of order, saith the Lord God, and not a house of confusion.
>
> Will I accept of an offering, saith the Lord, that is not made in my name?
>
> Or will I receive at your hands that which I have not appointed?
>
> And will I appoint unto you, saith the Lord, except it be by law, even as I and my Father ordained unto you, before the world was?
>
> I am the Lord thy God; and I give unto you this commandment—that no man shall come unto the Father but by me or by my word, which is my law, saith the Lord. (D&C 132:8–12.)

> I am the Lord thy God, and will give unto thee the law of my Holy Priesthood, as was ordained by me and my Father before the world was (D&C 132:28).

What I am saying is that, on the basis of what the Prophet Joseph Smith has said and what the Lord has said, we have no more right to alter the Lord's declaration about how he created man or how man fell and became mortal than we have to alter the revealed methods of baptism, ordination, and so on. The Creation and the Fall are as much a part of the plan of salvation as baptism or any of the ordinances are.

In seeking to understand the Creation, the Fall, and the Atonement in relation to the origin of man, we would do well to remember an observation made by the Prophet Joseph Smith during his King Follett discourse: "In the first place, I wish to go back to the beginning—to the morn of creation. There is the starting point for us to look to, in order to understand and be fully acquainted with the mind, purposes and decrees of the Great Elohim, who sits in yonder heavens as he did at the creation of this world. It is necessary for us to have an understanding of God himself in the beginning. *If we start right, it is easy to go right all the time; but if we start wrong, we may go wrong, and it be a hard matter to get right.*"[6]

The Prophet's declaration about the importance of getting started right and his warning about the dangers of getting started wrong invite all of us to look to the key passages of the scriptures that deal with the nature of God, the premortal existence, the Creation, the Fall, and the mission of Jesus Christ as the chief sources for our understanding of what took place. In this way we can discover what laws governed those events.

I once learned some fixed principles for myself in a geometry class. We learned, for instance, that there were unvarying rules for determining certain unknown measurements of a triangle. There are just two requirements: first, a person has to be given enough basic information about the triangle; second, he has to know the fixed principles involved. If these requirements are met, a person can discover the unknown or unstated measurements of a triangle as accurately as though they were stated. For example, it is a fixed rule that the sum of the three angles of a triangle is always 180 degrees. This sum never varies; it cannot vary. Thus, if a person is given the sizes of two angles of a triangle, he can compute the size of the third angle with perfect confidence of accuracy.

The Prophet Joseph used this same kind of reasoning and deduction in determining some doctrinal principles. For example, he concluded that Noah was baptized and ordained by the laying on of hands, even though the scriptures do not expressly so state. He knew how to arrive at the right conclusion because he knew the fixed principles involved. We read from the Prophet's teachings: "Now taking it for granted that the scriptures say what they mean, and mean what they say, we have sufficient grounds to go on and prove from the Bible that the gospel has always been the same; the ordinances to fulfill its requirements, the same, and the officers to officiate, the same; and the signs and fruits resulting from the promises, the same: therefore, as Noah was a preacher of righteousness he must have been baptized and ordained to the priesthood by the laying on of the hands, etc."[7]

On this same basis, I am saying that if we will listen and understand what the revelations and the Prophet Joseph are telling us about the fixed principles—about the laws of God that governed the Creation, the Fall, and the Atonement—we will have sufficient knowledge and comprehension of the eternal plan that we will not be seduced by, or drawn into an acceptance of, any false concept at the expense of gospel principles and the mission of Jesus Christ. If we don't know the doctrine or the scriptures, however, we might find ourselves making such trade-offs.

The scriptures do not always answer directly each question that might arise concerning a given topic. But if we know the principles involved we can generally arrive at an acceptable answer in the same way that we can determine the measurements of a triangle, or the way the Prophet concluded that Noah was baptized. We do this by first considering the known facts and formulas involved and then arriving at a conclusion based on those known principles. Then we should examine our conclusion to ensure that it does not run counter to other known principles. This is what makes scripture study fascinating and challenging. The more you learn the more you are *able* to learn, and whole areas of understanding open up to you that before were hidden.

However, in all of this we need to exercise caution. Our judgment must be guided by the known truths. The Prophet Joseph Smith warned: "A fanciful and flowery and heated imagination beware of; because the things of God are of deep import; and time, and experience, and careful and ponderous and solemn thoughts can only find them out. Thy mind, O man! if thou wilt lead a soul unto salvation, must stretch as high as the utmost heavens, and search into and contemplate the darkest abyss, and the broad expanse of eternity—thou must commune with God. How much more dignified and noble are the thoughts of God, than the vain imaginations of the human heart! None but fools will trifle with the souls of men."[8]

Theistic Evolution Not Consistent with Revelations

Speaking more specifically now, What is wrong with a belief in theistic evolution as an explanation for the origin of man? That is, what is erroneous about believing that God created Adam, or mankind, by the evolutionary process? I do not know of any passage of scripture that says categorically: "Organic evolution is wrong." But we can work out an answer by examining the principles involved. A verse from the book of Isaiah can serve as a kind of formula: "To the law and to the testimony: if they speak not according to this word, it is because there is no light in them" (Isaiah 8:20).

Probably the first signal we get that something might be wrong with the idea of organic evolution is that it omits the need for a fall of the kind described in the scriptures. The scriptures say that the fall of Adam introduced death and also reproduction (Moses 5:11; 6:48; 2 Nephi 2:22–25).

Furthermore, 2 Nephi 9:6–9 plainly says that the fall of Adam introduced two kinds of death—the spiritual kind and the physical kind—and thus laid the groundwork for a Savior who would need to atone for these two deaths. Several scriptures connect the mission of Jesus Christ directly to the fall of Adam. Consider the following:

> Adam fell that men might be; and men are, that they might have joy.
>
> And the Messiah cometh in the fulness of time, that he may redeem the children of men from the fall. (2 Nephi 2:25–26.)

> For as death hath passed upon all men, to fulfil the merciful plan of the great Creator, there must needs be a power of resurrection, and the resurrection must needs come unto man by reason of the fall; and the fall came by reason of transgression; and because man became fallen they were cut off from the presence of the Lord.
>
> Wherefore, it must needs be an infinite atonement. . . .
>
> . . . For behold, he suffereth the pains of all men, yea, the pains of every living creature, both men, women, and children, who belong to the family of Adam. (2 Nephi 9:6–7, 21.)

> Behold, he created Adam, and by Adam came the fall of man. And because of the fall of man came Jesus Christ, even

> the Father and the Son; and because of Jesus Christ came the redemption of man. (Mormon 9:12.)

> Because that Adam fell, we are; and by his fall came death; and we are made partakers of misery and woe. . . .
>
> Therefore I give unto you a commandment, to teach these things freely unto your children, saying:
>
> That by reason of transgression cometh the fall, which fall bringeth death, and inasmuch as ye were born into the world by water, and blood, and the spirit, which I have made, and so became of dust a living soul, even so ye must be born again into the kingdom of heaven, of water, and of the Spirit, and be cleansed by blood, even the blood of mine Only Begotten. (Moses 6:48, 58–59; see also vv. 49–54.)

> Wherefore, it came to pass that the devil tempted Adam, and he partook of the forbidden fruit and transgressed the commandment, wherein he became subject to the will of the devil, because he yielded unto temptation.
>
> Wherefore, I, the Lord God, caused that he should be cast out from the Garden of Eden, from my presence, because of his transgression, wherein he became spiritually dead. . . .
>
> But, behold, I say unto you that I, the Lord God, gave unto Adam and unto his seed, that they should not die as to the temporal death, until I, the Lord God, should send forth angels to declare unto them repentance and redemption, through faith on the name of mine Only Begotten Son. (D&C 29:40–42; see also 20:20–25.)

On the basis of the foregoing scriptures it appears that any theory or concept that lessens the importance of the fall of Adam or omits it from the plan of salvation, also lessens or omits, to the same extent, the redeeming mission of Jesus Christ. Hence, to erase or ignore the fall of Adam and its effects is to remove the need for the atoning blood of Jesus Christ.

Organic Evolution Is a Moral Issue

Let us examine what a person gives up if he denies or omits the fall of Adam from the plan. First of all, such a person says, in effect, that Adam did not introduce physical death or reproduction into this world, since these two processes, or conditions, would have been here on the earth and been operative before Adam was here; these processes would have been the means by which he got here. Taking this theoretical position is tantamount to disposing of the fall of Adam. The theory of evolution thus requires a reversal of the scriptures regarding physical death and also reproduction, and those who believe in evolution seem to accept this reversal without a whimper.

Second (and this seems very important), if one omits the Fall, it is but a short step to begin to deny man's spiritual, as well as his physical, fall. The scriptures teach that the fall of Adam not only brought physical death but also was the means of introducing sin and the consequent *spiritual* death—an alienation from the things of God—into the world. What happens when we omit the Fall? We also say that it was not Adam who introduced spiritual death! From a moral standpoint, if one omits the Fall as the source of sin, it is easy to rationalize sin right out of the picture and say that what the scriptures call sin, or transgression, really doesn't involve a moral infraction. Why? Because, according to this philosophy, sin has always been here and did not involve the breaking of a commandment of God.

It appears that, to be consistent, the evolutionist must deny not only that Adam brought about physical death and reproduction but also that he introduced sin and spiritual death. Even if an individual teacher who advocates this theory is willing to forgo the Fall as the source of physical death, is he also prepared to accept the moral responsibility of saying that sin is not sin? or of saying that man is not responsible and accountable for his own actions? Such teachings sound very much like the doctrine of Korihor. Someone who professes atheism would perhaps be willing to advocate this kind of philosophy, but how can a so-called believer do so? Although probably only a "believer" would be interested in the seeming compromise offered by theistic evolution, his acceptance of it would necessarily force him to deny what God has said about the origin of sin. Such a denial, it seems to me, creates an untenable position for a theistic evolutionist. It may be that the believer who accepts this theory has simply never thought it out to its logical, moral conclusions.

Are there *other* aspects of organic evolution that are incompatible with the plan of salvation? Yes, I believe there are. For instance, evolution functions on the concept of survival of the fittest and natural selection. It is jungle law. As such it is basically materialistic, animalistic, and earthy, and does not have its roots in mercy, justice, agency, or love. Since mercy, justice, agency, and love are attributes of God, it seems simply inconsistent with God's character that he would originate and implement a particular plan for the placement of man on this earth that did not have His attributes as its most prominent features. As I see it, organic evolution is therefore inconsistent with the character of God.

Sometimes we espouse a doctrine or belief not realizing what the full consequences or implications of that concept might be. If we begin with right and true principles—that is, the proper doctrinal framework—we will not collide with other right and true principles. But if we espouse a false concept, even if it seems at first to ease the tension between science and religion, we will find upon examining its broader implications that it comes into conflict with or contradicts some other known true principle. "If we start right, it is easy to go right all the time; but if we start wrong, we may go wrong, and it be a hard matter to get right." Because it is inconsistent with the latter-day scriptures, theistic evolution as an explanation for the origin of man seems to me to be founded on a false premise, and thus I feel this theory will, in the end, be an embarrassment and a millstone around the necks of those who espouse it.

Why the Lord Did Not Simply Create Man Mortal

Other questions that arise in association with theistic evolution include the following: Why didn't the Lord simply create man in a mortal, fallen state? Why cause him the trauma and difficulty of facing conflicting commandments? Did Adam obey God's will when he partook of the fruit? If so, why was he punished?

We do not yet have the complete story of the fall of Adam, nor do we know all of the elements and circumstances that were operative in that event—that is, in the process of Adam and Eve's becoming mortal. If we had more of the facts, I believe we would see that it was all accomplished in a very orderly way and according to eternal principles and procedures. Hidden behind the story of the rib and the forbidden fruit are some deeper meanings.

Consider these words from President Joseph Fielding Smith:

> Why did Adam come here? Not subject to death when he was placed upon this earth, there had to come a change in his body through the partaking of this element—whatever

> you want to call it, fruit—that brought blood into his body; and blood became the life of the body instead of spirit. And blood has in it the seeds of death, some mortal element. Mortality was created through the eating of the forbidden fruit, if you want to call it forbidden, but I think the Lord has made it clear that it was not forbidden. He merely said to Adam, if you want to stay here [in the garden] this is the situation. If so, don't eat it.[9]

One can tell that President Smith did not view the Fall as a tragic miscarriage of, or impediment to, the purposes of God. It was just the opposite—the Lord wanted Adam to fall. Mortality was an essential step in the progress of the human family. President Smith said he understood the Lord's words to Adam to mean that Adam was forbidden to stay in the garden if he ate a particular fruit—not that he was absolutely forbidden to eat the fruit in the first place. That clarifies a vital point, and I appreciate the spiritual insight of this great latter-day prophet and theologian.

Now let us consider the query, Why didn't God just create man mortal and thus save him the trauma and experience of a fall brought to pass through transgression and seemingly conflicting commandments? There are in the scriptures no one-sentence answers to this question, but we have been given enough knowledge concerning God's plan to think through a possible response. In the plan of salvation God does for human beings only what they cannot do for themselves. Man must do all he can for himself. The doctrine is that we are saved by grace, "after all we can do" (2 Nephi 25:23). If Adam and Eve had been created mortal, they would have been denied one of the steps in the process that they were capable of performing themselves. As we read in the Book of Mormon, man "brought upon himself" his own fall (Alma 42:12). Since the Fall was a necessary part of the plan of salvation, and since man was capable of bringing about the fallen condition himself, he was required—or rather it was his privilege—to take the necessary steps.

Furthermore, the Lord has told us that he does not create temporal or mortal conditions nor function on a mortal level. Notice this interesting statement:

> As the words have gone forth out of my mouth even so shall they be fulfilled, that the first shall be last, and that the last shall be first in all things whatsoever I have created by the word of my power, which is the power of my Spirit.

> For by the power of my Spirit created I them; yea, all things both spiritual and temporal—
>
> First spiritual, secondly temporal, which is the beginning of my work; and again, first temporal, and secondly spiritual, which is the last of my work—
>
> Speaking unto you that you may naturally understand; but unto myself my works have no end, neither beginning; but it is given unto you that ye may understand, because ye have asked it of me and are agreed.
>
> Wherefore, verily I say unto you that all things unto me are spiritual, and not at any time have I given unto you a law which was temporal; neither any man, nor the children of men; neither Adam, your father, whom I created.
>
> Behold, I gave unto him that he should be an agent unto himself; and I gave unto him commandment, but no temporal commandment gave I unto him, for my commandments are spiritual; they are not natural nor temporal, neither carnal nor sensual. (D&C 29:30–35.)

I take this statement and explanation by the Lord to be another of those universal fixed principles of eternity. Since the Lord works by law, I take it that he could not create Adam and Eve as mortals because in so doing he would have been creating man by a temporal, mortal law, an area in which he says he is not engaged. God did not need to create our first parents in a fallen condition anyway, because Adam and Eve, by their agency, were capable of bringing about the Fall quite effectively.

If God had created man mortal, then death, sin, and all the circumstances of mortality would be God's doing and would be eternal and permanent in their nature (see Ecclesiastes 3:14); whereas if man brings the Fall upon himself, he is the responsible moral agent, and God is able to rescue and redeem him from his fallen state. Moreover, Adam and Eve's having brought about the Fall themselves made them subject to punishment or reward for their actions. A little reflection upon these matters leads one to conclude that the Fall was accomplished in the very best possible way. As Lehi said about the Fall and the Atonement, "All things have been done in the wisdom of him who knoweth all things" (2 Nephi 2:24).

We can benefit from the observation of Elder Orson F. Whitney, who said, "The fall had a twofold direction—downward, yet forward."[10] It is as the Prophet Joseph Smith said: "Adam was made to open the way of the world."[11] Adam and Eve had the privilege of getting things under way by their own actions.

This is far better than their being created mortal and sinful. Here we might also observe that, since Adam opened the way of the world, it follows that there could not have been such worldly things as death, birth, sin, and reproduction going on before Adam's transgression—that is, before he opened the way.

Adam's Origin

I am in no position to speak for the Church or for the Brethren, but I want to express my personal belief on the subject of the creation of Adam. I believe that Adam's physical body was the offspring of God, literally (Moses 6:22); that he was begotten as a baby with a physical body not subject to death, in a world without sin or blood; and that he grew to manhood in that condition and then became mortal through his own actions. I believe that Adam's physical body was begotten by our immortal celestial Father and an immortal celestial Mother, and thus not into a condition of mortality, a condition which would have precluded Jesus from being the Only Begotten of the Father in the flesh (D&C 93:11)—*flesh* meaning *mortality*. Jesus' physical body was also begotten of the same celestial Father but through a mortal woman and hence into mortality.

Commenting on Luke 3:38 (''Adam, which was the son of God''), Elder Bruce R. McConkie wrote: ''This statement, found also in Moses 6:22, has a deep and profound significance and also means what it says. Father Adam came, as indicated, to this sphere, gaining an immortal body, because death had not yet entered the world. (2 Ne. 2:22.) Jesus, on the other hand, was the Only Begotten in the flesh, meaning into a world of mortality where death already reigned.''[12]

Evolution would place Adam's body as the offspring of animals, each generation having gradually evolved and improved in structure and in intelligence until a creature came into being that was more man-like than animal-like. This seems to me such a time-wasting process. We know that God can beget children: he is the Father of Jesus' body and has also begotten innumerable spirit children in his own likeness and image. Why would the Father resort to animal evolution to bring his very own family into the new world that he had created, rather than he and the heavenly mother doing it in just one generation by begetting Adam themselves? Surely we would not deny the heavenly parents the privilege of begetting their own children. If our heavenly parents were but spirits only, there might be some cause for expecting they would need an alternate way to produce Adam's body. But since they are tangible resurrected beings of flesh and bone, there seems to be no necessity to resort to the animals to produce bodies for Adam and Eve. How could Adam be called the son of God (Moses 6:22) if he were the offspring of animals?

Furthermore, if Adam were the product of animal evolution, it could hardly be said that he was created in the physical image of God; yet we know that the scriptures say man *was* created in God's image (Genesis 1:26–27). There is a very compelling passage in Mosiah that speaks of this same matter: "He [Abinadi] said unto them [the Nephites] that Christ was the God, the Father of all things, and said that he should take upon him the image of man, and it should be the image after which man was created in the beginning; or in other words, he said that man was created after the image of God" (Mosiah 7:27). It is easy to see the thrust of that passage: The image of man in which Christ appeared was the same image in which man was created in the beginning, the image of God. The particular wording of this verse calls for a single and standardized image for man all along from the beginning—a Godlike image, not an image barely removed from that of a brute.

Before leaving this subject, I would like to address one other related issue. There are those among the advocates of theistic evolution who do believe in a version of the fall of man. The scenario goes something like this: In the physical creation, God used the evolutionary process of natural selection and generation until an apelike animal was produced that was sufficiently advanced physically that God could place a man's spirit—namely, Adam's—into the body instead of an animal spirit, the latter having been used in all previous generations. This was the first man, these theorists claim, and he was immortal at this point; hence, when Adam subsequently fell, the effects of his transgression—death and the ability to produce children—applied only to man and not to the animals, those processes being already present in the animal kingdom.

Now, as I see it, a problem with this position is that it asks its adherents to accept the premise that advanced, wholly-mortal apelike beings (themselves subject to death and capable of reproducing) produced a man, Adam, who was not subject to death and who could not reproduce unless he transgressed in the garden. Thus, ironically, Adam had to transgress to become mortal like his apelike parents. This scenario seems to be an illogical situation from the standpoint of an evolutionist, whose emphasis is on the natural processes of reproduction and selection; the idea that Adam's mortal animal parents produced an immortal child seems to override, if not nullify, the natural evolutionary process.

These ideas thus raise more questions than they answer. How

does the theistic evolutionist account for Adam's unique deathless situation, if his body was completely the product of mortal animals? Why did Adam not inherit death and reproduction from his parents? Would a theistic evolutionist who advocates the above scenario be willing to suggest that the scriptural statements about Adam's deathless and childless state do not really apply to our first parents? To so state would be tantamount to rejecting the plain declarations of the scriptures; and if a person does that, what has happened to the "theistic" part of his theory? How many scriptures can one neglect and still have *theistic* evolution? Moreover, the scriptures that relate to this subject cannot be dismissed on the grounds that they are archaic or translated incorrectly: the scriptures that speak of the Fall and its effects upon mankind are latter-day scriptures found in the Book of Mormon, the Doctrine and Covenants, and the Pearl of Great Price.

Eternal Progression Not the Same as Organic Evolution

We frequently hear it said that the couplet "As man now is, God once was; as God now is, man may become" is an expression of evolution on such a grand scale that anyone believing in this statement should have no difficulty in accepting organic evolution. I agree that eternal progression is a kind of evolutionary process, but a little serious reflection will show that there is no parallel between that concept and organic evolution. Organic evolution is the change from a lower life-form to a higher life-form in a series of generations, involving a long line of different individuals. Eternal progression, on the other hand, is the process by which the same individual progresses from mortality to godhood. Organic evolution involves a change of species; eternal progression is change within the same species, for a spirit, a man, an angel, and a god are all of the same species, albeit in different stages of progression.

The Need for an Atonement

If we correctly view the creation of man and the fall of man according to the plan of God, the atonement of Jesus Christ falls right into place. The Fall and the Atonement are like two halves of a circle. Neither is complete without the other, nor can we understand the significance of either one unless we can see it in relation to the other. Together they make a *wholeness* or completeness that is not available if they are only viewed separately.

The first man, Adam, was created in an immortal, or deathless, condition, and by his transgression he fell. The Fall brought two deaths upon all mankind, neither of which man was able to pay for himself. "As in Adam all die, even so in Christ shall all be made alive" (1 Corinthians 15:22). The redemption is as broad in its influence as the Fall. Every person will die a physical death—none escape. Every person is shut out from the presence of God—none escape. Even little children who die would be shut out from the presence of God if no atonement had been made (Mosiah 3:16). Every person suffers two deaths, and every person is redeemed from both deaths. All will be raised from the grave; all will be brought back into the presence of God for the Judgment. (See Helaman 14:15–18; Mormon 9:12–13.)

Since the effects of the Fall dominate every mortal human being, redemption for mankind requires payment from One not dominated by the Fall, a condition which would enable this being to rescue man from what Jacob calls the "awful monster . . . death and hell"—the two deaths (2 Nephi 9:10). The unusual circumstances of the birth of Jesus Christ were the means by which a spirit being, a God (namely, Jehovah), could come into the world and obtain a physical body not dominated by death, yet capable of dying. That is, God the Father was the father of Jesus' physical body, making Jesus the Only Begotten of the Father in the flesh and the only one able to conquer death. Because of his parentage, Jesus could have lived forever on this earth. He would never have had to die—so he literally *gave his life* for us. Had he been dominated by death, his giving up his life at age thirty-three would only have meant his giving up time. But he actually gave his life to pay a debt contracted by Adam's transgression and the sins of all people. He shed his blood and gave his life in payment.

According to the scriptures, the fall of Adam placed us all in a position in which we cannot save ourselves. A Redeemer, a Savior, is absolutely necessary.

> Wherefore, all mankind were in a lost and in a fallen state, and ever would be save they should rely on this Redeemer (2 Nephi 10:6).
>
> The way is prepared from the fall of man, and salvation is free. . . .

> Wherefore, how great the importance to make these things known unto the inhabitants of the earth, that they may know that there is no flesh that can dwell in the presence of God, save it be through the merits, and mercy, and grace of the Holy Messiah. (2 Nephi 2:4, 8.)

> And now, ye see by this that our first parents were cut off both temporally and spiritually from the presence of the Lord; and thus we see they became subjects to follow after their own will. . . .
>
> And now, there was no means to reclaim men from this fallen state, which man had brought upon himself because of his own disobedience. . . .
>
> And now, the plan of mercy could not be brought about except an atonement should be made; therefore God himself atoneth for the sins of the world, to bring about the plan of mercy, to appease the demands of justice, that God might be a perfect, just God, and a merciful God also. (Alma 42:7, 12, 15. See also Mosiah 3:11, 16–17; Helaman 14:16–17; Ether 3:2.)

Since death, blood, and obedience were the mediums of exchange used in Christ's atonement, it follows that there is a one-to-one relationship between the fall of Adam and the atonement of Jesus Christ. According to the scriptures, Adam's transgression brought the Fall, and the Fall brought death, blood, and sin. Jesus paid the penalty and satisfied justice with his own death (the payment of his life) and his own blood and his own obedience. The effects of the Fall had no complete hold on him, either physically or morally, because he was sinless and genetically the Son of God. He overcame both kinds of death, bringing to pass the resurrection from physical death and the restoration of all people to the presence of God for judgment. It was in every sense a freewill offering, a ransom, a rescue, a redemption, performed by the only being capable of making such a payment. It was the sacrifice of a God, an infinite being (see Mosiah 13:28, 32; Alma 34:10–13; 42:15). This is what one of our Church hymns calls "redemption's grand design."[13]

If, as evolutionists seem to propose, mortality and death were original and perpetual conditions in the world, and if organic evolution was the process by which man came into being (without a fall in the scriptural sense), it seems illogical that eternal justice would require the sacrifice of a God for mankind's redemption. (For further discussions on the Atonement, see chapters 17 and 18 in this book.)

Summary and Conclusion

For the foregoing reasons, all of them taken from the teachings of the scriptures and the Brethren, I see the theory of organic evolution as contrary to the nature of God, insulting to the original status of man, and a subtle attack upon the mission of Jesus Christ. It may not seem so at first glance, but in terms of doctrine the theory of organic evolution is a concept that, if believed, would undercut the entire plan of salvation and our faith in the divinity and accomplishments of the Messiah. There must be a simple, straightforward way to make this situation evident to honest believers who espouse so-called theistic evolution, believers who may not realize they harbor a philosophy that is not only contradictory but also destructive. I do not think it is harmless. The end result is disaster, because the tenets of organic evolution are contrary to the plan of God.

In review, then, what are the universal truths that are given to us in the scriptures that would have bearing on this subject?

First, there is an eternal, perfect plan. Accepting this concept enables us to see the larger picture and prepares our minds against any false doctrine. This is especially so when one accepts the *whole* plan, with all of its parts extending from the premortal existence to the final judgment. To pick and choose, to alter and adapt, are not acceptable intellectual options when one is dealing with the plan of redemption. In other words, we should not "monkey" with the plan of salvation. The provisions of the plan are not negotiable.

Second, there is order in God's plan; there are certain fixed principles that were in place before the world was formed. Therefore, the plan does not change. This concept can be another major stabilizing influence in our gospel studies.

Third, what sin is and how it got into the world are moral issues. If a person accepts organic evolution as the explanation for the origin of man on this earth, it seems he has to reject the explanation for the origin of sin that is given in every one of the standard works. Because of the moral implications of such a course, it seems to me that most "believers" would not be eager to do this.

We are able to turn to the scriptures for a statement of the principles related to man's origin, but in some ways, with regard to this particular matter, we who live today are in a situation more critical than that of any other people. The high degree of scientific progress today, the sophisticated methods of gaining knowledge and formulating hypotheses, and the current advances in tests and measurements have all tended toward more complex hypotheses about man's origin than those with which Lehi, Jacob, Abinadi, Alma, or even Joseph Smith had to deal. Matters are complicated also because the scientific method is regarded so highly in our society.

Therefore, we have to diligently search to understand the revelations well enough to find adequate explanations. The doctrinal framework has been given to us in the scriptures and by the prophets of this dispensation for our guidance and use. It takes considerable effort to comprehend it, but if we ignore it, we are left to our own limited understanding. We cannot be content with a mediocre acquaintance with the plan of God. What we are challenged to do is to find a way, a simple way, to put the doctrinal issues so clearly before our hearers that those with faith in the revelations and in the atoning sacrifice of Jesus Christ will not unwittingly forsake the faith of our fathers—or of Elijah, Enoch, Nephi, and Joseph Smith—in order to try to be in harmony with what the world accepts.

Probably never before have believers in the scriptures had as great a need as they do now to grasp the iron rod of Lehi's dream to guide them through the subtle mists of darkness lest they wander in strange paths and become lost (see 1 Nephi 8:19–21, 24, 30). On scientific grounds, I cannot effectively answer the evolutionist, whether he be in or out of the Church; but I can see what the theological and moral issues are, and I can see that the theory of evolution is deeply entrenched in almost every discipline and field of study in which modern man is engaged. It is a very popular philosophy, but it is capable of eroding men's faith because it undercuts what God has revealed about the doctrine of Christ. The erosive effects of this theory are subtle, and it may not appear harmful to many at first. However, because of evolution's inherent opposition to the mission of the Messiah, it may possibly be that in connection with this subject, more than with any other, everyone must eventually and individually answer Pilate's question, "What shall I do then with Jesus which is called Christ?" (Matthew 27:22.)

Notes

1. *Teachings of the Prophet Joseph Smith*, comp. Joseph Fielding Smith (Salt Lake City: Deseret Book Co., 1976), pp. 324–25, italics added. Hereafter cited as *TPJS*.

2. *TPJS*, pp. 197–98.

3. *TPJS*, p. 198n.
4. *TPJS*, p. 198.
5. See *TPJS*, pp. 198–99.
6. *TPJS*, p. 343.
7. *TPJS*, p. 264.
8. *TPJS*, p. 137.
9. From a typescript, approved by President Smith, of an address given at the LDS Institute of Religion, Salt Lake City, Utah, 14 January 1961.
10. As found in Forace Green, comp., *Cowley and Whitney on Doctrine* (Salt Lake City: Bookcraft, 1963), p. 287.
11. *TPJS*, p. 12.
12. Bruce R. McConkie, *Doctrinal New Testament Commentary*, 3 vols. (Salt Lake City: Bookcraft, 1965–73), 1:95.
13. "How Great the Wisdom and the Love," *Hymns*, no. 195.

Chapter 14

THE DOCTRINE OF THE RESURRECTION

The doctrine of the resurrection from the dead—the doctrine that these very bodies in which we now reside will die and then be renewed to everlasting life—is a fundamental part of the gospel of Jesus Christ. I believe it is important and necessary to our faith that we understand what the scriptures say about it. And since one of the purposes of latter-day scripture is to clarify and bear witness to the central doctrines of the gospel, we shouldn't be surprised to find that the doctrine of the resurrection is clearly, repeatedly, and accurately taught in the first book of latter-day scripture published in this dispensation, namely, the Book of Mormon.

Anyone who has ever stood at the casket of a departed loved one, or who has visited the cemetery where a parent, child, husband, wife, or close friend is buried, has felt the heavy hand of death that is laid on all mankind because of the fall of Adam. Those who have had such experiences and who are also believers in the gospel of Jesus Christ undoubtedly have sensed the importance of the doctrine that every person, with no exceptions, who dies will rise from the dead with the same body and will continue with that body forever, never to die, grow old, or suffer physical pain again.

The Resurrection Taught in the Old Testament

The idea of a resurrection from the dead, that a dead body can be revived and restored to active, vibrant, healthy, and complete wholeness, is taught in all of the standard works. It is not as prominent in the Old Testament today as it once was, but we may rest assured that the ancient prophets of the Old Testament knew the doctrine and taught it plainly—it has simply been lost in the transmission from ancient times to our day. Apparently, most of the plainness about the resurrection has been deliberately taken out of the Old Testament.

In the King James Version of the Bible we read Job's testimony: "I know that my redeemer liveth, and that he shall stand at the latter day upon the earth." Job then prophesies of his own resurrection as follows: "And though after my skin worms destroy this body, yet in my flesh shall I see God: whom I shall see for myself, and mine eyes shall behold, and not another; though my reins be consumed within me." (Job 19:25–27.) Some modern translations render Job's words thus: "Without my flesh shall I see God," or, in other words, "I do not need this body." This is not the same testimony of the resurrection found in the King James Bible. The modern versions change Job's testimony of the resurrection to a denial of it.

In Isaiah 26:19 we find a clear prophetic declaration concerning the resurrection: "Thy dead men shall live, together with my dead body shall they arise. Awake and sing, ye that dwell in dust: for thy dew is as the dew of herbs, and the earth shall cast out the dead."

In the book of Ezekiel we read of that prophet's vision of the valley of dry bones. He saw that "the bones came together, bone to his bone," along with the sinews, flesh, skin, and breath, so that these persons lived again and stood upon their feet. The Lord then directed Ezekiel to say to the house of Israel: "Thus saith the Lord God; Behold, O my people, I will open your graves, and cause you to come up out of your graves. . . . and shall put my spirit in you, and ye shall live." (Ezekiel 37:1–14.)

To those of us who already believe and have a testimony that there will be a resurrection of the physical bodies of all mankind, these Old Testament scriptures seem clear enough. But that is because we have been tutored and taught by the clarity of latter-day revelation and by the Holy Ghost. Therefore, when we read these Old Testament scriptures we understand their doctrinal meaning. But many of our Christian and Jewish friends, who do not have the benefit of latter-day revelation and who do not enjoy the gift of the Holy Ghost, interpret these Old Testament verses differently. They see them as figurative, or allegorical, expressions or as something—anything—other than literal, plain-spoken declarations about a physical resurrection of the corporeal bodies of mankind. Many present-day Christians are not even sure that Jesus himself was resurrected with his physical body, and most of those who may believe Jesus had a physical resurrected body do not believe he still has that body today.

As Latter-day Saints we are a highly favored people in that we have not only all that the Bible has to say about the resurrection but also the additional, more detailed, and more specific testimonies from the Book of Mormon, the Doctrine and Covenants, the Pearl of Great Price, the Joseph Smith Translation, and the teachings of the latter-day prophets, particularly those of the Prophet Joseph Smith.

The Resurrection Taught in the New Testament

It is hard for the worldly-minded and those untutored in the things of the Spirit to believe that dead persons will be revived and come back to life. They think such a thing is "unreasonable" and fantastical. When Paul spoke to the philosophers on Mars' hill near the city of Athens, he had a very intellectual audience who worshipped "the Unknown God." These people often came together and "spent their time in nothing else, but either to tell, or to hear some new thing" (Acts 17:21). Paul proceeded to preach Jesus and the resurrection and told them: "[God] hath given assurance unto all men, in that he hath raised [Jesus] from the dead. And when they heard of the resurrection of the dead, some mocked: and others said, We will hear thee again of this matter." (Acts 17:31–32.)

Several years later during a hearing before King Agrippa and the Roman governor Festus, Paul encountered the same kind of worldly opposition to the resurrection. Paul praised Agrippa because, as Paul stated, "I know thee to be expert in all customs and questions which are among the Jews: wherefore I beseech thee to hear me patiently." In the course of his subsequent oration, Paul said to the king: "Why should it be thought a thing incredible with you, that God should raise the dead?" (Acts 26:3, 8.)

Paul proceeded to tell of his conversion and of his being visited by Jesus Christ on the road to Damascus (several years after the Crucifixion), and he testified that Jesus was raised from the dead. At this point, as Paul testified of the resurrection, Festus interrupted him and "said with a loud voice, Paul, thou art beside thyself; much learning doth make thee mad" (Acts 26:24).

As the above passages illustrate, the doctrine of the resurrection, concerning which the prophets have taught and testified, is simply not congruent with the learning and the philosophies of the world. The resurrection is something to which the world cannot relate empirically; it has to be understood by faith and by the Holy Ghost. Consequently it is not readily accepted or believed in the world. Paul's magnificent statement about the resurrection recorded in 1 Corinthians 15 apparently was written to convince the intellectuals of his day, those who trusted in reason, that the resurrection was logical, scriptural, and necessary. He said that his knowledge of the resurrection came by revelation but that the doctrine was reasonable even so. The testimony of the scriptures and of the Holy Spirit is that the resurrection of Jesus, and eventually of all mankind, is literal, historical, and factual truth. It really did happen to Jesus, it has already happened to many, and it will yet happen to many more. Everyone who has lived upon this earth is destined to come forth in the resurrection.

As we read the New Testament Gospels, we find that even the Apostles had difficulty at first believing in the resurrection of Jesus. He had told them it would occur three days (or upon the third day) after his death, but they were so close to the scene that it hardly seemed real to them. Believing things at a distance seems easier than believing those that are close at hand. Luke's account tells us that when the women found the stone rolled away from the tomb and the body of Jesus gone, "they were much perplexed." At that point they were told by two angels that Jesus had risen from the dead. Then (and not till then) did they remember that Jesus had told them that he would rise from the dead on the third day. The women hurried off and told these things to the eleven Apostles and others, but "their words seemed to them as idle tales, and they believed them not." (Luke 24:1–11.)

Later that same day, Jesus personally appeared to the Apostles, and they thought he was a spirit. So he said to them: "Why are ye troubled? and why do thoughts arise in your hearts? Behold my hands and my feet, that it is I myself: handle me, and see; for a spirit hath not flesh and bones, as ye see me have. And when he had thus spoken, he shewed them his hands and his feet." (Luke 24:38–40.)

There can be no doubt that at this point the Apostles could perceive that Jesus had been resurrected with a body of flesh and bones. They saw him; they touched him. Yet the next verse states: "And while they yet believed not for joy, and wondered, he said unto them, Have ye here any meat?" They then watched him eat food. (Luke 24:41–43.) It was hard for them to realize just what the reality was. They wanted to believe it, but it was difficult to do so.

Resurrection from the dead is miraculous; it seems unnatural in our mortal world. But it is a basic and fundamental doctrine of the gospel. It is one of the first principles of the gospel. Teaching the doctrine of the resurrection is as important as teaching faith, repentance, or baptism. The Prophet Joseph Smith said, "The Doctrines of the Resurrection of the Dead and the Eternal Judgment are necessary to preach among the first principles of the Gospel of Jesus Christ."[1] It is easy to see why this doctrine should be taught: The knowledge of a personal resurrection and of a personal judgment make faith, repentance, baptism, and receiving the gift of the Holy Ghost very important in our preparing for those great and inevitable events.

The Prophet Joseph stated that the resurrection of Jesus Christ is the center point of our hope for future happiness and that Jesus, having been resurrected himself, has the power to bring all people out of their graves to stand before him in judgment.[2]

With What Body Are the Dead Raised?

As mentioned earlier, 1 Corinthians 15 contains Paul's remarkable exposition on the resurrection, and much could be said concerning his great statement. However, for the moment I would like to focus on a particular verse from that chapter: "But some man will say, How are the dead raised up? and with what body do they come?" (v. 35.) During the remainder of the chapter Paul answers these two questions, launching into a discussion of the degrees of glory and referring to the resurrected body as a "spiritual body" (1 Corinthians 15:44). The word *spiritual* is used here to describe a condition. A resurrected body is a physical body in a *spiritual* condition, as contrasted to a mortal body which is also physical but is not in a spiritual condition; mortal bodies are subject to death and contain blood, but resurrected bodies will never die again and are, as President Joseph Fielding Smith explained, "quickened by the spirit and not the blood."[3]

The word *spiritual* is used in this same sense in a modern revelation that speaks of the physical resurrection: "For notwithstanding they die, they also shall rise again, a spiritual body. They who are of a celestial spirit shall receive the same body which was a natural body; even ye shall receive your bodies, and your glory shall be that glory by which your bodies are quickened." (D&C 88:27–28; see also Alma 11:45.)

With what body are the dead raised, then? They are raised with spiritual bodies, each person receiving in the resurrection "the same body which was a natural body."

These concepts were topics of discussion among the early Brethren in Nauvoo, particularly the question as to whether a person received his same bodily elements in the resurrection. Elder Orson Pratt observed that a man's body is constantly changing, losing old cells and producing new ones, and in the course of seven years a complete change takes place. This would seem to complicate the idea of a literal resurrection in which a person would receive his own bodily elements.

In a conference session on 7 April 1843, the Prophet responded to these observations. The report of the conference reads as follows:

> To a remark of Elder Orson Pratt's, that a man's body changes every seven years, President Joseph Smith replied: There is no fundamental principle belonging to a human system that ever goes into another in this world or in the world to come; I care not what the theories of men are. We have the testimony that God will raise us up, and he has the power to do it. If any one supposes that any part of our bodies, that is, the fundamental parts thereof, ever goes into another body, he is mistaken.[4]

We have only scant background on the situation that prompted the Prophet's public statement on the matter. However, thirty-one years later Elder Pratt gave a lecture in Ogden, Utah, in which he discoursed at length on matters pertaining to the resurrection, including the theory that a man's body changes every seven years, and it is clear that Elder Pratt's conclusions at this time were in harmony with the Prophet Joseph's statement.[5]

In discussing the Prophet Joseph's statement about the "fundamental parts," Elder Harold B. Lee cited the following explanation from a physician named Joseph S. Amussen:

> We have bodies that are composed of bone, muscle, fat, blood, lymph, nerves and tissues. In all these tissues there is a building up and breaking down of complex chemical compounds. These substances are made into tissues. They give form and beauty to the body, and also supply energy. They are derived from the elements in food, drink and air.
>
> These are not the fundamental parts of the body, however, for they are used and then discarded, and new substances come to take their place. This is not true of the fundamental parts. They never change. A person may fast for a certain period of time, and become very emaciated, "lose flesh" we say. People may live on their own tissues until they become almost "skin and bone," yet they live and can, when fed again, regain their former form and weight. During the fast, the fundamental parts of the body are not lost, but only the tissues that are taken into the body temporarily.[6]

It would be helpful if we had a more extensive explanation from the Prophet Joseph on what he meant by "fundamental parts." I have interpreted this to mean that there is something in each cell of a person's body that is uniquely the property of the owner of the body; hence, no matter what I eat, nothing else's fundamental parts ever become my fundamental parts, and no matter what becomes of my body, my fundamental parts never become the fundamental parts of any other living organism.

Consider this "fundamental parts" concept and how it may relate to things such as baby teeth, fingernails, toenails, whiskers, hair, or anything else we may lose or cut off throughout a lifetime. Obviously we don't want all those pieces of our bodies back; we don't want to end up with four-foot fingernails and so on. But whatever it is in the last joint of my fingers and toes that can produce a nail, I want back; and whatever it was on the top of my head that can produce hair, I want that fundamental part back, in good working order.

Each person obtains his own body in his mother's womb, and that body is precisely and exclusively his: there is something about that body that is his sole ownership not only now but also through all eternity. To be denied a body—as is the case with Lucifer—is everlasting damnation; or, in other words, if there were no resurrection, our fate would be everlasting damnation. In terms of eternity, we have barely begun to appreciate our mothers and what birth into mortality means to us.

President Brigham Young also spoke of these matters, and his remarks are in complete agreement with the teachings of the Prophet Joseph:

> The question may be asked, do not the particles that compose man's body, when returned to mother earth, go to make or compose other bodies? No, they do not. . . . Neither can the particles which have comprised the body of man become parts of the bodies of other men, or of beasts, fowls, fish, insect, or vegetables. They are governed by divine law and though they may pass from the knowledge of the scientific world, that divine law still holds, governs and controlls them. Man's body may be buried in the ocean, it may be eaten by wild beasts, or it may be burned to ashes, they may be scattered to the four winds, yet the particles of which it is composed will not be incorporated into any form of vegetable or animal life, to become a component part of their structure. . . . at the sound of the trumpet of God every parti-

> cle of our physical structures necessary to make our tabernacles perfect will be assembled, to be rejoined with the spirit, every man in his order. Not one particle will be lost.[7]

On an earlier occasion, President Young similarly testified, "The very particles that compose our bodies will be brought forth in the morning of the resurrection."[8] And, in an 1876 funeral sermon, Elder John Taylor stated: "All must come forth from the grave, some time or other, in the self-same tabernacles that they possessed while living on the earth."[9]

By way of a concluding statement on these matters, let us consider these words from President Joseph F. Smith:

> What a glorious thought it is . . . that those from whom we have to part here, we will meet again and see as they are. We will meet the same identical being that we associated with here in the flesh—not some other soul, some other being, or the same being in some other form, but the same identity and the same form and likeness, the same person we knew and were associated with in our mortal existence, even to the wounds in the flesh. Not that a person will always be marred by scars, wounds, deformities, defects or infirmities, for these will be removed in their course, in their proper time, according to the merciful providence of God. Deformity will be removed; defects will be eliminated, and men and women shall attain to the perfection of their spirits, to the perfection that God designed in the beginning.[10]

We note here that President Smith's statement that the body's scars, wounds, and deformities are still present at the moment of resurrection is a strong argument in favor of the concept that the dead are raised with the very same bodies they had in mortality. Such wounds and scars would not be present if resurrected bodies were fashioned from new materials.

The Book of Mormon a Witness for the Resurrection

Let us now turn to the Book of Mormon to see what it says about the important and interesting subject of the resurrection. If we want to read the account of Jesus' death and resurrection, we go to the books of Matthew, Mark, Luke, and John. But if we want to know why the death and resurrection of Jesus are so important and how those things apply to you and to me, we go to the Book of Mormon.

We should expect the Book of Mormon to teach much about the resurrection, because the very purpose and mission of the Book of Mormon is to testify of Jesus Christ. The Book of Mormon contains the fulness of the everlasting gospel. It could not be a witness for Christ if it did not teach the doctrine of the resurrection.

Five thousand years ago the Lord revealed to the prophet Enoch what the fundamental and basic content of the Book of Mormon would be. He did not mention history, or culture, or geography. He mentioned one thing: The book would testify of Jesus Christ's resurrection and the resurrection of all mankind. Recorded in the book of Moses, this statement about the Book of Mormon is part of the Lord's description of latter-day events preceding the Second Coming: "And righteousness will I send down out of heaven; and truth will I send forth out of the earth, to bear testimony of mine Only Begotten; his resurrection from the dead; yea, and also the resurrection of all men; and righteousness and truth will I cause to sweep the earth as with a flood, to gather out mine elect from the four quarters of the earth, unto a place which I shall prepare, an Holy City . . . and it shall be called Zion, a New Jerusalem" (Moses 7:62).

The doctrine of the resurrection is taught by every major prophet in the Book of Mormon. Some form of the word *resurrection* occurs 83 times in the book, and variations of the phrase "rise from the dead" occur several times also. The word *resurrection* comes from the root words *re* and *surge*. It is a resurgence, and means to get up again, an "uprising." Note the similarity to the word *insurrection*, which is a political "uprising."

Lehi, Jacob, and Benjamin on the Resurrection

In examining what the Book of Mormon teaches us about the doctrine of the resurrection, we begin with father Lehi's discourse recorded in 2 Nephi 2. This discourse is actually a blessing Lehi gave to his son Jacob. Speaking of the mission and sacrifice of the Messiah, Lehi states: "Wherefore, how great the importance to make these things known unto the inhabitants of the earth, that they may know that there is no flesh that can dwell in the presence of God, save it be through the merits, and mercy, and grace of the Holy

Messiah, who layeth down his life according to the flesh, and taketh it again by the power of the Spirit, that he may bring to pass the resurrection of the dead, being the first that should rise'' (2 Nephi 2:8).

Note that Lehi says Jesus is the ''first that should rise'' in the resurrection. There are accounts in the scriptures of persons who were brought back to life before Jesus' resurrection, but these people were restored to mortality only. Elijah healed a boy, as did Elisha, and Jesus raised from the dead at least three people: the son of the widow of Nain, Jairus' twelve-year-old daughter, and Lazarus. But these were not resurrections in the real sense. All of these people certainly died again. Jesus was the first to rise from the dead with an immortal body.

In the Book of Mormon record, father Lehi continues to explain that at the time of creation there was no death and that, had there been no fall, all things that were created would have continued forever and had no end (2 Nephi 2:22). The fall of Adam introduced sin and death. Lehi then declares that the Messiah would come to ''redeem the children of men from the fall'' (2 Nephi 2:26). Lehi shows the close relationship between the Fall and the Atonement.

Later, as recorded in 2 Nephi 9, Jacob—who had become a prophet and who was destined to be one of the greatest doctrinal teachers of the Book of Mormon—explains in considerable detail about the need for a resurrection. First, he testifies of the reality of the resurrection: ''For I know that ye have searched much, many of you, to know of things to come; wherefore I know that ye know that our flesh must waste away and die; nevertheless, in our bodies we shall see God'' (2 Nephi 9:4). Note that the language here is similar to that of Job's testimony. The Book of Mormon thus seems to confirm that the Job passage is accurate as it appears in the King James Version.

Next, Jacob states specifically why there is a need for a power of resurrection:

> For as death hath passed upon all men, to fulfil the merciful plan of the great Creator, there must needs be a power of resurrection, and the resurrection must needs come unto man by reason of the fall; and the fall came by reason of transgression; and because man became fallen they were cut off from the presence of the Lord.
>
> Wherefore, it must needs be an infinite atonement—save it should be an infinite atonement this corruption could not put on incorruption. Wherefore, the first judgment which

> came upon man must needs have remained to an endless duration. And if so, this flesh must have laid down to rot and to crumble to its mother earth, to rise no more.
>
> O the wisdom of God, his mercy and grace! For behold, if the flesh should rise no more our spirits must become subject to that angel who fell from before the presence of the Eternal God, and became the devil, to rise no more.
>
> And our spirits must have become like unto him, and we become devils, angels to a devil, to be shut out from the presence of our God, and to remain with the father of lies, in misery, like unto himself. (2 Nephi 9:6–9.)

The Fall brought upon all mankind not only a physical death but also a spiritual death. This second type of death meant that the spirit was separated from God and could not return to his presence. Thus, without the atonement of Christ, because of the Fall the physical bodies of all people would "rot" and "crumble" to the earth and their spirits would become devils. The atonement of Jesus Christ automatically redeems all people from both of these deaths that came upon them because of Adam, and brings them back into the presence of God for the Judgment (see Helaman 14:15–18; Mormon 9:13).

Continuing, Jacob describes death as an awful monster:

> O how great the goodness of our God, who prepareth a way for our escape from the grasp of this awful monster; yea, that monster, death and hell, which I call the death of the body, and also the death of the spirit.
>
> And because of the way of deliverance of our God, the Holy One of Israel, this death, of which I have spoken, which is the temporal, shall deliver up its dead; which death is the grave.
>
> And this death of which I have spoken, which is the spiritual death, shall deliver up its dead; which spiritual death is hell; wherefore, death and hell must deliver up their dead, and hell must deliver up its captive spirits, and the grave must deliver up its captive bodies, and the bodies and the spirits of men will be restored one to the other; and it is by the power of the resurrection of the Holy One of Israel.
>
> O how great the plan of our God! For on the other hand, the paradise of God must deliver up the spirits of the righteous, and the grave deliver up the body of the righteous; and the spirit and the body is restored to itself again, and all

> men become incorruptible, and immortal, and they are living souls, having a perfect knowledge like unto us in the flesh, save it be that our knowledge shall be perfect.
>
> Wherefore, we shall have a perfect knowledge of all our guilt, and our uncleanness, and our nakedness; and the righteous shall have a perfect knowledge of their enjoyment, and their righteousness, being clothed with purity, yea, even with the robe of righteousness.
>
> And it shall come to pass that when all men shall have passed from this first death unto life, insomuch as they have become immortal, they must appear before the judgment-seat of the Holy One of Israel; and then cometh the judgment, and then must they be judged according to the holy judgment of God. (2 Nephi 9:10–15.)

These words clearly establish the physical resurrection of all mankind, of everyone who belongs to the family of Adam. The resurrection is as broad as the Fall, "for as in Adam all die, even so in Christ shall all be made alive" (1 Corinthians 15:22).

Another valuable source of information about the resurrection is Mosiah 3. In this chapter King Benjamin teaches the doctrine he said an angel had taught him. After telling of the divinity of Jesus Christ, the Lord Omnipotent who would "come down from heaven," Benjamin explains that Jesus would suffer and bleed at every pore and that he would be taken by men and be crucified. Benjamin then testifies that Jesus "shall rise the third day from the dead; and behold, he standeth to judge the world." (Mosiah 3:2–10.)

Abinadi on the Resurrection

Later in the Book of Mormon record, Abinadi the prophet testifies of the resurrection of Jesus and of all mankind. He points out that the Messiah who will come to atone for man's sins is none other than God himself—the creator of the world. Lehi, Nephi, Jacob, and Benjamin teach this concept also (see 1 Nephi 19:7–10; 2 Nephi 9:5; Mosiah 3), but Abinadi seems to drive it home even more thoroughly.

Abinadi says that the redemption will be made by God himself. He also says that God will bring to pass the resurrection of the dead.

> For behold, did not Moses prophesy unto them concerning the coming of the Messiah, and that God should redeem

> his people? Yea, and even all the prophets who have prophesied ever since the world began—have they not spoken more or less concerning these things?
>
> Have they not said that God himself should come down among the children of men, and take upon him the form of man, and go forth in mighty power upon the face of the earth?
>
> Yea, and have they not said also that he should bring to pass the resurrection of the dead, and that he, himself, should be oppressed and afflicted? (Mosiah 13:33–35.)

These words are reminiscent of those found in the book of Isaiah, quoted earlier in this chapter: "Thy dead men shall live, together with my dead body shall they arise" (Isaiah 26:19).

Further on in the account, Abinadi testifies:

> But behold, the bands of death shall be broken, and the Son reigneth, and hath power over the dead; therefore, he bringeth to pass the resurrection of the dead.
>
> And there cometh a resurrection, even a first resurrection; yea, even a resurrection of those that have been, and who are, and who shall be, even until the resurrection of Christ—for so shall he be called.
>
> And now, the resurrection of all the prophets, and all those that have believed in their words, or all those that have kept the commandments of God, shall come forth in the first resurrection; therefore, they are the first resurrection. (Mosiah 15:20–22.)

Then, near the end of his oration, Abinadi explains:

> And now if Christ had not come into the world, speaking of things to come as though they had already come, there could have been no redemption.
>
> And if Christ had not risen from the dead, or have broken the bands of death that the grave should have no victory, and that death should have no sting, there could have been no resurrection.
>
> But there is a resurrection, therefore the grave hath no victory, and the sting of death is swallowed up in Christ.
>
> He is the light and the life of the world; yea, a light that is endless, that can never be darkened; yea, and also a life which is endless, that there can be no more death.
>
> Even this mortal shall put on immortality, and this corruption shall put on incorruption, and shall be brought to

> stand before the bar of God, to be judged of him according to their works whether they be good or whether they be evil. (Mosiah 16:6–10.)

For this plain talk and for calling the people to repentance, Abinadi was taken and bound by the wicked priests of Noah, who caused this valiant prophet to suffer death by fire.

Amulek on the Resurrection

In the book of Alma we find the prophet Amulek's teachings on the resurrection, some of which are among the clearest Book of Mormon statements on this doctrine. In speaking of the Son of God, Amulek says:

> And he shall come into the world to redeem his people; and he shall take upon him the transgressions of those who believe on his name; and these are they that shall have eternal life, and salvation cometh to none else.
>
> Therefore the wicked remain as though there had been no redemption made, *except it be the loosing of the bands of death; for behold, the day cometh that all shall rise from the dead and stand before God, and be judged according to their works.*
>
> Now, there is a death which is called a temporal death; and the death of Christ shall loose the bands of this temporal death, that all shall be raised from this temporal death.
>
> The spirit and the body shall be reunited again in its perfect form; both limb and joint shall be restored to its proper frame, even as we now are at this time; and we shall be brought to stand before God, knowing even as we know now, and have a bright recollection of all our guilt.
>
> Now, this restoration shall come to all, both old and young, both bond and free, both male and female, both the wicked and the righteous; and even there shall not so much as a hair of their heads be lost; but every thing shall be restored to its perfect frame, as it is now, or in the body, and shall be brought and be arraigned before the bar of Christ the Son, and God the Father, and the Holy Spirit, which is one Eternal God, to be judged according to their works, whether they be good or whether they be evil.
>
> Now, behold, I have spoken unto you concerning the death of the mortal body, and also concerning the resurrection of the mortal body. I say unto you that this mortal body

> is raised to an immortal body, that is from death, even from the first death unto life, that they can die no more; their spirits uniting with their bodies, never to be divided; thus the whole becoming spiritual and immortal, that they can no more see corruption. (Alma 11:40–45, italics added.)

Note particularly that Amulek says everyone, with no exceptions, will be resurrected. Then he explains that the resurrection means that the spirit and the body are reunited. He also says that when thus joined, the spirit and the body will never be separated again. Resurrected beings do not die again. They are not reincarnated. The question often arises, Is Jesus the Savior of other worlds? The answer is yes. Did he suffer and die and resurrect on those other worlds? The answer is no. A resurrected being's spirit and body cannot be separated ever again—as the scriptural passage above specifies. Will the sons of perdition be resurrected? Yes. Will they die again? According to this passage of scripture, no.

Aaron on the Resurrection

Later in the book of Alma, Aaron, son of Mosiah, teaches the plan of redemption to the king of the Lamanites, and explains about the fall of Adam, the atonement of Christ, and the resurrection from the dead:

> And Aaron did expound unto him the scriptures from the creation of Adam, laying the fall of man before him, and their carnal state and also the plan of redemption, which was prepared from the foundation of the world, through Christ, for all whosoever would believe on his name.
>
> And since man had fallen he could not merit anything of himself; but the sufferings and death of Christ atone for their sins, through faith and repentance, and so forth; and that he breaketh the bands of death, that the grave shall have no victory, and that the sting of death should be swallowed up in the hopes of glory; and Aaron did expound all these things unto the king. (Alma 22:13–14.)

Alma on the Resurrection

Further on in the book of Alma, Alma himself teaches the doctrine of the resurrection to his son Corianton in these words:

> Behold, there is a time appointed that all shall come forth from the dead. Now when this time cometh no one knows; but God knoweth the time which is appointed.
>
> Now, whether there shall be one time, or a second time, or a third time, that men shall come forth from the dead, it mattereth not; for God knoweth all these things; and it sufficeth me to know that this is the case—that there is a time appointed that all shall rise from the dead.
>
> Now there must needs be a space betwixt the time of death and the time of the resurrection.
>
> And now I would inquire what becometh of the souls of men from this time of death to the time appointed for the resurrection?
>
> Now whether there is more than one time appointed for men to rise it mattereth not; for all do not die at once, and this mattereth not; all is as one day with God, and time only is measured unto men.
>
> Therefore, there is a time appointed unto men that they shall rise from the dead; and there is a space between the time of death and the resurrection. And now, concerning this space of time, what becometh of the souls of men is the thing which I have inquired diligently of the Lord to know; and this is the thing of which I do know.
>
> And when the time cometh when all shall rise, then shall they know that God knoweth all the times which are appointed unto man. (Alma 40:4–10.)

Alma says he does not know all of the details, but he makes it clear that there will be a resurrection of all mankind sooner or later. He speaks of the resurrection as a kind of restoration: "The soul [spirit] shall be restored to the body, . . . every limb and joint" and every hair. All things shall be "restored to their proper and perfect frame." (Alma 40:23.)

Alma also explains the relationship of the Fall and the Atonement and the resurrection as follows:

> And thus we see that all mankind were fallen, and they were in the grasp of justice; yea, the justice of God, which consigned them forever to be cut off from his presence.
>
> And now, the plan of mercy could not be brought about except an atonement should be made; therefore God himself atoneth for the sins of the world, to bring about the plan of mercy, to appease the demands of justice, that God might be a perfect, just God, and a merciful God also. . . .

> . . . And mercy cometh because of the atonement; and the atonement bringeth to pass the resurrection of the dead; and the resurrection of the dead bringeth back men into the presence of God; and thus they are restored into his presence, to be judged according to their works, according to the law and justice. (Alma 42:14–15, 23.)

We should note here that, although many scriptures make it clear that the resurrection involves both the body and the spirit, the teachings of Jacob, Amulek, and Alma focus our attention more fully upon the fact that the resurrection is absolutely essential to both the body and the spirit, that neither the body nor the spirit could be saved without the other. These prophets tell us that the resurrection is as much a benefit to the spirit as it is to the body. This fact gives more depth to our understanding of such passages as Doctrine and Covenants 45:17 and 138:50, wherein the thought is expressed that after death the spirit looks upon the absence of its body as a type of bondage. Likewise we learn from Doctrine and Covenants 93:33–34 that a fulness of joy can be obtained only when the spirit and the body are joined inseparably.

In a related vein, the Prophet Joseph Smith taught:

> We came to this earth that we might have a body and present it pure before God in the celestial kingdom. The great principle of happiness consists in having a body. The devil has no body, and herein is his punishment. He is pleased when he can obtain the tabernacle of man, and when cast out by the Savior he asked to go into the herd of swine, showing that he would prefer a swine's body to having none.[11]
>
> Perhaps there are principles here that few men have thought of. No person can have this salvation except through a tabernacle.
>
> Now, in this world, mankind are naturally selfish, ambitious and striving to excel one above another; yet some are willing to build up others as well as themselves. So in the other world there are a variety of spirits. Some seek to excel. And this was the case with Lucifer when he fell. He sought for things which were unlawful. Hence he was sent down, and it is said he drew many away with him; and the greatness of his punishment is that he shall not have a tabernacle. This is his punishment.[12]

We should also note at this point in our discussion that Alma and several Book of Mormon prophets frequently speak of a divine plan, and it is known among them by such names as the plan of salvation, the plan of redemption, the great plan, and the plan of mercy. These prophets see the plan of salvation as a unified and functional whole. To them, the Creation, the Fall, the Atonement, the Resurrection, and the Judgment are each part of the foreordained plan of God rather than isolated, separate, independent, and unrelated occurrences. Hence, the Book of Mormon prophets consider all of these events under such umbrella terms as *redemption* or *salvation*. Perhaps that is why Nephi, Lehi, Benjamin, and others do not feel a need to specify certain details, since when they speak of *atonement* or *redemption* they mean to convey all that those terms include.

Unmistakable Evidence of Christ's Resurrection

The greatest record establishing that Jesus literally received his body from the grave is found in chapter 11 of 3 Nephi, which recounts how Jesus Christ came to the land Bountiful on the American continent, showed his body to the gathered multitude, and let them feel with their hands that his body was tangible and real. In the early part of this chapter, the record states that the people—hearing a voice from heaven declaring that Jesus was the Father's Beloved Son, in whom he was well pleased—looked up toward the heavens,

> and behold, they saw a Man descending out of heaven; and he was clothed in a white robe; and he came down and stood in the midst of them; and the eyes of the whole multitude were turned upon him, and they durst not open their mouths, even one to another, and wist not what it meant, for they thought it was an angel that had appeared unto them.
>
> And it came to pass that he stretched forth his hand and spake unto the people, saying:
>
> Behold, I am Jesus Christ, whom the prophets testified shall come into the world.
>
> And behold, I am the light and the life of the world; and I have drunk out of that bitter cup which the Father hath

given me, and have glorified the Father in taking upon me the sins of the world, in the which I have suffered the will of the Father in all things from the beginning.

And it came to pass that when Jesus had spoken these words the whole multitude fell to the earth; for they remembered that it had been prophesied among them that Christ should show himself unto them after his ascension into heaven.

And it came to pass that the Lord spake unto them saying:

Arise and come forth unto me, that ye may thrust your hands into my side, and also that ye may feel the prints of the nails in my hands and in my feet, that ye may know that I am the God of Israel, and the God of the whole earth, and have been slain for the sins of the world.

And it came to pass that the multitude went forth, and thrust their hands into his side, and did feel the prints of the nails in his hands and in his feet; and this they did do, going forth one by one until they had all gone forth, and did see with their eyes and did feel with their hands, and did know of a surety and did bear record, that it was he, of whom it was written by the prophets, that should come.

And when they had all gone forth and had witnessed for themselves, they did cry out with one accord, saying:

Hosanna! Blessed be the name of the Most High God! And they did fall down at the feet of Jesus, and did worship him. (3 Nephi 11:8–17.)

Later during this visit, Jesus announced to the Nephites that he was going also to the lost tribes of Israel to show them his body (3 Nephi 17:4). No doubt an experience similar to that recorded in 3 Nephi, with people touching the wounds in the Savior's body, will be found in the yet-to-be-obtained records of the lost tribes.

Summary and Conclusion

Although all the standard works testify of the reality of the resurrection, nowhere is this doctrine more clearly or more forcefully taught than in the Book of Mormon. What does the Book of Mormon say about the resurrection? At least the following:

1. The resurrection is needed because of the fall of Adam, which brought both temporal and spiritual death. Death is an

"awful monster," but the resurrection redeems all people from that monster by bringing all mankind out of the grave and back into the presence of God.

2. Without the atonement of Christ there would be no resurrection. Jesus had power over death because he was more than a mortal man. He was a God in his flesh as well as in his spirit.

3. *Resurrection* means the reuniting of the spirit and the physical body on a permanent basis.

4. The resurrection pertains to more than the physical body. It involves the redemption of the spirit as well. Without the resurrection no one could return to the presence of God, and all persons would become devils.

5. Jesus was the first to rise in the resurrection.

6. All mankind will be resurrected.

7. Not all will be resurrected at the same time. The righteous come forth before the wicked, and those (of the righteous) who lived before Christ come forth before those (of the righteous) who live after Christ.

8. There is a period of waiting between the time of death and the time of resurrection. During this period the spirit is in paradise or in darkness, meaning spirit prison.

9. The Creation, the Fall, death, the Atonement, the resurrection, and the Judgment are all necessary and are all part of a divine, merciful, and eternal plan of God. Rather than speaking of these events as independent and unrelated, the Book of Mormon ties all of them together. The resurrection is shown to be a necessary part of the plan of redemption.

10. Resurrected bodies are tangible and solid, and can be felt and handled by mortal men.

11. After his resurrection Jesus Christ personally appeared to a multitude of about twenty-five hundred people on the American continent and invited them to feel his hands, feet, and side. The people did so and knew for a surety that he was the God of Israel, who had been slain and had risen again.

12. After the resurrection of Jesus occurred, in America many deceased Saints rose from their graves and appeared to many. Samuel prophesied concerning these events, and the fulfillment of his prophecy was recorded at Jesus' special request.

13. Resurrected beings never die again.

14. All mankind will be judged after the resurrection of the body.

15. All of the prophets taught the gospel and testified of Jesus Christ, which means they also taught the doctrine of the resurrection.

As mentioned earlier, the Lord revealed to Enoch that a basic purpose of the record we call the Book of Mormon would be to testify of the resurrection of Christ and the resurrection of all mankind. Thus, the grand declaration that Jesus Christ is a God, that he has redeemed mankind from the fall of Adam, that he rose from the tomb, and that he brought about a physical resurrection of all mankind is profusely taught in the Book of Mormon. The Doctrine and Covenants and the teachings of the Prophet Joseph Smith offer further refinements and clarifications about the resurrection, but the Book of Mormon presents the fundamental message of the resurrection so plainly that anyone who wants to know the doctrinal basics of this subject can learn them well from that source.

Notes

1. *Teachings of the Prophet Joseph Smith*, comp. Joseph Fielding Smith (Salt Lake City: Deseret Book Co., 1976), p. 149. Hereafter cited as *TPJS*.
2. See *TPJS*, p. 62.
3. Joseph Fielding Smith, *Doctrines of Salvation*, comp. Bruce R. McConkie, 3 vols. (Salt Lake City: Bookcraft, 1954–56), 2:284.
4. *History of the Church* 5:339.
5. See Orson Pratt, in *Journal of Discourses* 16:353–68. Hereafter cited as *JD*.
6. As cited in Harold B. Lee, *Youth and the Church* (Salt Lake City: Deseret Book Co., 1970), p. 183; the source for the quote from Joseph S. Amussen is the *Improvement Era* 30 (June 1927): 703–4.
7. Brigham Young, "The Resurrection," 1875 discourse printed in the *Elders' Journal* 1 (July 1904): 153.
8. Brigham Young, in *JD* 8:28.
9. John Taylor, in *JD* 18:333.
10. Joseph F. Smith, *Gospel Doctrine* (Salt Lake City: Deseret Book Co., 1939), p. 23.
11. *TPJS*, p. 181.
12. *TPJS*, p. 297.

PART IV

The Savior

Chapter 15

JESUS THE MASTER TEACHER

There is no doubt that Jesus is the greatest teacher and the greatest example the world has ever known. This is because he is the greatest being that has lived on this earth. He was literally a God living among mortal men. He is the very creator of the planet on which we live, the creator of the stars we see in the heavens. He is the firstborn Son of God in the spirit, the Only Begotten of the Father in the flesh. He atoned for Adam's fall and for our own sins. He is our only Savior and the final judge of mankind.

An idea put forth by Earl V. Pullias of the University of Southern California has become popular among several modern educators. He said, "One can be no greater as a teacher than he is as a person."[1] President Harold B. Lee expressed a corollary to this: "You cannot lift another soul until you are standing on higher ground than he is. . . . You cannot light a fire in another soul unless it is burning in your own soul. You teachers, the testimony that you bear, the spirit with which you teach and with which you lead, is one of the most important assets that you can have, as you help to strengthen those who need so much, wherein you have so much to give."[2] Jesus is the greatest of all teachers because he is the greatest of all persons. He stood on the higher ground and excelled in every way.

Jesus was not simply a dispenser of information. He was an inspirer and mover of men. To the meek, the humble, and the repentant he was always a friend. To the proud and the haughty he was a disturbing influence. In debate he was superb. No one could refute his argument; no one could fail to see the force of his message. There were times when no enemy dared question him any further. He was strong in his assertions and declarations. Had Jesus been a mere "pushover," the Jewish leaders never would have viewed him as a threat to their system. Finally, since they could not silence him, they plotted to remove him from the scene altogether.

Factors Necessary for Great Teaching to Occur

It seems to me that in order for great teaching to occur—teaching that may approach, in some small degree, the caliber of the Savior's—certain things have to take place. I can think of at least five.

First, teachers must have something important to teach. In the case of teachers in the Church, that something is the gospel of Jesus Christ; it is the most important subject matter in the world. Gospel teachers are engaged in the most important work possible, for their teaching could have a more lasting effect, change more people's lives, and do more good in the world than national political conventions or summit conferences.

Second, teachers ought to be excited about what they are teaching. They must understand the importance of and feel a purpose for the instruction. If they don't feel the need for teaching a particular subject, they won't be very enthusiastic and might, by their neglect, give a negative impression about the subject.

Third, teachers must have somebody to whom they can give the message.

Fourth, teachers must have an effective way of communicating. This area includes such things as a teacher's vocabulary, methods, and use of examples, objects, models, and audiovisual aids. It also includes a teacher's ability to recognize the opportune time for teaching and to give the proper level of instruction, all based on the readiness of the learner. The material must be appropriate for the occasion, and it should be conveyed in so plain a manner that no one can misunderstand. Gospel instructors must teach by the Spirit so that they not only inform but also inspire; when they testify of the truth of what they have taught, their words go into the hearts of their listeners and not just the heads.

Fifth, teachers, especially gospel teachers, must have a desire to improve, to grow in knowledge and in skill, so as to become more effective.

Gospel teachers who desire to be most effective in all of the above areas, as well as gospel students who desire to better understand the Master and his message, will find it helpful to consider Jesus' example as the Master Teacher. Using the books of Matthew, Mark, Luke, and John—which are testimonies about Jesus—let us look at some of the events in Jesus' mortal ministry and see what we can learn about him as a teacher. We will supplement the Gospel accounts with latter-day scriptures, which provide a clearer understanding of the Savior and his mission. The Joseph Smith

Translation, for instance, makes Jesus a more vivid figure than is the case in other Bible versions.

Jesus' Teaching Was an Organized Plan

Jesus came to earth to accomplish several major tasks (see the accompanying chart). Thus, to Jesus teaching was not an end in itself; it was a way of accomplishing his purposes. Teaching was a means to advance the gospel and to establish the kingdom of God on the earth.

The record of Jesus' ministry shows that he followed an organized plan. During the first year, he taught the multitudes, most of whom had already been introduced to the gospel by John the Baptist. From among the many who followed Him, Jesus chose those whom he would make his leaders. After calling the Twelve and the Seventy, his efforts were directed less toward preaching to the masses and more toward training these new officers. The Sermon on the Mount, for example, was given primarily to the disciples, at a missionary preparation meeting, and not so much as a public discourse. Jesus soon sent the Twelve and the Seventy on missions. This gave them valuable experience at a time when Jesus was still on earth to counsel them. To properly train the teachers was of prime importance in building the kingdom, and Jesus tended to it personally. No doubt the missionary practices of the early Church were patterned after the methods that Jesus taught and demonstrated to his disciples. The Savior spent the last two years of his ministry training those who would be the leaders in the Church. The last week of his mortal life he spent instructing the Twelve and testifying boldly against the dealings of the Jewish religious leaders. His entire ministry was orderly and purposeful, directed toward accomplishing his mission on the earth.

Jesus' Teaching Methods

In making a list of Jesus' teaching methods I came to realize that his methods were adapted to the particular need of the occasion (see section entitled "Jesus' Teaching Methods" in the accompanying chart).[3] Our basic source for information on how Jesus taught is the text of the four Gospels; and while they are effective testimonies, they are not complete biographies and therefore often lack supporting details. For instance, we all know that without uttering a word a person can communicate much through his facial expression, a raised eyebrow, a wink, a gesture, a movement of the body, and so forth. Generally these types of communication, any of which the Savior might have employed, go unrecorded and therefore unperceived in the sacred record. I recall, however, a passage in the Gospel of Mark that says that Jesus "looked round about on them [the Pharisees] with anger" (Mark 3:5). In the Book of Mormon account of the Savior's visit to the American continent, we read that Jesus "did smile upon" the people (3 Nephi 19:25, 30). In each of these instances, the Lord's countenance conveyed a message in addition to any words spoken.

We cannot avoid wondering how many more times the Savior enhanced a teaching situation with a glance, a step forward, a raised hand, a louder or softer tone of voice, an inflection or emphasis on a word, a rapidly spoken phrase, a long silent pause, a quick retort, and so on. Undoubtedly Jesus' entire personality—all that he was physically, mentally, spiritually, and emotionally—served to convey the particular teaching of the moment. As was the case with Jesus, the live teacher can be the most effective audiovisual aid there is.

Let us now examine in some detail some of the teaching methods used by Jesus, those methods that *can* be gleaned from the scriptural record.

Simple Declarations, the Use of Miracles, and the Surprise Element

Jesus repeatedly turned ordinary events into teaching experiences. Often, perhaps most often, Jesus said simply and straightforwardly what he meant. The Sermon on the Mount seems to be a good example of that. Some who heard the sermon were "astonished" with the forthrightness of it, for he spoke "as one having authority from God, and not as having authority from the scribes" (JST, Matthew 7:36–37). Having studied much, the scribes were learned, and when attempting to teach they could quote a myriad of sources and give a waterfront of opinions, but they had no clear declaration as to what was really right. Jesus didn't teach his disciples in that manner. He gave the answer; he declared the doctrine in simple, direct terms and spoke with the authority of God. The people perceived the difference between him and the scribes and were astonished.

Another teaching technique of the Savior was the performance of miracles. We are impressed with the wide variety of his miracles.

Jesus the Master Teacher

Major Tasks of Jesus' Ministry

A study of the four Gospels reveals that the Savior used a variety of teaching methods in his ministry. Although he was the Master Teacher, for him teaching was not an end in itself but a means to an end. Everything he did contributed to the purpose of his life on earth. Thus, he used various communicative methods to accomplish the work of his ministry, the major tasks of which were:

1. To bear witness of the gospel (John 7:7; 9:39–41; 15:22; 18:37).
2. To show mankind the only true way toward eternal salvation (John 14:6).
3. To establish the kingdom of God among men on the earth by restoring the gospel, ordaining and training Church leaders, and converting the honest in heart (Luke 1:32–33; Mark 3:14; Luke 4:18–19).
4. To withstand all temptations and live without sin (Matt. 4:3–11; Heb. 2:4–18; 4:15; Alma 7:10–13; *Lectures on Faith* 5:2).
5. To testify against wickedness and false traditions (JST, John 7:24; Matt. 15:3–6; Mark 7:9–13; 2 Ne. 10:3–5).
6. To make an atonement with his blood and give his life for the world (Luke 24:45–58; John 10:15; Mosiah 3:16–19; D&C 38:4; 45:3–5).
7. To bring to pass the resurrection of all mankind from the dead (John 5:25–29; 2 Ne. 8; 9:21–22; Morm. 9:13).

Jesus' Teaching Methods

Following is a listing of Jesus' most notable teaching methods. At first glance some of the items may not seem to be teaching methods at all; but a closer look at each real-life event—keeping in mind the precise tasks that constitute the Savior's ministry—readily brings the reader to an awareness that these are teaching situations, and Jesus' responses to the situations constitute his teaching methods. Hence we find that he:

1. Used simple declaration (Matt. 5, 6, 7; John 7:14–18).
2. Spoke with forthrightness and authority (Matt. 7:28–29).
3. Performed miracles as a teaching activity (Matt. 9:1–8; 21:18–22; Mark 2:1–12; 6:51–52).
4. Used gentle subtlety (John 4:15–19).
5. Quoted from the Old Testament (Matt. 19:3–6; 22:31–32; John 10:34).
6. Appealed to the Old Testament for precedents (Matt. 12:1–8).
7. Used logic (Matt. 10:10–12; 12:9–14, 22–28; Mark 3:22–26; Luke 6:6–11; 13:14–17).
8. Used irony (Matt. 9:10–13; Mark 2:15–17; Luke 5:27–32; John 8:39–44).
9. Used colorful, attention-getting figures of speech (Matt. 18:6; 23:13–33; Mark 14:21; Luke 7:24–28; John 5:14; 5:35; 6:35).
10. Employed object lessons (Matt. 18:1–6; 22:16–22; Luke 5:4–10).
11. Asked questions (Matt. 16:13–15; Luke 7:24–26; 22:35; 24:13–26).
12. Asked questions of those who asked him questions (Luke 10:25–28).
13. Bargained by means of questions (Matt. 21:23–27).
14. Used invective and censure. Used witty reply and repartee. (Matt. 22:15–46; John 4:16–19; 10:31–32.)
15. Candidly corrected those who were in error (Matt. 22:29).
16. Used debate and argument, beyond mere discussion (John 7, 8).
17. Spoke consoling words (Mark 5:36; Luke 7:43–50; 8:48; John 8:10–11).
18. Taught with the Spirit (Luke 24:25–32; John 3:34).
19. Taught by example (Matt. 4:19; John 10:27; 13:15).
20. Taught with parables (JST, Matt. 13:1–52; 21:34; Luke 15:1–32; 16:1–31).
21. Was selective in what he taught to different groups (Matt. 7:6; 13:10–11).
22. Sometimes posed a problem (Matt. 17:24–25; 22:41–46; Luke 7:40–42).
23. Refused to give signs (Matt. 12:38–40).
24. Changed the subject, thus avoiding the full force of the issue (Matt. 22:30–31).
25. Prophesied (Matt. 12:36–42; 24:3–51).
26. At least one time refused to say anything (Luke 23:7–11).

He healed people of diseases and also of physical, structural ailments such as a withered hand, blindness, deafness, and the inability to speak. He cast out devils, calmed storms, multiplied food, walked on water, got a coin out of a fish's mouth, cursed a tree, reattached a severed ear, and raised persons from the dead. These acts demonstrated that he had power over diseases, over the unseen world of the spirits, and over the world of nature and physical things, including the weather. They showed that he could overcome the law of gravity and that he could even restore life to dead bodies. He cured broken hearts and healed souls as well as mended physical bodies. The wide scope of these activities surely taught his disciples that "all power" was given him "both in heaven and on earth" (D&C 93:17; Matthew 28:18). Jesus spoke to the elements, and they obeyed.

Jesus used the miracle of curing a man of palsy as a teaching device (Mark 2:1–12; Matthew 9:1–8). The man, lying on a bed, was let down through the roof of a house into the midst of a crowd of people. Although it was evident that the man was suffering from a physical ailment and was unable to walk, Jesus' first words to him were, "Son, thy sins be forgiven thee." This greatly agitated the scribes who were sitting there, and they reasoned in their hearts: "Why doth this man [Jesus] thus speak blasphemies? who can forgive sins but God only?" Jesus then said to them, "Is it not easier to say, Thy sins be forgiven thee, than to say, Arise and walk?" (JST, Matthew 9:5; see also JST, Mark 2:7.) It is as if he had said to them, "You cannot determine through mortal sight whether his sins are forgiven, but you can perceive whether he gets up and walks." Then Jesus made this clarifying statement as to his purpose: "But that ye may know that the Son of man hath power on earth to forgive sins, (he saith to the sick of the palsy,) I say unto thee, Arise, and take up thy bed, and go thy way into thine house." It is very clear from the way this miracle is reported, particularly in the Joseph Smith Translation, that Jesus used the healing of the man's body, which they who were witnesses could perceive with their eyes, to illustrate His ability to heal a soul, which they could not see. This miracle was a teaching device. It surely worked well, for the people were all amazed and said, "We never saw it on this fashion." I suppose you could say it was a case of moving from the known to the unknown, from the visible to the invisible, from the physical to the spiritual dimension.

Jesus also used gentle subtlety—the surprise element. He said to the woman at Jacob's well, "Go, call thy husband, and come hither." The woman answered, "I have no husband." Jesus said,

"Thou hast well said, I have no husband: for thou hast had five husbands; and he whom thou now hast is not thy husband: in that saidst thou truly." The woman said unto him, "Sir, I perceive that thou art a prophet." (John 4:16–19.)

Jesus' use of this teaching technique was a part of his delivering the real message of this instructional moment. Sitting at a well where people came to draw water and utilizing this setting to make a comparison between earthly water and the "living water," Jesus taught the woman that he was the Messiah. He said that if someone drank the water drawn from the well, that person would thirst again; but a person who drank the water He had to give would never thirst again. The woman doubted he could provide such water, because he had neither rope nor bucket and the well was deep. She also asked him if he thought he was greater than Jacob himself, who gave them the well. The whole episode compares secular things to spiritual. The woman was engrossed in the worldly things—the flesh, the natural water, the rope, the bucket. She could hardly grasp the idea of the "living water," and even when she began to believe, her response was that she would like some of that special kind of water so that she would never have to come again to the well to draw. She was still thinking in physical terms. It took some time before she could appreciate that the "living water" Jesus could give would be like a *flowing* well "springing up unto everlasting life." (John 4:6–15.)

Use of Scriptures, Logic, and Irony

Jesus taught from the scriptures. He read from them, quoted them, and explained them to his hearers. Numerous occasions are recorded in which he quoted Isaiah, Moses, or the Psalms, or cited events from the book of Kings. He often reminded his audience of events recorded in the Old Testament, using scriptural accounts of what David, or Moses, or Abraham had done in order to provide an example or establish a precedent. He also used the Old Testament to teach doctrine, the laws governing marriage and divorce, the doctrine of the resurrection, and particularly his own messiahship.

Jesus also used logic or reasoning as a teaching method. The scriptural record shows him using plain "common sense" to arrive at conclusions about proper daily behavior. For example, once Jesus was in the synagogue on the Sabbath day, and a man with a withered hand was present. The Pharisees, anticipating that Jesus would heal the man, questioned the Master: "Is it lawful to heal on the sabbath days?" As was their custom, they were seeking a chance to accuse and find fault with him. Jesus reasoned with them: "What man shall there be among you, that shall have one sheep, and if it fall into a pit on the Sabbath day, will he not lay hold on it, and lift it out? How much then is a man better than a sheep? Wherefore it is lawful to do well on the sabbath days." Then he healed the withered hand—and he did it right then and there, where everyone could see him do it. (Matthew 12:9–14; see also Luke 6:6–11.) The Pharisees were so frustrated by his power, because it exposed the shallowness of their own reasoning, that they "were filled with madness; and communed one with another what they might do to Jesus" (Luke 6:11).

Later, perhaps the same day, he cast an evil spirit out of a man, and many people observed the change that came over him that was healed. The Pharisees said, "This fellow doth not cast out devils, but by Beelzebub the prince of devils." Again Jesus used logic or common sense to help them arrive at a proper understanding, saying: "Every kingdom divided against itself is brought to desolation; and every city or house divided against itself shall not stand: and if Satan cast out Satan, he is divided against himself; how shall then his kingdom stand? And if I by Beelzebub cast out devils, by whom do your children cast them out?" (Matthew 12:22–27.)

Jesus sometimes used irony, satire, or adroit sarcasm when dealing with the Pharisees, Sadducees, and scribes. On one occasion he showed no objection when, while he and his disciples were eating, publicans and sinners came and sat down with them. The Pharisees saw a chance to find fault with this, so they asked the disciples, "Why eateth your Master with publicans and sinners?" Jesus knew their intentions and replied, "They that be whole need not a physician, but they that are sick. . . . I am not come to call the righteous, but sinners to repentance." (Matthew 9:10–13; Mark 2:15–17; Luke 5:27–32.)

A casual reading may not uncover the force of the Savior's remarks above, but a little meditation on the subject will do so. Who in this world does not need the teachings and saving power of Jesus? Who among all mankind is truly righteous without the gospel of Christ? Can anyone be redeemed without the Redeemer? Is there any other way? Is there any other salvation? When Jesus said he was sent only to the sick, that was true; but who among all mankind is not sick? Were the complaining, self-righteous Pharisees spiritually whole and well? Were not they sinners also? Unquestionably they were sicker and in greater need of Jesus' healing influence than were those "sinners" whom they despised. When

Jesus said to the Pharisees, "I am not come to call the righteous, but sinners to repentance," he was in fact condemning the Pharisaic brand of self-righteousness which had blinded their eyes and hardened their hearts to the reality of their own sinful condition.

Another instance of Jesus' use of this type of language is found in the context of his giving the parables of the lost sheep, the piece of silver, and the prodigal son (Luke 15:1–32). The setting was as follows: The publicans and the sinners drew near to hear Jesus teach; the Pharisees and scribes murmured, saying, "This man receiveth sinners, and eateth with them." Jesus then told the Pharisees and scribes a parable wherein a man, who had one hundred sheep and lost one of them, left the ninety-nine in the wilderness to go find that one lost sheep. Having found him, the man rejoiced mightily over the recovery. Jesus' rebuke of the self-righteous attitude of the Pharisees then came in these words: "I say unto you, that likewise joy shall be in heaven over one sinner that repenteth, more than over ninety and nine just persons, which need no repentance."

If we were to take this last statement literally, it would put a premium on sin. The comment about heaven's having more joy over one sinner than over ninety-nine righteous persons is not a simple, straightforward declaration of fact; it is a rebuke of the Pharisees' self-important, self-righteous attitude, because they were certain they needed no repentance for themselves. They were "righteous," all right—*self*-righteous! Are we really to believe there is more joy in heaven over one sinner that repents than over ninety-nine truly righteous persons such as Enoch, Abraham, the brother of Jared, Nephi, and Joseph Smith? What tremendous odds—ninety-nine to one! In considering Jesus' statement to the Pharisees, the words of the Old Testament prophet Samuel come to mind: "Hath the Lord as great delight in burnt offerings and sacrifices, as in obeying the voice of the Lord? Behold, to obey is better than sacrifice." (1 Samuel 15:22.) What the Savior was really saying to the Pharisees was, in effect, "There is more joy in heaven over one of these despised publicans who honestly repents than there is over ninety-nine self-righteous persons like you, who in your own estimation need no repentance."

Note how the Prophet Joseph Smith interpreted the Savior's words on this occasion:

> The hundred sheep represent one hundred Sadducees and Pharisees, as though Jesus had said, "If you Sadducees and

> Pharisees are in the sheepfold, I have no mission for you; I am sent to look up sheep that are lost; and when I have found them, I will back them up and make joy in heaven." This represents hunting after a few individuals, or one poor publican, which the Pharisees and Sadducees despised.
>
> . . . Like I say unto you, there is joy in the presence of the angels of God over one sinner that repenteth, more than over ninety-and-nine just persons that are so righteous; they will be damned anyhow; you cannot save them.[4]

It may bother some to hear that Jesus would speak this way, because it is at variance with the popular misconception that he was timid and colorless in his personality and spoke only pleasant things. I think the record given in the New Testament is quite clear but has often been misread and misinterpreted. Irony, sarcasm, and satire are literary forms that, when used in a live setting, are usually unmistakable in their meaning. The words say one thing but mean another, and a correct understanding of them is dependent on sound and context. When these words are reduced to writing, however, the background and context are often lost; as a result, the force of the conversation is also lost, and the careless reader may even arrive at just the opposite meaning for a particular passage. Such has been the case many times with these examples we have been discussing.

The four Gospels do not present a single instance in which Jesus was impatient, critical, or unkind with people who were humble, teachable, and willing to change their lives. He mingled with publicans and sinners, and he forgave transgressions on condition of repentance. He cast out devils, healed the lame, raised the dead, fed the hungry, opened the eyes of the blind, gave hearing to the deaf, and restored the sick to health—if they but had the faith that he could do these things. But he was a terror to the workers of iniquity and to the deceptive, the self-righteous, the hypocritical. In dealing with the repentant he was the gentle yet firm Messiah. To the proud, the haughty, and the arrogant, he was absolutely indomitable and irrepressible, and a threat to their craftiness.

Jesus was capable of having tremendous physical and emotional impact on those with whom he met and dealt. When they saw and heard him, many people thought he was one of the Old Testament prophets come to earth again—perhaps Elijah or Jeremiah (Matthew 16:14; Mark 8:27–29; Luke 9:18–19). He was as powerful as the truth that he taught.

Use of Colorful Speech and Object Lessons

Jesus used colorful, attention-getting figures of speech. We find these in his conversations with his disciples, in his teachings to the multitudes, and in his censures of the Jewish rulers. Let us consider some examples. When he called fishermen into his service he said, "I will make you fishers of men" (Matthew 4:19). If a person knowingly gives offense, said Jesus, "it were better for him that a millstone were hanged about his neck, and that he were drowned in the depth of the sea" (Matthew 18:6). That is, it would have been better for the man to have died than to have committed the sin. Of Judas, who betrayed him, Jesus said, "It had been good for that man if he had not been born" (Matthew 26:24).

Jesus praised John the Baptist in colorful language, calling him a "burning and a shining light," a man "much more than a prophet" (John 5:35; Luke 7:26). James and John he surnamed the "sons of thunder" (Mark 3:17), while the Jewish rulers he called "hypocrites," "child[ren] of hell," "blind guides," and described them as being "like unto whited sepulchres, . . . full of dead men's bones," a "generation of vipers" (Matthew 23:13, 15, 16, 27, 33).

To a man who had been cured of a physical ailment, Jesus said, "Sin no more, lest a worse thing come unto thee" (John 5:14), not meaning that every physical ailment is the direct result of sin, but rather that sin leads to a loss of salvation, a loss worse than any physical affliction. Of those Pharisees and scribes who had such great inconsistency in their beliefs, he said that they "strain at a gnat, and swallow a camel" (Matthew 23:24). To his disciples he declared, "If thy hand offend thee, cut it off. . . . If thy foot offend thee, cut it off. . . . And if thine eye offend thee, pluck it out." (Mark 9:43–47.) The Joseph Smith Translation makes it clear that these are figurative expressions having reference to friends and associates, it being better to be without present friends and companions if they are the kind who would lead us astray.

In bearing testimony of himself and his messiahship, Jesus employed effective imagery, declaring, "I am the bread of life" (John 6:35). He also said, "I am the door of the sheepfold. All that ever came before me who testified not of me are thieves and robbers." (JST, John 10:7–8.) And further, "Many prophets and righteous men have desired to see those things which ye see, and have not seen them; and to hear those things which ye hear, and have not heard them" (Matthew 13:17). "The queen of the south," the Savior testified, "shall rise up in the judgment with the men of this generation, and condemn them: for she came from the utmost parts of the earth to hear the wisdom of Solomon; and, behold, a greater than Solomon is here'' (Luke 11:31); likewise, he declared, the ''men of Nineve shall rise up in the judgment with this generation, and shall condemn it: for they repented at the preaching of Jonas; and, behold, a greater than Jonas is here'' (Luke 11:32).

Whether by the means of figurative language or through the use of bold declaration, Jesus repeatedly testified that he was the Messiah. After bearing such a testimony to a gathering of Jews, he said, ''If ye believe not that I am he, ye shall die in your sins'' (John 8:23–24). There is no question that the message came through, for the Jews later asked, ''Art thou greater than our father Abraham?'' Jesus replied, ''Abraham rejoiced to see my day. . . . Before Abraham was, I am.'' The Savior was saying, in effect, ''Yes, I am greater than Abraham; I am the Lord.'' According to the record, the Jews ''took . . . up stones to cast at him.'' (See John 8:53–59.) That they tried to stone him indicates they got the message that Jesus claimed to be the Messiah, the Son of God, the great Jehovah. This is further certified by what some taunters said to him at the cross. They ''reviled him, wagging their heads,'' and said: ''If thou be the Son of God, come down from the cross.'' (Matthew 27:39–40.) And the chief priests, scribes, and elders said, ''He trusted in God; let him deliver him now, if he will have him: for he said, I am the Son of God'' (Matthew 27:43). There can be no doubt that Jesus was successful in putting his point across to both saint and sinner.

Jesus used objects, models, or visual aids to reinforce his words. When a group of fishermen had fished all night and caught nothing, Jesus then told them to cast their nets in again. When they did so, the nets came up full of fish. All were astonished, and then Jesus, with his object lesson vividly in place, said to Peter, ''Fear not; from henceforth thou shalt catch men.'' (Luke 5:4–10.) The purpose of a model, object, or visual aid is to increase the learner's perception. Jesus did this on occasion with persons who were blind or deaf. Sometimes, if the person was deaf, Jesus put his fingers into the person's ears, and thus the person not only saw Jesus but also felt him (see Mark 7:33). If the person was blind, Jesus might put his hands over the person's eyes or place clay on them. Hence, although the blind person could not see, he could hear Jesus and feel his touch, and this would increase the person's perception. (See Mark 8:22–25; John 9:6.) I don't know all the reasons why Jesus did these things, but it appears that one of his purposes was to increase the perception, attention, and experience of the afflicted person.

On another occasion, when his disciples asked, "Who is the greatest in the kingdom of heaven?" he set a little child before them and declared that, to become great, a person must become converted and be as humble as a little child. He also warned against offending "one of these little ones which believe in me." The word which is translated "offend" in the King James Version needs some clarification. To offend does not mean, in this case, simply to displease the child or to make it unhappy, but literally it means to "cause to stumble" or lead away from the gospel. Jesus' statement about offending little children is a warning against false teachings, and it is a warning that teachers must be concerned about the influence they have on students. The gospel teacher who plants doubt in place of faith in the minds of students, who criticizes the Brethren, or who makes light of sacred things and fosters a spirit of cynicism risks the possibility of offending the Lord's "little ones." So exercised was Jesus on this point that he said, as mentioned earlier, "Whoso shall offend one of these little ones which believe in me, it were better for him that a millstone were hanged about his neck, and that he were drowned in the depth of the sea." (Matthew 18:1–6.) Such descriptive language tells us that the Lord cannot be pleased by the teacher who is cynical and who, by example, teaches others to be the same. He called the false doctrines of such teachers the "leaven of the Pharisees and of the Sadducees," and warned us to beware of it (Matthew 16:6, 12). He said that a student receiving this kind of faithless doctrine becomes "twofold more the child of hell" than he was before he was taught (JST, Matthew 23:12). It is better that the sheep have no shepherd than that they be in the care of wolves. One of the problems with a cynic is that he feels little if any responsibility for the consequences of what he gives to others. Such a teacher is a wolf in sheep's clothing. The scriptural image of a wolf to describe a false, cynical leader is well chosen, for the word *cynic* itself comes from a word meaning "doglike." You can visualize this kind of teacher running around with his nose to the ground, sniffing out something to complain about or some cherished belief to discredit.

Asking Questions and Reproving the Wayward

We mentioned earlier that Jesus could turn ordinary events into teaching situations. One way that he did that was by asking questions. In this way he could get people talking and involved. For example, he once asked the Twelve, "What was it that ye disputed among yourselves by the way?" They had been disputing over "who should be the greatest" among them. As soon as he could get them talking or at least thinking about it, then he could teach them. In this instance he taught them that "if any man desire to be first, the same shall be last of all, and servant of all." (Mark 9:33–35.) On another occasion he asked the Twelve, "Whom do men say that I the Son of man am?" (Matthew 16:13.) In this case Jesus was making a point clear by the means of contrast, as if he had said, "Who do *other* men say I am, and who do *you* say I am?" Later, on the day of his resurrection, as he walked along the road to Emmaus with two of his disciples (who didn't recognize him), he asked, "What manner of communications are these that ye have one to another, as ye walk, and are sad?" One of them replied, "Art thou only a stranger in Jerusalem, and hast not known the things which are come to pass there in these days?" And Jesus asked, "What things?" Then the disciples rehearsed the matter of the crucifixion of Jesus and of the reported resurrection, about which they seemed to have some doubt. Through these questions Jesus set up the structure for a whole afternoon's discussion of the mission of the Messiah, and this gave him the opportunity to teach of his atonement and to show that the scriptures testified of him. The experience caused the disciples' hearts to burn within them. (Luke 24:13–35.)

Sometimes he asked questions in response to those who asked him questions. When "a certain lawyer" asked, "Master, what shall I do to inherit eternal life?" Jesus said unto him, "What is written in the law? how readest thou?" When the man then answered his own question from the scriptures, Jesus said, "Thou hast answered right." (Luke 10:25–28.)

At least one time Jesus bargained with his antagonists by means of questions. The Jewish rulers wanted to know by what authority he acted and taught and who gave him that authority. Just the day before he had driven the money changers out of the temple, so at this point the rulers were very much aware of him and sensitive to his actions. When they inquired regarding his authority he said, "I also will ask you one thing, which if ye tell me, I in like wise will tell you by what authority I do these things." He then asked them to tell him by what authority John the Baptist did his work—was it of heaven or of men? This type of question forced them into a dilemma. He knew it would. If they admitted John's authority was of God, he would say, "Why did ye not then believe him?" If they said John's authority was of man, the people who received John as a prophet would, they feared, react against them. So they attempted to save face, saying, "We cannot tell." Jesus promptly replied: "Neither tell I you by what authority I do these things." However, he did tell them that John came to them "in the way of righteousness" and that the publicans and harlots, if they believed John, would go into heaven before they (the Jewish rulers) would. (Matthew 21:23–32.)

Many of the examples of the teaching situations Jesus encountered, as recorded in the scriptures, were adversarial in nature, because they arose while Jesus labored with the hard-hearted, cynical, and conniving Jewish rulers. Some might wonder why Jesus engaged in this combative activity with those who were so opposed to him. Why didn't he just ignore them? He didn't because this type of confrontation actually constituted part of his mission. Note this explanation from the Prophet Joseph Smith:

> The Melchizedek High Priesthood [is] no other than the Priesthood of the Son of God. . . . It is also the privilege of the Melchizedek Priesthood, to reprove, rebuke, and admonish, as well as to receive revelation. . . .
>
> I frequently rebuke and admonish my brethren, and that because I love them, not because I wish to incur their displeasure, or mar their happiness. Such a course of conduct is not calculated to gain the good will of all, but rather the ill will of many; . . . the higher the authority, the greater the difficulty of the station; but these rebukes and admonitions become necessary, from the perverseness of the brethren, for their temporal as well as spiritual welfare. They actually constitute a part of the duties of my station and calling.[5]

Given these statements from the Prophet, we can conclude that it was necessary that Jesus, as one possessing all the powers of the Melchizedek Priesthood, testify against sin and wickedness and rebuke those responsible for that wickedness. Had he failed to do so, the wayward and the wicked would not have been challenged to repent in this life, nor would they be left without excuse in the Day of Judgment. This act of reproving is a prerogative of those holding the keys; the rest of us, therefore, had best not use this method so directly.

For the disciples and the believers Jesus performed acts of kindness; he talked to them about prayer, explained the need they had for the Holy Ghost, and taught them in the synagogues and in the courtyard of the temple. To the woman with an issue of blood, he said, "Be of good comfort: thy faith hath made thee whole; go in peace" (Luke 8:48). To the woman who bathed his feet with her tears and dried them with her hair, he said, "Thy sins are forgiven. . . . Thy faith hath saved thee." (Luke 7:48–50.)

Teaching by the Spirit and by Example

Jesus taught with the Spirit. When he quoted the law, and the prophets, and the Psalms in all things concerning himself, the people's hearts burned within them (see Luke 24:25–32). It was the Spirit that made this happen. When Peter testified that he knew that Jesus was the Christ, the Son of God, Jesus said, "Flesh and blood hath not revealed it unto thee, but my Father which is in heaven" (Matthew 16:13–18). Here the phrase "flesh and blood" represents the learning of man through worldly methods, through the mortal senses. Learning from "my Father in heaven" represents learning by the Spirit, by revelation. There is an essential difference between the knowledge of the world and the knowledge of the Spirit: knowledge obtained through revelation saves one's soul; worldly knowledge, even if correct, cannot cleanse the soul nor qualify one for the celestial kingdom. The Spirit reveals things absolutely essential to one's salvation, things that cannot be learned through the mortal, physical senses. Such things are learned through the Spirit, or they are not learned at all.

The Jewish leaders thought a person had to go to their school in order to learn to preach. This is illustrated by the amazement of the Jewish rulers over Jesus' endless wisdom. He had not gone through their training and curriculum, nor had he attended their schools, and yet he knew so much about the scriptures and about men and things. Once, in what appears to be a mixture of surprise and dismay over Jesus' success as a teacher, the rulers marvelled and cried out, "How knoweth this man letters, having never learned?" In response Jesus said, "My doctrine is not mine, but his that sent me." (John 7:15–16.) It was not that Jesus had "never learned," but that his learning came from the Father, by revelation, rather than from the schools and philosophies of the worldly wise. The Pharisees and Sadducees may have had facts, but they were without the conviction and witness of the Holy Ghost, and thus they were "ever learning, and never able to come to the knowledge of the truth" (2 Timothy 3:7). Without the Spirit they could not understand the things of God, even when they read the scriptures. The record says that the Father gave Jesus the Spirit without measure (John 3:34). The Savior taught by the power of the Holy Spirit; it had been with him all his life, and it gave him divine wisdom, even by the age of twelve years.

Jesus also taught by example. He prepared himself for his ministry and for the work he had to do. He fasted, he prayed, he read the scriptures, and he taught. Those who knew him would have observed the things he did and would have learned from them. Even though he was the Son of God and was divine, he would not have had the spiritual power he did unless he had been obedient and worked to develop it. When the disciples could not cast out a certain type of evil spirit, Jesus cast it out and told them why they had been unable to do this: their faith was not strong enough. He explained to them that such acts required prayer and fasting. (Matthew 17:14–21.) Does not this episode show us that it was by fasting and prayer that Jesus obtained his power and spiritual strength?

Use of Parables

No discussion of Jesus as a teacher would be complete without mention of his parables. We have already referred to several of the parables that Jesus directed to the Jewish rulers, and we noted that these had an element of censure and condemnation in them. The parables of instruction to the multitudes—such as the parables of the sower, the ten virgins, the talents, and the pearl of great price—contain a little less of this element, but they are, nonetheless, somewhat hidden in their meaning. It is possible that many of the Pharisees and scribes, and also the multitudes, did not at first receive the full impact of the message he spoke to them in parables, even when he chided them through the stories. Jesus used parables not for the purpose of making the spiritual points crystal clear, but as a device to conceal and shadow the deeper meaning from the proud, the lazy, and the self-righteous. The parable of the sower illustrated this through a description of different kinds of soils. The soils represented the different degrees of spiritual readiness and productivity of the people.

Although many have thought that the parables were intended to make the truths of the kingdom easily available, really the parables were intended to conceal the finer points of doctrine from those who did not value them. When the disciples asked Jesus why he spoke to the multitudes in parables, he replied: "Because it is given unto you to know the mysteries of the kingdom of heaven, but to them it is not given. . . . Therefore speak I to them in parables: because they seeing see not; and hearing they hear not, neither do they understand." (Matthew 13:10–13.)

The Prophet Joseph Smith said: "I have a key by which I understand the scriptures. I enquire, what was the question which drew out the answer, or caused Jesus to utter the parable?"[6] The context shows that the parables were given to the multitudes and to the Jewish rulers, not to the disciples. For example, Jesus introduced the parable of the wicked husbandmen with these words: "And again, hear another parable; for unto you that believe not, I speak in parables; that your unrighteousness may be rewarded unto you" (JST, Matthew 21:34). You may have noticed that, by contrast, there are no parables in 3 Nephi, an account of the Savior's ministry among a righteous people.

I know it is common among teachers in and out of the Church to misuse the parables, and many fail to note what Jesus said about why he used them. But the New Testament is quite clear on this matter. I have noticed that if you already know the doctrine, you can usually find it somewhere in a parable, but it is next to impossible to learn it for the first time from the parable alone as the source. Jesus was selective in what he taught to different groups. He did not give away the mysteries to those who had no interest in them and who would not search for, meditate upon, and live worthy of the higher truths. Jesus' purpose in withholding information can be viewed, on one hand, as merciful, because his doing so prevented the people from receiving information they were unprepared for and upon which they would have been judged later. But, on the other hand, it was also an act of justice. No man is saved in ignorance, especially willful ignorance. The rule is, as the Savior stated, "Ask, and it shall be given you; seek, and ye shall find; knock, and it shall be opened unto you: for every one that asketh receiveth; and he that seeketh findeth; and to him that knocketh it shall be opened" (Matthew 7:7–8). Jesus did not refuse to teach the unbelieving, the indifferent, and the rebellious who would not seek; rather, he gave them the lesser part because of their lack of readiness. No doubt they would eventually reach a time when they would regret their slothfulness and pride and mourn their lost opportunity—if not in this life, then in the spirit world. We too may experience such regrets if we fail to seek diligently the things of the kingdom. The principle of readiness is basic in the psychology of teaching and is nowhere better illustrated than in Jesus' use of parables.

I have a love for the New Testament, especially as it has been made plainer through latter-day revelation and the teachings of the Brethren. There is a joy in learning about the Savior. My heart and mind have been made glad by the knowledge of the Lord Jesus Christ, his compassion, his courage, his humility, his manliness, and his masterful ability to teach. In the best sense of the word, he is a hero. I have a testimony by the Spirit that he is real. He is the Son of God; yet, I marvel, even in his greatness he has time for smaller things. He knows each of us; he knows our names and our joys, weaknesses, and trials. He knows, and he cares. There is so much about him that "I scarce can take it in."[7] He is our Savior, the great Exemplar, the Master Teacher.

Notes

1. Earl V. Pullias, *Toward Excellence in College Teaching* (Dubuque, Iowa: W. C. Brown Co., 1963), p. 44.
2. Harold B. Lee, "Stand Ye in Holy Places," *Ensign* 3 (July 1973): 123.
3. The idea for this section of the chart was first suggested to me several years ago by a master's thesis written in 1951 by Glenn L. Pearson, a former Brigham Young University faculty member, entitled "Missionary Methods and Doctrines of the Primitive Church as Determined by a Study of the New Testament." Through the years I have continued to learn about the Savior's teaching methods, and in this chart I have enlarged, adapted, and rearranged the material Brother Pearson presented originally in his thesis.
4. *Teachings of the Prophet Joseph Smith*, comp. Joseph Fielding Smith (Salt Lake City: Deseret Book Co., 1976), pp. 277–78. Hereafter cited as *TPJS*.
5. *TPJS*, pp. 111–13.
6. *TPJS*, pp. 276–77.
7. "How Great Thou Art," *Hymns*, no. 86.

Chapter 16

SERMON ON THE MOUNT AND IN BOUNTIFUL: COMPARISONS

The word of the Lord is always precious and will be the most meaningful to us when we understand it in relation to the setting in which it was originally given. President Brigham Young said:

> Do you read the Scriptures, my brethren and sisters, as though you. . . . stood in the place of the men who wrote them? If you do not feel thus, it is your privilege to do so, that you may be as familiar with the spirit and meaning of the written word of God as you are with your daily walk and conversation, or as you are with your workmen or with your households.
>
> The people on every hand are inquiring, "What does this scripture mean, and how shall we understand this or that passage?" Now I wish, my brethren and sisters, for us to understand things precisely as they are, and not as the flitting, changing imagination of the human mind may frame them.[1]

It is in this light and for the purpose spoken of by President Young that I wish to present some parallels between the Savior's sermon in Bountiful to the Nephites, as recorded in 3 Nephi in the Book of Mormon, and a similar sermon, the Sermon on the Mount, recorded in the book of Matthew in the New Testament. Our primary sources for this study are, of course, the Book of Mormon and the New Testament. Fortunately, we have not only the King James Version of the New Testament but also the Joseph Smith Translation, which gives us many additional insights and points of understanding. We will pursue our subject, then, with the assurance that the Joseph Smith Translation gives the best account of the biblical sermon and that the Book of Mormon gives a correct account of the Nephite sermon. With this sure scriptural foundation we can make some useful comparisons and contrasts.

The Settings

There are at least three notable differences between the setting of the Nephite sermon and that of the Sermon on the Mount:

1. The sermon to the Nephites was given to a mixture of people; there was a multitude of believers, and among them were also twelve special disciples who had been called to be the Lord's personal representatives in the Americas.[2] The Sermon on the Mount recorded in Matthew, on the other hand, was given to a small number of believers, primarily the Twelve Apostles whom Jesus had chosen in the Holy Land.

2. The Sermon on the Mount was a missionary-oriented discourse preparatory to Jesus' sending forth the Twelve to preach. The Nephite sermon was directed to the multitude, only portions of it being pointed specifically to the twelve Nephite disciples.

3. The Sermon on the Mount was given prior to the Lord's atonement and death, before he had completely fulfilled the law of Moses. The Nephite sermon was delivered after the Atonement—the multitude consisting of those who had been spared in the great destruction that had taken place in the Americas a few weeks earlier at Jesus' death—and thus after the fulfillment of the law of Moses.

Since one sermon was to the Nephites and the other was primarily to the Jewish Twelve, and since the sermons were given in differing circumstances and for different purposes, both cultural and doctrinal differences are apparent in the content of these two extensive discourses. The best understanding of the Sermon on the Mount is likely to be gained from the Joseph Smith Translation because it not only restores lost doctrinal concepts but also preserves, better than any other version of the Bible, the Jewish background and original setting of the sermon. Likewise, the best understanding of the Nephite sermon can be gained from studying the context in which it appears in the Book of Mormon. Thus there is something to be gained not only in examining the similarities but also in noting the contrasts between the two sermons.

The Beatitudes

The Beatitudes as given in the Nephite sermon consist of at least eleven statements, each containing the word *blessed,* meaning a condition of happiness or spiritual well-being. The Book of Mormon account of the Beatitudes adds certain spiritual elements not found in the King James Version, such as "Blessed are the poor in spirit *who come unto me*" and "Blessed are all they who do hunger and thirst after righteousness, for they shall be filled *with the Holy Ghost*" (3 Nephi 12:3, 6, italics added). Many already know of these significant additions and have benefited from studying them. We should also be aware that the Joseph Smith Translation of Matthew 5 contains the same clarifications, a fact which indicates that Jesus spoke these same things to the Jewish Twelve; but these concepts were lost in the transmission of the biblical text and thus were missing from the King James Version.

This leads to an additional important feature of the Beatitudes that I want to point out: These choice, brief statements are not separate, disjointed platitudes; each has a relationship to the others. Let us look at them from the more complete list given in the Nephite sermon and in the Joseph Smith Translation. The Beatitudes deal first with a person's relationship to God. They speak of such things as faith in Jesus Christ, repentance, baptism, forgiveness of sins, and receiving the Holy Ghost. (These particular features are missing from the King James Version.) The emphasis then shifts to a person's feelings about himself, or those feelings that spring from within. For example: Blessed are the poor in spirit, those who mourn, those who are meek, and those who hunger and thirst after righteousness. Then the emphasis shifts to a person's attitude toward others. For example: Blessed are the peacemakers. And finally a fourth emphasis appears—how a person should handle other people's attitudes toward himself. Thus, blessed are all they who are persecuted for righteousness' sake or who are reviled and persecuted falsely.

This particular sequence of the Beatitudes follows a pattern seen in other scriptures, scriptures which describe one's relationship first to God, then to oneself, and then to one's fellowmen. Note the similar arrangement in the Ten Commandments. The first four commandments deal with man's relationship to God: man is to have no other gods and no graven images; he is not to take the name of God in vain; and he is to honor the Sabbath day. The fifth refers to one's parents, a commandment which is a good transition between the earlier commandments and those that follow. The last five commandments deal with man's relationship to his fellowman: man is not to kill, commit adultery, steal, lie, or covet. (See Exodus 20.) This type of organized sequence gives additional meaning to the Beatitudes and to the Ten Commandments that would not be perceivable if each beatitude or each commandment were separate and unrelated to the others. This sequence is also in harmony with Jesus' declaration that the first great commandment is to love God with all one's heart and that the second is to love one's neighbor as oneself (see Matthew 22:34–40).

A similar pattern can be seen in the sequence of the Articles of Faith. These begin with statements about the Godhead and man's relationship to God; then move on to principles regarding personal behavior, such as baptism and ordination; and finally end with declarations on general behavior, such as in article thirteen about virtue, honesty, doing good to all men, and so on. Such unity and harmony in the Lord's teachings enhance their spiritual impact on us; we see a much deeper meaning in the principles than we would if they were presented in an unrelated form.

In the incomplete way that the Beatitudes are listed in the King James Version, the first category—a person's relationship to God—is missing. It was, therefore, quite essential that the Joseph Smith Translation restore two beatitudes about faith, repentance, baptism, and the Holy Ghost. It was equally significant that these were placed at the beginning of the list in their proper doctrinal sequence. (See JST, Matthew 5:3–4.)

Scribes and Pharisees

The Nephite sermon, unlike the Sermon on the Mount, has no mention of scribes or Pharisees. This is to be expected, since the institution of scribes and Pharisees among the Jews began during the Babylonian captivity, several decades after Lehi's colony left Jerusalem. As a consequence, much of the cultural milieu so prominent in Judaism in New Testament times was not found among the Book of Mormon people.

The Law of Moses

In the Sermon on the Mount, Jesus tells his disciples that he has not "come to destroy the law, . . . but to fulfil" it. Certain aspects of the law of Moses are then specified. (See Matthew 5:17–47.) In the biblical sermon Jesus states that the law *will* be fulfilled; in the Book of Mormon sermon the Savior states three times that the law is *already* fulfilled (see 3 Nephi 12:17–20, 46). The emphasis on the fulfillment of the law of Moses caused such wonderment among the Nephite people that, following the sermon, Jesus gave an extended explanation about the fulfillment of the law (see 3 Nephi 15:2–9).

The biblical sermon contains no such explanation, although the Joseph Smith Translation contains an interesting alteration in Matthew 5:21–22 (modifying Matthew 5:19–20) that indicates the future fulfillment of the law of Moses: "Whosoever shall do and teach these commandments of the law until it be fulfilled, the same shall be called great."

"Be Ye Therefore Perfect"

In Matthew 5:48 Jesus states: "Be ye therefore perfect, even as your Father which is in heaven is perfect." A stronger statement is found in the Nephite sermon: "I would that ye should be perfect *even as I, or* your Father who is in heaven is perfect" (3 Nephi 12:48, italics added). The change in wording in the Nephite sermon is probably due to the fact that Jesus had been resurrected by that time and thus had become like the Father in every way.

Although the Joseph Smith Translation renders the verse somewhat differently than the King James Version, it does not add the comment about Jesus' own perfection. Surely this reflects the difference between Jesus' mortal state at the time of the biblical sermon and his resurrected, exalted condition at the time of the Nephite discourse.

The Lord's Prayer

In the Nephite sermon, the sample prayer, commonly known as the Lord's Prayer, is given to the multitude. However, in the Sermon on the Mount, the prayer is given primarily to the Twelve. This distinction has a certain bearing upon some notable differences between the two versions of the prayer.

"Thy kingdom come." The biblical account of the prayer includes the phrase "Thy kingdom come" (Matthew 6:10). The Nephite sermon does not contain this phrase (see 3 Nephi 13:9–10), evidently because the kingdom of God had already come to the Nephites. The record itself makes this clear, since it shows that the Nephites had prophets among them who were baptizing, conferring the Holy Ghost, and doing many things that pertain to the kingdom.

"Give us this day our daily bread." This phrase is found in the biblical sermon (Matthew 6:11) but not in the Nephite one. This is ap-

parently due to the difference in the circumstances of the two sermons. The biblical sermon was given primarily to the Twelve, and they were to leave their normal, secular employ and "take . . . no thought" (Matthew 6:34) for food, clothing, and such temporalities —meaning that they were not to labor at occupations as other men did for the necessities of life. Therefore it was particularly appropriate for them to pray for their "daily bread," that is, for the bread of the day. The Nephite sermon does not contain this plea because the prayer was given as an example to the multitude, who were to labor for bread as all members of the Church are obliged to do. They were to earn a temporal living.

This last example serves to emphasize the distinction not only between the two sermons but also between the special calling of the Apostles and the duties of regular members of the Church. Thus it is that we really cannot appreciate fully either sermon until we compare them.

"He Taught Them as One Having Authority"

The King James Version states that at the conclusion of the Sermon on the Mount the people were astonished, for Jesus had taught them "as one having authority, and not as the scribes" (Matthew 7:29). The Joseph Smith Translation states that Jesus taught "as one having authority *from God,* and not as *having authority from* the scribes" (JST, Matthew 7:37, italics added). The Nephite sermon does not have this comment in any form, since there were no such scribes among the Nephites. As to the authority of Jesus, however, the Nephite record continues with several expressions from the Savior stating his authoritative position: "I am he that gave the law, and I am he who covenanted with my people Israel; therefore, the law in me is fulfilled, for I have come to fulfil the law; therefore it hath an end. . . . I am the law, and the light. Look unto me, and endure to the end, and ye shall live." (3 Nephi 15:5, 9.)

Conclusion

If a person made only a superficial or casual study of the scriptures, he might suppose that Joseph Smith, in providing a more complete rendering of the Sermon on the Mount for his Bible translation, simply superimposed the sermon from 3 Nephi. But a deeper investigation shows that the Joseph Smith Translation of chapters 5 through 7 of Matthew presents an independent, fresh, and informative account of its own. The same careful search likewise reveals that the Nephite sermon is a fresh and independent discourse, totally adapted to the particular situation of the Nephite people to whom it was given.

Notes

1. Brigham Young, *Discourses of Brigham Young*, sel. John A. Widtsoe (Salt Lake City: Deseret Book Co., 1941), p. 128.

2. Nowhere does the Book of Mormon label the twelve American disciples as Apostles, even though the twelve in Jerusalem were called Apostles. However, in the Wentworth Letter, dated 1 March 1842, Joseph Smith apparently refers to the twelve Nephite disciples as Apostles (see *History of the Church* 4:538).

Chapter 17

THE DOCTRINE OF THE ATONEMENT

At one time there was a program on the BYU campus called the "Last Lecture Series." The idea was that if you had one last opportunity to deliver a lecture, what would you choose to say? For years I have mulled that over in my mind and wondered what I would select to talk about in such a setting. Probably I would say something about family and friends and the blessing of working at BYU in the company of good people. However, the subject of the Atonement would also be very high on my priority list of topics to cover in a last lecture. I can't think of any subject that I have tried harder to master and to understand and to develop the ability to explain. To learn the charity, generosity, power to rescue, and the pardoning mercy of God, as set in order by the Atonement, is the greatest of all studies.

Barriers to an Understanding of the Atonement

As I have taught various gospel subjects, I have encountered three main topics concerning which there is much misunderstanding among students—namely, the plates and internal structure of the Book of Mormon, the scattering and gathering of Israel, and the doctrine of the Fall and the Atonement.

As a teacher I have witnessed some of the barriers that prevent students from coming to a proper understanding of the Atonement. One of the difficulties is that most people are neither theologians nor even doctrine-oriented. Many seem to object to linking scriptural passages together to form a concept. They generally want to see it all said in one brief passage of scripture rather than shaped through bringing several passages together and building from point to point.

It seems to be the common mode of mankind not to search for careful, precise, and specific information about doctrinal items. It appears that many are content with only casual, approximate information. Nephi wrote of his feelings about much of mankind: "They will not search knowledge, nor understand great knowledge, when it is given unto them in plainness, even as plain as word can be" (2 Nephi 32:7).

Although many of the young people now among us are the brightest and the most faithful youth we have ever seen, this same barrier to understanding also hinders many of them, for it is not the common practice of mankind to search doctrine.

The "Very Points" of Doctrine

Let us look at some passages of scripture that I think speak of learning the gospel with precision rather than approximation. All of these scriptures use some form of the phrase "points of doctrine."

Nephi said: "And at that day shall the remnant of our seed . . . come to the knowledge of their Redeemer and the *very points of his doctrine*, that they may know how to come unto him and be saved" (1 Nephi 15:14, italics added).

Speaking to his son Corianton, Alma said: "And now behold, my son, do not risk one more offense against your God upon *those points of doctrine*, which ye have hitherto risked to commit sin" (Alma 41:9, italics added).

And in Helaman 11:22–23 we read: "They had peace in the seventy and eighth year, save it were a few contentions concerning the points of doctrine which had been laid down by the prophets. And in the seventy and ninth year there began to be much strife. But it came to pass that Nephi and Lehi, and many of their brethren *who knew concerning the true points of doctrine*, having many revelations daily, therefore they did preach unto the people, insomuch that they did put an end to their strife in that same year." (Italics added.)

During the Savior's visit to the Nephites he said: "There shall be no disputations among you . . . concerning *the points of my doctrine*, as there have hitherto been" (3 Nephi 11:28, italics added). And later Jesus declared that the gospel would be taught to the Gentiles so that "they may repent and come unto me and be baptized in my name and know of *the true points of my doctrine*, that they may be numbered among my people, O house of Israel" (3 Nephi 21:6, italics added).

The same terminology appears also in the Doctrine and Covenants, wherein the Lord affirms that the Book of Mormon shall bring people to the "true points of my doctrine, yea, and the only doctrine which is in me" (D&C 10:62; see also v. 63).

What is a "point of doctrine"? One dictionary defines a *point* as a "penetrating detail, a precise concept; a prominent or important item; the 'telling part' of an argument or discussion; the salient feature; the precise thing; the 'turning point.' " Such is the meaning of a *point* of doctrine as contrasted to a teaching that is vague, undefined, ambiguous, uncertain, fuzzy, foggy, obscure, or unfocused. As I reflect on the scriptural passages above, I hear the Lord saying that he expects us to learn the very points of his doctrine and that the Book of Mormon is the principal means he has provided by which we are to learn them. The Book of Mormon cannot be the "most correct of any book on earth" and be wrong on the most important doctrines of the gospel.

It is my observation that the points of doctrine given to us in the Book of Mormon and other latter-day scripture will answer all the major doctrinal questions that have been raised during, and as the result of, the Apostasy—those questions which have been the focus of the great church councils from the Nicene Council to Vatican II.

Use of the Right Words

If we use the right words it will help us better understand doctrines such as the Atonement. In this way we can avoid ambiguity. President Ezra Taft Benson has spoken on at least two occasions about the importance of using the right words in gospel teaching:

> It is important that in our teaching we make use of the language of holy writ. Alma said, "I . . . do command you in the language of him who hath commanded me" (Alma 5:61).
>
> The words and the way they are used in the Book of Mormon by the Lord should become our source of understanding and should be used by us in teaching gospel principles.[1]
>
> King Benjamin caused that his three sons "should be taught in all the language of his fathers." (Mosiah 1:2.) They needed to understand and use the language of holy writ. If they didn't know the right words, they wouldn't know the plan.[2]

In a 1940 letter the First Presidency gave directions along this same line to the Church Educational System. This was a sequel to the "Charted Course" statement issued just two years earlier in 1938. Following is an excerpt from that letter of the First Presidency, dated 17 February 1940 and addressed to Franklin L. West, commissioner of Church Education:

> Teachers will do well to give up indoctrinating themselves in the sectarianism of the modern "Divinity School Theology." If they do not, they will probably bring themselves to a frame of mind where they will be no longer useful in our system. The most brilliant of them will find enough in the Gospel to tax all their brilliancy, even genius. The heights and depths of the Gospel have yet to be sounded.
>
> The teachers will not teach ethics or philosophy, ancient or modern, pagan or so-called Christian; they will as already stated teach the Gospel and that only, and the Gospel as revealed in these last days.
>
> In their teaching, the teachers will use the verbiage and terminology which have become classic in the Church. They will not use terms and concepts which, though in one sense, are susceptible of being applied to the Church and Church doctrines, yet which, in another sense, are completely misleading. . . .
>
> The *Gospel* should be spoken of as *the Gospel*, God's revealed truth.[3]

In summarizing the above instructions of the First Presidency, Commissioner West wrote to J. Wyley Sessions, chairman of the Division of Religion at Brigham Young University: "In a general way, they said that we should use our own terminology and avoid as far as we can the terminology used by the sectarian churches. It was suggested that the . . . 'Department of Sacred Scripture' might be called the 'Department of Latter-day Scripture'; that the 'Department of Practical Christianity' be called the 'Department of Church Organization and Activities.' "[4]

The words of President Benson, coupled with the words of an earlier First Presidency, remind us of Paul's instruction to the Corinthians given more than nineteen hundred years ago:

> Now we have received, not the spirit of the world, but the spirit which is of God; that we might know the things that are freely given to us of God.

> Which things also we speak, not in the words which man's wisdom teacheth, but which the Holy Ghost teacheth; comparing spiritual things with spiritual.
>
> But the natural man receiveth not the things of the Spirit of God: for they are foolishness unto him: neither can he know them, because they are spiritually discerned. (1 Corinthians 2:12–14.)

It is important that we use the language of the scriptures in our gospel teaching. If we will use direct words and the terminology of the scriptures, our teachings will be clear and our meanings unmistakable.

Consider the following example of the use of terminology. I find it is important to make a distinction between the words *spirit* and *spiritual*. It is better, for instance, to refer to the organization of our spirit bodies as the *spirit* creation rather than the *spiritual* creation. *Spirit* is a better word in this case because it has a more definite and limited meaning: it can only refer to the creation of spirits. Now, we say that the fall of Adam brought two kinds of death—physical death and *spiritual* death. The use here of the word *spiritual* rather than *spirit* helps us understand that spiritual death is a condition, not the actual death of the spirit being; it is a death as to the things of righteousness, a separation from the presence of God. Furthermore, the word *spiritual* can refer to many things. For example, we know that the condition of man and animals in the Garden of Eden was physical, tangible, solid, and real, but not mortal; therefore, it is spoken of as a *spiritual* condition (see D&C 88:26–28 for a similar use of the term *spiritual*). Hence, if we used the word *spiritual* to refer to the premortal creation of spirits, we would engender confusion in others' minds if we used it again to refer to conditions in the Garden of Eden. Thus it is necessary for clarity that we make some careful distinctions in our use of words like *spirit* and *spiritual*.

Does It Matter?

I think we need to understand the Fall and the Atonement in the way that the scriptures teach them so that we can teach, when required, the proper concepts to others with a clear and certain sound, detect false doctrine and incorrect views when expressed by others, and benefit from the influence such understanding will have on our own perspective and zeal.

Nephi said he had great joy in proving what he knew about Christ:

> Behold, my soul delighteth in proving unto my people the truth of the coming of Christ; for, for this end hath the law of Moses been given; and all things which have been given of God from the beginning of the world, unto man, are the typifying of him.
>
> And also my soul delighteth in the covenants of the Lord which he hath made to our fathers; yea, my soul delighteth in his grace, and in his justice, and power, and mercy in the great and eternal plan of deliverance from death.
>
> And my soul delighteth in proving unto my people that save Christ should come all men must perish. (2 Nephi 11:4–6.)

Thus, I think it *does* matter whether we are clear and precise in our gospel teaching and learning; and I think it *is* important that we learn well the salient points of the gospel. I, for one, do not want to harbor and accumulate wrong concepts in my own thinking that I will have to unlearn when I enter the spirit world. I want to make those adjustments now, in this life, and learn the "very points of his doctrine" from the scriptures and from the Brethren, and thus gain whatever correct information and view*points* I can about life here and hereafter.

In dealing with doctrinal topics we can benefit if we examine and compare several reliable sources. The key is to analyze. Frequently there are parts within a single source that are sufficiently ambiguous that they could be interpreted in more than one way. The value of analyzing corroborating witnesses is that often a second or third source sheds enough light on a concept that it will help delimit and define an otherwise ambiguous passage. We use the second or third witnesses, then, to *control* our interpretation.

In studying gospel doctrines, I have found it helpful to take a particular scriptural passage and isolate every separate thought and idea in that passage. One way of doing this is to number every new element or thought as it occurs in the passage. Then one can compare these concepts with those found in what seems to be a parallel passage. It is startling how quickly this process of analysis can bring to light both the differences and the parallels between the passages.

Various Dimensions of the Atonement

The atonement of Jesus Christ is multidimensional: it involves not only the payment of a debt but also elements of love and of service. A study of the Atonement that omitted any of these dimensions would necessarily be fragmentary; the doctrines of the gospel do not have much meaning in abstract theory standing separate and apart from people. Therefore, as the Atonement shows us, we must have love for one another and teach the importance of service and recognize the condescension of God. If it were not for his love and condescension, Jesus would never have made an atonement. I like this statement from Nephi: "He doeth not anything save it be for the benefit of the world; for he loveth the world, even that he layeth down his own life that he may draw all men unto him. Wherefore, he commandeth none that they shall not partake of his salvation. . . . For he doeth that which is good among the children of men." (2 Nephi 26:24, 33.)

On the other hand, if we fail to establish the doctrinal foundation, our teaching about the Atonement can degenerate into ethical and philosophical humanism. The divine element is preserved and kept in focus only through setting forth the doctrinal foundation of the great plan of redemption, which existed in the mind of God before the creation of the world and which was carried out through the Creation, the fall of Adam, and the atonement of Jesus Christ. The plan of salvation is not limited to just the first principles and the temple ceremony. The plan of salvation includes and incorporates the whole transaction—including the grand premortal council, the Creation, the Fall, the Atonement, all of the gospel principles and ordinances, the resurrection, the Judgment, exaltation, and so on.

The Inherited Effects of the Fall of Adam

Let's look at some of the precise things that are said about the effect the fall of Adam has had on mankind. It is necessary to have some idea of the Fall in order to appreciate the Atonement. There are several specific places in the scriptures that deal with the fall of Adam (or the fall of man), and these passages are our best sources. Most of them are in the Book of Mormon, but there are some key passages also in the Doctrine and Covenants and the Pearl of Great Price.

As I see it, the chief sources for information on the Fall and its relationship to the Atonement are 2 Nephi 2; 2 Nephi 9; Mosiah 3; Mosiah 12–16; Alma 34; Alma 42; Helaman 14; Mormon 9; Doctrine and Covenants 29; Moses 5–6; and Romans 5. There are, of course, many other individual passages in the scriptures that address this topic, but these chapters have impressed me as being the most direct, containing, as they do, the "very points" of the doctrine. The prophets whose teachings are in these chapters are Lehi, Jacob, Benjamin, Abinadi, Amulek, Alma, Samuel the Lamanite, Moroni, Joseph Smith, Enoch, and Paul. They all teach the same basic doctrine (there are no contradictions among them), but they do not all emphasize the same particular things. Analyze their words, isolate and number the individual ideas, and you will find that each prophet clarifies some particular point more distinctly than the others do. In this chapter we will examine a sampling of the teachings of these prophets.

Lehi and Jacob on the Fall and the Atonement

In 2 Nephi 2 we read the teachings of Lehi about the Fall and the Atonement, from which I have isolated the following six items:

1. Adam and Eve were driven out of the Garden of Eden because they partook of the forbidden fruit (v. 19).
2. All mankind were "lost, because of the transgression of their parents" (v. 21).
3. Without the Fall, all things would have remained as they were created (v. 22).
4. Without the Fall, Adam and Eve would have had no children (v. 23).
5. The Messiah would come to redeem mankind from the Fall (v. 26).
6. Because of the atonement of the Messiah mankind is free to act (v. 26).

Among the things Lehi does not say about the Fall and the Atonement in this chapter of the Book of Mormon are the following:

1. He does not define death, and he does not use the term *spiritual death*.
2. He does not specifically mention physical death as distinct from spiritual death.
3. He does not define what he means when he speaks of mankind's being "lost."

4. He does not define or explain what would make the Messiah able to redeem mankind, or how the Redeemer would accomplish it.
5. He does not use words that refer directly to man's spirit.

We cannot suppose Lehi didn't know of these things; we simply have to recognize that he used broad terms and that these unspoken and unexplained details are encompassed in his use of such words as *fall, lost,* and *redemption*. Thus, chapter 2 of 2 Nephi constitutes one of the greatest philosophical statements about good, evil, law, agency, happiness, misery, God, man, and the devil ever recorded, and it contains the plainest declaration that Adam and Eve would have had no children without the Fall. But in speaking of those things, Lehi leaves many of the details undefined.

Lehi's son Jacob, however, supplies some very pointed definitions in 2 Nephi 9. He uses specific words like *death of the body, resurrection, spirit, hell, grace, paradise, spiritual death,* and *infinite atonement.* Among other things, Jacob specifies the following concerning the Fall and the Atonement:

1. An infinite atonement is needed to overcome the Fall (v. 7).
2. Without an infinite atonement, there would be no resurrection of the bodies of men (v. 7).
3. Without an infinite atonement, the spirits of all men would become devils, forever miserable; that is, they would not just be subject to the devil, but they would actually become devils (vv. 8–9).
4. Because of the Atonement, all mankind will be resurrected, meaning that each person's spirit will be restored to its own physical body again (vv. 10–13).
5. After the resurrection, all mankind will be judged of God (v. 15).
6. The Redeemer, who will die for mankind, is also the Creator (v. 5). (Jacob mentions this but does not dwell on it at length.)
7. All of these things are according to an eternal plan of the great Creator (vv. 6, 13).

Jacob may not have known any more about the plan of salvation than Lehi did, but in his recorded sermon Jacob defined some of the points more distinctly. Yet Lehi, as we have his words recorded in 2 Nephi 2, covered some fundamental things that Jacob did not cover in his talk as given in 2 Nephi 9. Thus it is that we need both chapters.

King Benjamin on the Fall and the Atonement

In Mosiah 3, King Benjamin gives a lengthy statement about the Fall and the Atonement, citing words which he said he learned from an angel. Benjamin extensively defines and identifies the Redeemer and his mission as follows:

1. The Lord God Omnipotent will come to dwell among men in a tabernacle of clay and be the Savior (vv. 5–11).
2. The Redeemer will be called Jesus Christ (vv. 8, 12, 18).
3. The Redeemer will bleed from every pore (v. 7).
4. He is the Creator (v. 8).
5. His mother will be named Mary (v. 8).
6. He will be crucified (v. 9).
7. He will rise from the dead the third day (v. 10).
8. His blood atones for the fall of Adam (v. 11).
9. Nothing would save man if it were not for the atonement of the Lord's blood (v. 15).
10. His blood redeems little children (v. 16).
11. There is no other way or means of salvation (v. 17).

Three times Benjamin mentions the fallen condition experienced by all persons by reason of their being descendants of Adam: he refers to "those who have fallen by the transgression of Adam" (Mosiah 3:11); speaking of children, he says that "in Adam, or by nature, they fall" (Mosiah 3:16); and he declares that "the natural man is an enemy to God, and has been from the fall of Adam" (Mosiah 3:19). In his doctrinal exposition, father Lehi implies this kind of inheritance from Adam, but Jacob and Benjamin are the ones who spell it out.

There are three other strong declarations in the Book of Mormon stating that mankind inherits the effects of the fall of Adam. Note the expression of the brother of Jared as he pleaded with the Lord for help: "Now behold, O Lord, and do not be angry with thy servant because of his weakness before thee; . . . because of the fall our natures have become evil continually" (Ether 3:2). The second statement comes from Alma, who said: "Now we see that Adam did fall by the partaking of the forbidden fruit, according to the word of God; and thus we see, that by his fall, all mankind became a lost and fallen people" (Alma 12:22). And from Samuel the

Lamanite we have the following: "For all mankind, by the fall of Adam . . . , are considered as dead, both as to things temporal and to things spiritual" (Helaman 14:16).

The Atonement and Little Children

The matter of mankind's having inherited the fall of Adam is a fundamental doctrine of the gospel, but to much of traditional Christianity it is a major stumbling block. Since about the fourth century, Catholic doctrine has held that because children inherit the fall from Adam they are thus born in sin. This belief is based primarily on a misinterpretation of two verses from Romans, which read: "Wherefore, as by one man sin entered into the world, and death by sin; and so death passed upon all men, *for that all have sinned*. . . . For as by one man's disobedience many *were made sinners*, so by the obedience of one shall many be made righteous." (Romans 5:12, 19, italics added.)

These verses were wrongly interpreted by Augustine and others to mean that all mankind *sinned* in Adam and that, therefore, children are born in original sin. This resulted in the development of the practice of infant baptism, since infants were considered legally to be sinners by inheritance.

Some today, not feeling comfortable with this traditional Christian doctrine of the depravity of children, have rejected the concept of the Fall altogether, and so speak glowingly of the inherent goodness of man. Either extreme position does not accurately represent the teachings of the scriptures, especially the teachings of the Book of Mormon. The restored gospel takes a position between the two extremes, not denying either but showing how the matter is handled by the Atonement.

Regarding this topic the Lord told Mormon: "Little children are whole, for they are not capable of committing sin; wherefore the curse of Adam is taken from them in me, that it hath no power over them" (Moroni 8:8). Note that here the fall of Adam or its influence—the Lord even calls it a "curse"—is not denied, but its damning effect on little children is shown to be blocked by the intercessory power of the Atonement. The curse is real, but the Atonement prevents it from occurring.

This is the same concept taught by King Benjamin, who explains that children, as well as adults, have need of the Atonement because of the fall of Adam: "And even if it were possible that little children could sin they could not be saved; but I say unto you they are blessed; for behold, as in Adam, or by nature, they fall, even so the blood of Christ atoneth for their sins" (Mosiah 3:16). Moreover, we read in modern revelation that "every spirit of man was innocent in the beginning; and God having redeemed man from the fall, men became again, in their infant state, innocent before God" (D&C 93:38). And a succinct expression of this influence and power of the Atonement is found in the second article of faith: "Men will be punished for their own sins, and not for Adam's transgression."

These scriptures say that if it were not for the atonement of Christ, all members of the human family, upon coming into this world as infants, would be lost because of the fall of Adam. Hence we can see why the idea that calls for infant baptism is so erroneous: it sets aside the atonement of Christ as though it had no such power to redeem little children.

Since the Bible is not clear on this very important provision of the Atonement, we see the great need that exists for the enlightening teachings of the Book of Mormon. In a world that generally does not understand the work of Jesus Christ, the Nephite scripture is an indispensable tool for making known the "very points" of Christ's doctrine.

The power of the Atonement to redeem little children is also dealt with in Joseph Smith's translation of Matthew 18. The topic under discussion here is who is the greatest in the kingdom of heaven. Jesus tells the Twelve that they must become as little children, he places a child in their midst as an object lesson, and then he declares that his mission is to save mankind. Now, in the King James Version, Matthew 18:11 reads as follows: "For the Son of man is come to save that which was lost." However, the Joseph Smith Translation adds to that a most important teaching: ". . . and to call sinners to repentance; but these little ones have no need of repentance, and I will save them." This significant clarification is in harmony with the teachings of the Doctrine and Covenants and the Book of Mormon on the power that the Atonement has to intercede for children as they are affected by the transgression of Adam. Such a doctrine is much needed in those circles where traditional Christian views are still held.

The correct doctrine is that mankind has inherited the *effects* of the Fall, but not the sin associated with it. There is a great difference between inheriting only the results or effects of the sin and inheriting the sin itself. Since they only inherit its effects, little children have no accountability or responsibility for original sin. Thus, because of the atonement of Christ, babies are born innocent so far as the law of God is concerned, but babies inherit the effects of the Fall inasmuch as they are out of the presence of God and are subject to physical death. All human beings, though innocent at birth, are destined to die; they cannot prevent it. Nor can they reclaim even one soul from death after it has occurred. Little children are not subject to death because of any sin of their own—it is a biological inheritance from Adam.

Even Adam himself was not held responsible for his original transgression in the Garden of Eden; yet the results and effects of that sin passed upon him when he entered mortality to exactly the same extent that they pass upon each of us as an inheritance from Adam. In mortality Adam was in just the same condition as we are. The Atonement automatically covered the transgression which brought the Fall, and Adam was held responsible to repent only for the transgressions he may have committed when in mortality. This is the plain teaching of the prophet Enoch, as recorded in the book of Moses:

> And [God] called upon our father Adam by his own voice, saying: I am God; I made the world, and men before they were in the flesh.
>
> And he also said unto him: If thou wilt turn unto me, and hearken unto my voice, and believe, and repent of all thy transgressions, and be baptized, even in water, in the name of mine Only Begotten Son, who is full of grace and truth, which is Jesus Christ, the only name which shall be given under heaven, whereby salvation shall come unto the children of men, ye shall receive the gift of the Holy Ghost, asking all things in his name, and whatsoever ye shall ask, it shall be given you.
>
> And our father Adam spake unto the Lord, and said: Why is it that men must repent and be baptized in water? And the Lord said unto Adam: Behold I have forgiven thee thy transgression in the Garden of Eden.
>
> Hence came the saying abroad among the people, that the Son of God hath atoned for original guilt, wherein the sins of the parents cannot be answered upon the heads of the children, for they are whole from the foundation of the world. (Moses 6:51–54.)

Here we note that Adam was told he must repent of and be baptized for all his transgressions committed in mortality, but he was already forgiven of the transgression committed in the Garden of Eden.

The Divinity of Jesus Christ

When the prophet Abinadi comes on the scene in the Book of Mormon (see Mosiah 11–17), he teaches the same doctrine as the earlier prophets but with a little different emphasis and choice of words. His predecessors mention once or twice that the Redeemer is also the Creator, the Lord Omnipotent, but Abinadi hammers at it so emphatically that the reader cannot miss it.

Abinadi cites the Ten Commandments, which he says *God* gave to Moses on Mount Sinai (Mosiah 12:33–13:24) and then explains the following:

1. God himself shall make an atonement for mankind (Mosiah 13:28). (Thus Abinadi identifies the Savior as the God who gave Moses the commandments.)
2. Without the Atonement, which God himself shall make, man must perish (Mosiah 13:28).
3. No one can be saved without the redemption of God (Mosiah 13:32).
4. Moses prophesied that God would redeem his people (Mosiah 13:33).
5. All the prophets have spoken more or less about these things; they have said that God himself should come down and take upon him the form of man (Mosiah 13:33–34).
6. God himself shall come down among men and redeem his people (Mosiah 15:1).
7. And thus God will break the bands of death (Mosiah 15:8).
8. The Redeemer (whom Abinadi has repeatedly identified as "God himself") shall be called Christ (Mosiah 15:21).

Abinadi was not the first to declare that Christ is God, but he certainly emphasized the fact more often and with more clarity than the others did. This got him into trouble with a corrupt generation of Nephites, as King Limhi explained: "And because he said unto them that Christ was the God, the Father of all things, and said that he should take upon him the image of man, and it should be the image after which man was created in the beginning; or in other words, he said that man was created after the image of God, and that God should come down among the children of men, and take upon him flesh and blood, and go forth upon the face of the earth

—and now because he said this, they did put him to death'' (Mosiah 7:27–28).

Later in the Book of Mormon record, the prophet Amulek speaks eloquently about the atonement of Jesus Christ. We will isolate only two items here.

First, Amulek says that without an atonement ''all mankind must unavoidably perish'' (Alma 34:9). He does not define what *perish* means, but because we have read the words of Jacob in 2 Nephi 9:6–9, we know that in this context *perish* means that the physical body would decay with never a chance for resurrection and that the spirit of each person would become a devil, forever miserable.

Second, Amulek defines the atonement of Christ in a most remarkable manner: ''It is expedient that there should be a great and last sacrifice; yea, not a sacrifice of man, neither of beast, neither of any manner of fowl; for it shall not be a human sacrifice; but it must be an infinite and eternal sacrifice'' (Alma 34:10). My guess is that most people, on first consideration, would think of Jesus' sacrifice as a human sacrifice, the sacrifice of a man as opposed to one of animals. But Amulek's words hold us to a different explanation: A human sacrifice would not have been adequate, since it would not have been infinite; redemption required the sacrifice of a God.

We have come a long way in the ''points of doctrine'' since we started with 2 Nephi 2. The writings of the prophets after Lehi and Nephi do not contradict anything written earlier, but they clarify, focus, and control our understanding and interpretation of the earlier teachings.

Thus, in the Book of Mormon, Christ is God. He is not simply a mortal, a great teacher, a friend of mankind. He is God. I have been surprised to find that the Book of Mormon never identifies Jesus as the firstborn spirit, man's Elder Brother. In the Book of Mormon, he isn't so much man's brother as he is man's God.

Jesus the Only Begotten of the Father in the Flesh

Jesus' condition in mortality was unique (see accompanying chart). Being the Son of a mortal mother and of an immortal Father, he inherited the effects of the Fall without being dominated by them as we are. If Jesus had been subject to death as we are, then in dying at age thirty-three he would have been only giving up his *time*, for eventually he would have died anyway. But the scriptures say he gave his *life*.

Thus I see it as one of the "very points" of doctrine that we accept Jesus Christ as the Only Begotten Son of God in the flesh, who would not have had to die physically or spiritually except as he willed to do so as part of the atoning sacrifice (see John 5:26; 10:17–18; Helaman 5:11). He died a physical death on the cross, and he died a "spiritual death" in the Garden of Gethsemane (as well as on the cross) when he took upon himself the sins of all mankind. Note these words of President Brigham Young:

> The Father withdrew His spirit from His Son, at the time he was to be crucified. Jesus had been with his Father, talked with Him, dwelt in His bosom, and knew all about heaven, about making the earth, about the transgression of man, and what would redeem the people, and that he was the character who was to redeem the sons of earth, and the earth itself from all sin that had come upon it. The light, knowledge, power, and glory with which he was clothed were far above, or exceeded that of all others who had been upon the earth after the fall, consequently at the very moment, at the hour when the crisis came for him to offer up his life, the Father withdrew Himself, withdrew His Spirit, and cast a veil over him. This is what made him sweat blood. If he had had the power of God upon him, he would not have sweat blood; but all was withdrawn from him, and a veil was cast over him, and he then plead with the Father not to forsake him. "No," says the Father, "you must have your trials, as well as others."[5]

Clearly, a great deal rested on Jesus' birth, life, suffering in Gethsemane, death on the cross, and resurrection. Brigham Young said: "Had he [Jesus] refused to obey his Father, he would have become a son of perdition."[6] Why is this so? Because an eternal law had been broken, creating a debt no mortal could pay. Had Jesus sinned he would have lost his capacity to mend a broken eternal law. He and all mankind would have been left without a remedy.

"Even So in Christ Shall All Be Made Alive"

It seems that many people do not understand the meaning of Paul's words, "As in Adam all die, even so in Christ shall all be made alive" (1 Corinthians 15:22). Most think it only pertains to

Jesus Christ and Mortal Man: Parentage

Mortal Man

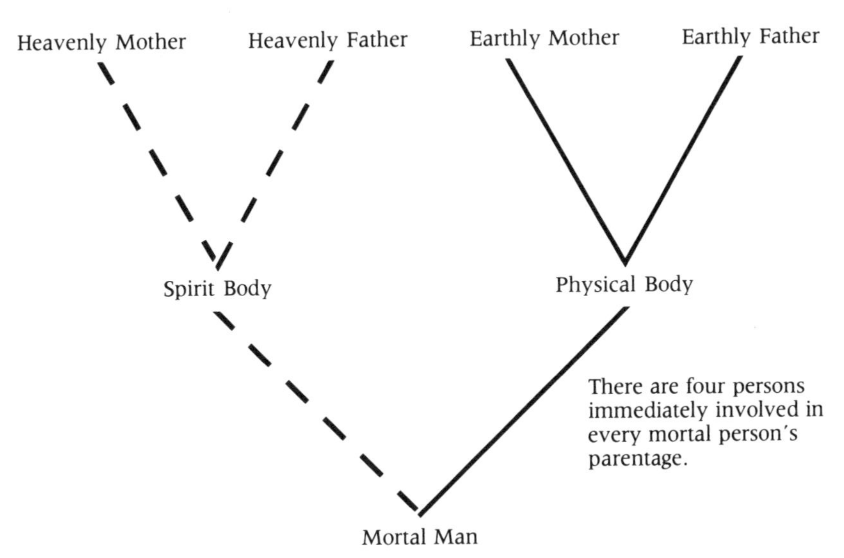

Jesus

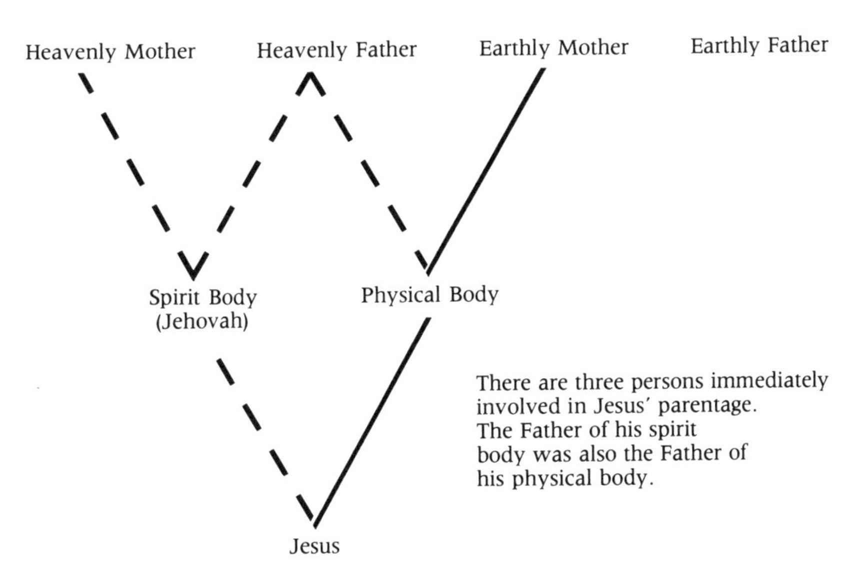

Because we are the spirit children of heavenly parents, we each have the spark of divinity within us. Consider the divinity of Jesus Christ as it relates to not only his spirit but also his physical body. Because of his status as the Only Begotten in the flesh (D&C 93:11), Jesus had power over death, a power that none of us has. He had life in himself (John 5:26; 10:17–18; Helaman 5:11).

the death of the body and the resurrection of the body. In truth, Paul's statement covers both physical death and spiritual death. As in Adam all die a physical and a spiritual death, so in Christ shall all be made alive, that is, be redeemed from both the physical death and the spiritual death. The Atonement is as broad in its influence as the Fall.

Because of Christ, all mankind, with no exceptions, will be redeemed from those two deaths. That is, every human being will be resurrected from the dead and every human being will be restored to the presence of God. All that was lost in the Fall will be restored by the Atonement. I have found that many do not understand that. There is a prevailing idea that although the resurrection is free, only those who repent and obey the gospel will ever return to the presence of God. Those who adhere to this idea, however, seem to have missed a very essential point and fundamental concept of the Atonement, and that is that Jesus Christ has redeemed all mankind from *all* the consequences of the fall of Adam.

The scriptures teach that every person, saint or sinner, will return to the presence of God after the resurrection. It may be only a temporary reunion in his presence, but justice requires that all that was lost in Adam be restored in Jesus Christ. Every person will return to God's presence, behold his face, and be judged for his own works. Then, those who have obeyed the gospel will be able to stay in his presence, while all others will have to be shut out of his presence a second time and will thus die what is called a second spiritual death.

See how clearly this is taught by Samuel the Lamanite:

> For behold, he surely must die that salvation may come; yea, it behooveth him and becometh expedient that he dieth, to bring to pass the resurrection of the dead, that thereby men may be brought into the presence of the Lord.
>
> Yea, behold, this death bringeth to pass the resurrection, *and redeemeth all mankind from the first death—that spiritual death*; for all mankind, by the fall of Adam being cut off from the presence of the Lord, are considered as dead, both as to things temporal and to things spiritual.
>
> But behold, the resurrection of Christ redeemeth mankind, yea, *even all mankind, and bringeth them back into the presence of the Lord.*
>
> Yea, and it bringeth to pass the condition of repentance, that whosoever repenteth the same is not hewn down and cast into the fire; but whosoever repenteth not is hewn down

> and cast into the fire; and there cometh upon them *again* a spiritual death, yea, a *second death*, for they are cut off *again* as to things pertaining to righteousness. (Helaman 14:15–18, italics added.)

Similarly, Moroni wrote:

> Behold, [God] created Adam, and by Adam came the fall of man. And because of the fall of man came Jesus Christ, even the Father and the Son; and because of Jesus Christ came the redemption of man.
>
> And because of the redemption of man, which came by Jesus Christ, they are brought back into the *presence of the Lord*; yea, this is wherein *all men* are redeemed, because the death of Christ bringeth to pass the resurrection, which bringeth to pass a redemption from an endless sleep, from which sleep all men shall be awakened by the power of God when the trump shall sound; and they shall come forth, both small and great, and all shall stand before his bar, being redeemed and loosed from this eternal band of death, which death is a temporal death.
>
> And then cometh the judgment of the Holy One upon them; and then cometh the time that he that is filthy shall be filthy still; and he that is righteous shall be righteous still; he that is happy shall be happy still; and he that is unhappy shall be unhappy still. (Mormon 9:12–14, italics added.)

The two passages above also give an insight into Jacob's words: "Wo unto all those who die in their sins; for they shall return to God, and behold his face, and remain in their sins" (2 Nephi 9:38).

President Joseph Fielding Smith wrote on this topic, and in so doing he quoted something Elder Orson Pratt had said on the subject. Hence, the following excerpt from President Smith's writings is a testimony from both of them:

> Christ's sacrifice and death did two things for us: it brought unto us *unconditional salvation* and *conditional salvation*. Sometimes we refer to these as *general salvation* and *individual salvation*. I am going to read what Orson Pratt said in relation to this. It is one of the clearest statements I know about. It is very concise and well thought out. . . .
>
> ". . . Universal redemption from the effects of *original sin*, has nothing to do with redemption from our *personal sins*; for

the original sin of Adam and the personal sins of his children, are two different things. . . .

"The children of Adam had no agency in the transgression of their first parents, and therefore, they are not required to exercise any agency in their redemption from its penalty. They are redeemed from it without faith, repentance, baptism, or any other act, either of the mind or body.

"*Conditional redemption* is also universal in its nature; it is offered to all but not received by all; it is a universal gift, though not universally accepted; its benefits can be obtained only through faith, repentance, baptism, the laying on of hands, and obedience to all other requirements of the gospel.

"*Unconditional redemption* is a gift forced upon mankind which they cannot reject, though they were disposed. Not so with conditional redemption; it can be received or rejected according to the will of the creature.

"Redemption from the original sin is without faith or works; redemption from our own sins is given through faith and works. *Both are the gifts of free grace*; but while one is a gift *forced* upon us unconditionally, the other is a gift merely *offered* to us conditionally. The redemption of the one is *compulsory*; the reception of the other is *voluntary*. Man cannot, by any possible act, prevent his redemption from the fall; but he can utterly refuse and prevent his redemption from the penalty of his own sins."[7]

Frequently, when I am teaching a class and we have read and discussed 2 Nephi 2 and 9, I quote for the students Paul's statement, "As in Adam all die, even so in Christ shall all be made alive," and then ask them, "What death did Adam bring?" Students seem to have no difficulty in understanding the idea that Adam brought two deaths—the physical, meaning the death of the body, and the spiritual, meaning our separation from the presence of God. Then I ask, "What did the atonement of Jesus Christ bring?" They readily respond that it brought about mankind's resurrection from the grave; but they seem to have difficulty in grasping the idea that Jesus also redeemed all mankind from the spiritual death and that every one of us is going to be in the presence of God again, if only for the Judgment. Although most students can explain that the Atonement makes it possible for us to work out our salvation by faith, repentance, and so forth, they often slide right past this concept that we will be redeemed from *all* the effects of the Fall, and seem to feel that no one is going to return to God's presence except the righteous. While it is true that not all people will remain permanently in the presence of the Lord, it is equally true that all will return to his presence for judgment; thus, in our discussions I do not think we are justified in leaving out this critical part of the redemption process. This is one of the "very points" of doctrine taught in the Book of Mormon, a point that a person ought to know.

An Alternate Plan?

Was there an acceptable alternate plan, or alternate savior, if Jesus had not fulfilled his mission? This question may seem unimportant or even unnecessary, but it has some strong implications. Judging from the general life-style of mankind, or even of churchkind, many people must feel either that salvation is not worth struggling for or that there is more than one way to gain salvation. The real question is this: Is acceptance of the gospel of Jesus Christ mandatory or is it optional? Will the billions of people who have lived on the earth without a knowledge of Christ have to come to a knowledge of the very points of his doctrine before they can be saved? Is the gospel of Christ the only way or just the *best* way, the quickest way? We know that the creation of the world and the fall of Adam were parts of the divine plan, but does that mean that there were alternate ways by which man could have become mortal, the system used on this earth simply being only one of them? Or is the gospel—that process of creation, fall, and atonement that leads to the redemption and exaltation of mankind—the only absolute and workable way?

What would have happened if Jesus had not come? or if he had come to earth but not been obedient to the end and not accomplished the Atonement? Was there then an alternate plan, another savior, a backup man?

Several years ago I discussed this topic with a group of teachers, and I noted that they were strongly of the opinion that if Jesus had failed, there would have been another way to accomplish salvation. They acknowledged that any other way probably would have been harder without Jesus, but, they said, man could have eventually saved himself without Jesus if Jesus had failed. Thus—although I don't think any of us had at that time searched out the logical implications of our thoughts—these teachers were saying, in effect, that Jesus Christ was a convenience but not an ultimate necessity. I countered by quoting Acts 4:12, wherein are recorded the words of Peter: "Neither is there salvation in any other: for there is none other name under heaven given among men, whereby we must be saved." Their retort was that Peter said this *after* the atonement and resurrection of Christ were accomplished facts, and that therefore there is *now* no other way; but if Jesus had failed to make the Atonement, they reasoned, there would have to have been and would be an alternate way.

At that time I was not as well acquainted with the Book of Mormon and the book of Moses as I am now, and I had not thought this subject out completely; hence, while I protested their conclusion, I could not in the moment of the encounter think of a scriptural rebuttal. I was certain they were wrong, but I lacked the immediate ammunition to refute them. However, if I had known then what I know now, I would have called these teachers' attention to the scriptural items discussed below.

Looking at things chronologically, we find that Moses 6:52 is the earliest known reference stating that there is no other name other than Jesus Christ by which salvation is obtained. In this passage Enoch recounts a conversation between the Lord and father Adam. The Lord tells Adam that he must "be baptized, even in water, in the name of mine Only Begotten Son, . . . which is Jesus Christ, the only name which *shall* be given under heaven, whereby salvation shall come unto the children of men" (italics added).

Next we have 2 Nephi 25:20: "There *is* none other name given under heaven save it be this Jesus Christ, . . . whereby man can be saved" (italics added).

Then 2 Nephi 31:21: "There *is* none other way nor name given under heaven whereby man can be saved in the kingdom of God" (italics added).

But the very clearest expression of this concept is given by King Benjamin, quoting the words of an angel from heaven: "There *shall be* no other name given nor any other way nor means whereby salvation can come unto the children of men, only in and through the name of Christ" (Mosiah 3:17, italics added). Later this same King Benjamin gives some additional particulars: "This *is* the means whereby salvation cometh. And there *is* none other salvation save this which hath been spoken of; neither are there any conditions whereby man can be saved except the conditions which I have told you." (Mosiah 4:8, italics added.)

The value of these passages is that they were spoken *before* the Atonement had taken place. This gives them an additional force and focus that they might not have if they had been spoken afterwards. (See also Mosiah 5:8; Alma 38:9; Helaman 5:9.) In my estimation, these are some of the "very points" of doctrine that are clarified for us in the Book of Mormon and other latter-day scriptures, if we just believe the scriptures mean what they say. All of this is in harmony with and gives substance to Jesus' words to Thomas: "I am the way, the truth, and the life: no man cometh unto the Father, but by me" (John 14:6; see also 3 Nephi 27:1–8; D&C 18:23; 109:4).

Hymns Reinforce Doctrine of Atonement

Many of our Church hymns reinforce the "very points" of doctrine we have discussed in this chapter. These hymns can enrich and reinforce our understanding of these subjects. Following are some excerpts from the hymnbook that are pertinent to the doctrine of the Atonement:

Behold the great Redeemer die,
A broken law to satisfy.[8]

For us the blood of Christ was shed;
For us on Calvary's cross he bled,
And thus dispelled the awful gloom,
That else were this creation's doom.[9]

How infinite that wisdom,
The plan of holiness,
That made salvation perfect
And veiled the Lord in flesh,
To walk upon his footstool
And be like man, almost,
In his exalted station,
And die, or all was lost.[10]

He died in holy innocence,
A broken law to recompense. . . .
This sacrament doth represent
His blood and body for me spent.[11]

He shed a thousand drops for you,
A thousand drops of precious blood.[12]

His precious blood he freely spilt;
His life he freely gave,
A sinless sacrifice for guilt,
A dying world to save. . . .
How great, how glorious, how complete,
Redemption's grand design,
Where justice, love, and mercy meet
In harmony divine![13]

I marvel that he would descend from his throne divine
To rescue a soul so rebellious and proud as mine. . . .
I think of his hands pierced and bleeding to pay the debt!
Such mercy, such love, and devotion can I forget?[14]

I believe in Christ; he ransoms me.
From Satan's grasp he sets me free.[15]

Conclusion

In my opinion, the kind of faith necessary for salvation—the kind of faith spoken of in the *Lectures on Faith*—cannot be achieved if one views Jesus Christ's atonement, his excruciating pain, his bleeding at every pore, as simply an act of major convenience. As I read the Book of Mormon I perceive the message that the Fall's effects on all of us, coupled with our own sins, are so severe and dominating that, unless we are redeemed by One more powerful than all mankind combined, we will not be redeemed at all. The power of redemption is not in fallen man. I believe that saving faith requires a person to be completely convinced that he is entirely dependent upon Jesus Christ, and him only, for every shred of salvation. Without the Savior all is lost. The slightest reservation about the absolute necessity of Christ's atonement is injurious to one's spiritual health and to one's perfect faith and knowledge. I see no compromise on this point. Our relation to Christ is crucial, not casual. It is a necessity, not an option. May we diligently study and learn the "very points" of doctrine regarding the Atonement that we might develop and maintain that faith in Christ that leads to salvation.

Notes

1. Ezra Taft Benson, "The Book of Mormon and the Doctrine and Covenants," *Ensign* 17 (May 1987): 84.

2. Ezra Taft Benson, "Worthy Fathers, Worthy Sons," *Ensign* 15 (November 1985): 36.

3. As cited in Ernest L. Wilkinson, Leonard J. Arrington, and Bruce C. Hafen, *Brigham Young University: The First One Hundred Years,*

4 vols. (Provo, Utah: Brigham Young University Press, 1975–76), 2:381–82, italics in original.

4. As cited in Wilkinson, Arrington, and Hafen, *First One Hundred Years* 2:383.

5. Brigham Young, in *Journal of Discourses* 3:206.

6. Brigham Young, in *Journal of Discourses* 10:324.

7. Joseph Fielding Smith, *Doctrines of Salvation*, comp. Bruce R. McConkie, 3 vols. (Salt Lake City: Bookcraft, 1954–56), 2:9–10, italics in original; the source for the quote from Orson Pratt is the *Millennial Star* 12 (March 1, 1850): 69.

8. "Behold the Great Redeemer Die," *Hymns*, no. 191.

9. "While of These Emblems We Partake," *Hymns*, no. 173.

10. "O God, the Eternal Father," *Hymns*, no. 175.

11. "God Loved Us, So He Sent His Son," *Hymns*, no. 187.

12. "He Died! The Great Redeemer Died," *Hymns*, no. 192.

13. "How Great the Wisdom and the Love," *Hymns*, no. 195.

14. "I Stand All Amazed," *Hymns*, no. 193.

15. "I Believe in Christ," *Hymns*, no. 134.

Chapter 18

THE PRICE OF REDEMPTION

The word *redemption* means to make a purchase, to be ransomed, to be liberated, to be rescued, to be delivered. In religious terms we speak of redemption as our deliverance from death and from the consequences of our sins. But, as the word *redemption* implies, such deliverance comes at a price and with an obligation.

And what was that price? we might ask. What made necessary the redemption of mankind from death and sin? Why was Jesus Christ particularly qualified to deliver us, and what did it cost him to become our Redeemer? What will it cost us to be redeemed? What would have been the fate of mankind had there been no Redeemer? The answers to these questions are basic to the gospel, and without some understanding of them we might not realize what the gospel is; conversely, if we come to understand what the price of redemption was, our gratitude for what Jesus has done for us will increase manyfold.

To answer the above questions, then, we will consider some relevant passages from the New Testament. However, since our ultimate purpose is to get at the truth and to understand things as they really are, we will feel free to use all of the standard works, not only to confirm what is in the New Testament but also to clarify and supplement it. The Book of Mormon, the Doctrine and Covenants, the Pearl of Great Price, and the Joseph Smith Translation of the Bible are clearer, more detailed, and therefore superior to the King James Version of the New Testament in declaring the doctrinal aspects of the Savior's mission. It is often the case that the New Testament tells *what* Jesus did, whereas latter-day revelation explains *why* he did it and gives a more significant purpose to his words and actions.

We should use all the correct information we can find in discussing the mission of Jesus Christ. Thus it is impossible for a person to gain a thorough understanding of the mission of Jesus Christ and his atonement if he does not consult and study latter-day revelation. You cannot get such an understanding from the New Testament alone in any language. Why is this? As has been shown in other chapters in this book, the problem with the Bible is not one of language and translation—it is the absence of an adequate and complete manuscript. Hence we need latter-day revelation to teach us what we need to know.

The Nature of the Four Gospels

Another brief observation concerning the New Testament record is in order here. Our basic sources for the mortal life and ministry of Jesus are the four books commonly known as the Gospels—Matthew, Mark, Luke, and John. The present title for each of these reads "The Gospel According to . . ." followed by the name of the particular writer—St. Matthew, St. Mark, and so forth.[1] Furthermore, it has become customary to think of these books as biographies or life histories of Jesus. They are in a sense biographical, but they are much more than that.

The Joseph Smith Translation emphasizes the *doctrinal* nature of these books, giving them the titles, "The *Testimony* of St. Matthew," "The *Testimony* of St. Mark," and so on. Such titles give these records a different character than if they were mere biographies, because a testimony has more to do with the nature, the purpose, and the significance of the Savior than with the details of his daily life. Notice also that in Doctrine and Covenants 88:141 the Lord refers to John's record as a testimony rather than a biography. Of course there are some biographical details in the Gospels, but they are incidental rather than central.

Let me illustrate the nature of the four Gospels in a little different way. Jesus lived on this earth about thirty-three years. The books of Matthew, Mark, Luke, and John combined deal with only thirty-one days of those thirty-three years. That is, only thirty-one days of his mortal life are specified in the four books taken together. That would be a very meager biography or life history of anyone, let alone anyone as important as the Savior. However, these records do give considerable information as to *who* Jesus is—including his parentage, why he came to earth, the circumstances of his birth, his baptism, what he said, what he did, his sufferings, his atonement, his death, his burial, his resurrection from the dead, and his ascension into heaven. These are the things essential for a testimony. Other topics such as eating habits, favorite foods, color of hair, clothing, tone of voice, physical build, and the size of the house in which he lived are relatively unimportant when compared to the doctrinal things.

The Story Begins in Premortal Life

In order to comprehend why mankind's redemption was necessary and why Jesus was qualified to bring about that redemption, we must first consider the events of the premortal life. In that life, we understand, the Savior was selected as our Redeemer. We knew him there; hence our first acquaintance with Jesus began many thousands of years before we were ever born into mortality.

I think we often miss the real issue of the contention in premortality that eventually led to the War in Heaven. We talk about it as though Lucifer were going to force everybody to obey. He said, "I will redeem all mankind, that one soul shall not be lost" (Moses 4:1), and we interpret that as meaning that he was proposing forced obedience.

It seems strange to me that a third of all the spirits that had the potential to be born into this world would have favored a plan based on forced obedience. Most of us do not like to be forced. As I see it, the real issue was not so much one of force as it was that Lucifer said he would *guarantee* salvation for his spirit brothers and sisters. He promised salvation without excellence, without effort, without hard work, without individual responsibility. That is the lie he promulgated in the pre-earth councils.

That so-called shortcut to salvation captivated many gullible and lazy spirits. They wanted something for nothing. We have certain aspects of that in our society today: something is offered for nothing (a free lunch, we sometimes call it), and certain kinds of subsidies promise to guarantee the reward without the effort. With his something-for-nothing offer, then, Lucifer led away many spirits.

But individual progress does not come that way. Only by serious and strenuous exertion do we improve in character and in spiritual growth. In our society we still come in contact with many who are influenced by this erroneous philosophy advocated by the rebellious in the premortal life. They think they can achieve salvation and exaltation without a struggle. We are still fighting the War in Heaven with the same participants and the same issues, but we are fighting it on new territory.

Having ascertained that the devil's program was based on a false promise of excellence without effort, we can better appreciate the plan of our Father and His Chosen Son—a plan that would require real struggle on our part in order to do our best in this world to overcome our weaknesses and to obtain redemption from the effects of mortality. Such a redemption would be made possible through the sacrifice and merits of our Redeemer, Jesus Christ. It is in view of the premortal life and the issues fought in the War in Heaven, then, that everything else in the ministry of Jesus and in the gospel must be understood. If we overlook the premortal life, we never get the clear perspective necessary in mortality to understand the gospel of redemption.

Upon learning in the premortal life about the plan of redemption, no doubt many of us labored as missionaries for the Savior, going among the spirits to persuade others to choose the Savior and following him in preparing for earth life. Elder Orson Pratt, discussing the conditions that existed in the premortal world that finally led to the War in Heaven, the appointment of some to special callings, and also the expulsion of many spirits, said:

> It is not likely that the final decision of the contending armies took place immediately. Many, no doubt, were unsettled in their views, unstable in their minds, and undecided as to which force to join: there may have been, for aught we know, many deserters from both armies: and there may have been a long period before the division line was so strictly drawn as to become unalterable. Laws, without doubt, were enacted, and penalties affixed, according to the nature of the offences or crimes: those who altogether turned from the Lord, and were determined to maintain the cause of Satan, and who proceeded to the utmost extremities of wickedness, placed themselves without the reach of redemption: therefore, such were prohibited from entering into a second probationary state, and had no privilege of receiving bodies of flesh and bones. . . .
>
> Among the two-thirds who remained, it is highly probable that there were many who were not valiant in the war, but whose sins were of such a nature that they could be forgiven through faith in the future sufferings of the Only Begotten of the Father, and through their sincere repentance and reformation. We see no impropriety in Jesus offering himself as an acceptable offering and sacrifice before the Father to atone for the sins of His brethren, committed, not only in the second, but also in the first estate. Certain it was, that the work which Jesus was to accomplish, was known in the Grand Council where the rebellion broke out; it was known that man would sin in his second estate: for it was upon the

> subject of his redemption that the assembly became divided, and which resulted in war. . . .
>
> If all the two-thirds who kept their first estate were equally valiant in the war, and equally faithful, why should some of them be called and chosen in their spiritual state to hold responsible stations and offices in this world, while others were not? If there were none of those spirits who sinned, why were the Apostles, when they existed in their previous state, chosen to be blessed "with all spiritual blessings in heavenly places in Christ?" All these passages seem to convey an idea, that there were callings, choosings, ordinances, promises, predestinations, elections, and appointments, made before the world began.[2]

We now have a veil of forgetfulness drawn over our minds, and we do not remember the details of those premortal events; yet the spiritual capacity that we developed in the pre-earth life has come with us into mortality, and when we hear the gospel preached it strikes a familiar note. We are learning again principles we once knew; that previously developed spiritual capacity responds to every true doctrine that is taught to us when the doctrine is properly presented. Our main business in this world, then, is to continue that spiritual development we started so long ago, and this we will do by faith in that same Jesus whom we knew and loved and obeyed in our premortal life.

The Need for Mankind's Redemption

With the broader perspective given us by a knowledge of the premortal life, we can see that a wise Heavenly Father has ordained all the necessary steps leading to the redemption and exaltation of his children. Let us now consider the particular earthly events that set in motion this process of redemption. Here we will be answering the question, What made necessary the redemption of mankind from death and sin?

In John 3:16–17 we read: "For God so loved the world, that he gave his only begotten Son, that whosoever believeth in him should not perish, but have everlasting life. For God sent not his Son into the world to condemn the world; but that the world through him might be saved." The Bible provides us with this great statement about how we, without the Savior, would surely perish. Paul also discusses these things in 1 Corinthians and in Romans, but not as clearly as we would like. It takes the Book of Mormon, the Doctrine and Covenants, and the Pearl of Great Price to explain more fully why we would have perished. We would have perished because of the fall of Adam; we could not save ourselves from either his fall or our own sins.

There is passage after passage in the Book of Mormon and in other latter-day scriptures indicating that the fall of Adam brought death upon mankind, two kinds of death: the death of the body and the death of the spirit, this second kind of death being a separation from things of righteousness—an alienation from the things of God. Because of the Fall, Adam and Eve and all of their posterity suffered both of these deaths. Thus, if there were no act of redemption made by someone who was not subject to those deaths—or, in other words, if there were no atonement made by Jesus Christ—then mankind would everlastingly remain subject to those two deaths and could not be redeemed. And so it was absolutely critical that the Lord come into the world and work out an atonement.

Let's take a look at some of the plain statements in the Book of Mormon on Adam's fall and the resulting need for mankind's redemption. In a missionary situation, Alma said:

> Now we see that Adam did fall by the partaking of the forbidden fruit, according to the word of God; and thus we see, that by his fall, all mankind became a lost and fallen people.
>
> And now behold, I say unto you that if it had been possible for Adam to have partaken of the fruit of the tree of life at that time, there would have been no death, and the word would have been void, making God a liar, for he said: If thou eat thou shalt surely die.
>
> And we see that death comes upon mankind, yea, the death which has been spoken of by Amulek, which is the temporal death; nevertheless there was a space granted unto man in which he might repent; therefore this life became a probationary state; a time to prepare to meet God; a time to prepare for that endless state which has been spoken of by us, which is after the resurrection of the dead. (Alma 12:22–24.)

And in Alma 22:13–14 we read of another missionary situation in which these doctrines are clearly stated:

> And Aaron did expound unto him [Lamoni's father] the scriptures from the creation of Adam, laying the fall of man

> before him, and their carnal state and also the plan of redemption, which was prepared from the foundation of the world, through Christ, for all whosoever would believe on his name.
>
> And since man had fallen he could not merit anything of himself; but the sufferings and death of Christ atone for their sins, through faith and repentance, and so forth; and that he breaketh the bands of death, that the grave shall have no victory, and that the sting of death should be swallowed up in the hopes of glory; and Aaron did expound all these things unto the king.

Finally, we note an excerpt from the words of Nephi's younger brother Jacob. Jacob is one of the great doctrinal preachers of the Book of Mormon. He is one of the greatest theologians in all scripture. It would be hard to measure one prophet against another, but some have gifts in one direction and others have gifts in another; and Jacob had a great insight into, as well as a great facility of expression to explain, the Atonement.

> For as death hath passed upon all men, to fulfil the merciful plan of the great Creator, there must needs be a power of resurrection, and the resurrection must needs come unto man by reason of the fall; and the fall came by reason of transgression; and because man became fallen they were cut off from the presence of the Lord.
>
> Wherefore, it must needs be an infinite atonement—save it should be an infinite atonement this corruption could not put on incorruption. Wherefore, the first judgment which came upon man must needs have remained to an endless duration. (2 Nephi 9:6–7.)

The "first judgment which came upon man" was "thou shalt surely die" (Moses 3:17). It involved both deaths, the death of the body and the death as to things pertaining to righteousness, or the spiritual death.

Jesus saved mankind from these deaths, the consequences of the fall of Adam. We cannot have a proper understanding of the need for a Savior if we do not believe in the fall of Adam. And we should go one step further and accept that the creation of the world was done with the view in mind that there would be a fall and with the provision of a Savior from before the foundation of the world.

The fall of Adam was no surprise to heaven. God wanted it done. He provided the Savior before the Fall ever occurred.

Jesus the Designated Redeemer

Having come thus far in our discussion, we are now prepared to consider the reasons why Jesus was qualified to redeem mankind.

Jesus was the divinely appointed Beloved Son of God the Father, and he was born of Mary into mortality. In many ways—in the incidentals such as eating and talking and the wearing of clothes—he was like other men. But in parentage, being sired by the Eternal Father himself, he was vastly different from all others. It was necessary that he be different from others so that he could make a payment for the transgression of Adam and for everyone's personal sins.

Every other person born into the world has been subject to the fall of Adam and therefore subject to death. Only Jesus was able to give his life but remain undominated by death. Thus, when he chose to die, not being subject to death either by Adam's fall or by any sins of his own, he could shed his blood and give his life as an offering for others. He could also rise from the dead with a perfect, glorified physical body. No one else could do that. Here again the Book of Mormon gives the clearest explanations regarding these matters, as evidenced by the following words of Amulek:

> And now, behold, I will testify unto you of myself that these things are true. Behold, I say unto you, that I do know that Christ shall come among the children of men, to take upon him the transgressions of his people, and that he shall atone for the sins of the world; for the Lord God hath spoken it.
>
> For it is expedient that an atonement should be made; for according to the great plan of the Eternal God there must be an atonement made, or else all mankind must unavoidably perish; yea, all are hardened; yea, all are fallen and are lost, and must perish except it be through the atonement which it is expedient should be made.
>
> For it is expedient that there should be a great and last sacrifice; yea, not a sacrifice of man, neither of beast, neither of any manner of fowl; for it shall not be a human sacrifice; but it must be an infinite and eternal sacrifice.

> Now there is not any man that can sacrifice his own blood which will atone for the sins of another. Now, if a man murdereth, behold will our law, which is just, take the life of his brother? I say unto you, Nay.
>
> But the law requireth the life of him who hath murdered; therefore there can be nothing which is short of an infinite atonement which will suffice for the sins of the world. (Alma 34:8–12.)

Thus we see that Jesus was indeed qualified to be the Redeemer of mankind. But what were the specific costs to the Savior as he fulfilled this redemptive role?

Jesus' Spiritual Preparation

Even though Jesus was the Son of God by divine appointment, he had to keep the commandments and be sinless in order to make an atonement that would benefit others. He had to remain sinless, even as he was tempted and could sense the pull and attraction of sin. Note Paul's words: "For verily he took not on him the nature of angels; but he took on him the seed of Abraham." That means that he did not come into this world with a wall around him that would shield him from pain and sorrow and temptation; rather, he came with the feeling, warmth, concern, and sensitivity common to other human beings. "Wherefore in all things it behoved him to be made like unto his brethren, that he might be a merciful and faithful high priest in things pertaining to God, to make reconciliation for the sins of the people. For in that he himself hath suffered being tempted, he is able to succour them that are tempted." (Hebrews 2:16–18.) Paul also wrote that Jesus "was in all points tempted like as we are, yet without sin. Let us therefore come boldly unto the throne of grace, that we may obtain mercy, and find grace to help in time of need." (Hebrews 4:15–16.)

As recorded in the Book of Mormon, around 124 B.C. King Benjamin stated that an angel had told him the Savior "shall suffer temptations, and pain of body, hunger, thirst, and fatigue, even more than man can suffer, except it be unto death; for behold, blood cometh from every pore, so great shall be his anguish for the wickedness and the abominations of his people" (see Mosiah 3:2–7).

Jesus did not attain to the marvelous ability to resist temptation and avoid sin simply by virtue of his being the Son of God. He had to practice the righteous way of life that leads to that strength and character. Such a capacity and status is not achieved instantly. The preparation for Jesus, and for us, began in the premortal existence. Indeed, it was during that earlier time that we, by our faith in Jesus' future atonement and our compliance with the plan of redemption, progressed to the point that we were permitted to be born into this world as little children, innocent before God.

Jesus' Life One of Self-Denial

The Prophet Joseph Smith taught that Jesus "descended in suffering below that which man can suffer; or, in other words, suffered greater sufferings, and was exposed to more powerful contradictions than any man can be."[3] Because Jesus knew more he felt more; he understood more; he suffered more; and he could be tempted more than any other person. It seems that the number and severity of the temptations that one experiences are in proportion to one's knowledge and perception. A person with greater capacity may be called on to endure greater temptations. On the other hand, the joys and the rewards for that same person are also greater.

Jesus was obedient to the Father. He said, "The Father hath not left me alone; for I do always those things that please him" (John 8:29). Jesus drew strength from his Father the same way that we can draw strength from Jesus. He used a vivid description when he said that his disciples were to take up the cross and follow him. What does it mean to take up one's cross? We find out from the Joseph Smith Translation: "Then said Jesus unto his disciples, If any man will come after me, let him deny himself, and take up his cross, and follow me. And now for a man to take up his cross, is to deny himself all ungodliness, and every worldly lust, and keep my commandments." (JST, Matthew 16:25–26.)

The above passages of scripture show that Jesus denied himself of things that his mortal nature may have desired and yet were wrong for him; and he became spiritually strong as a result of that denial. The question that each of us has to answer for himself sometime in his lifetime (and the sooner the better) is whether the spirituality that can be gained is worth the required self-denial. The Savior says it is; the scriptures say it is; and I say it is. But apparently most people in the world do not think the sacrifice is worth it, for we observe that human beings in general do not deny themselves of very many things. Apparently many do not feel that a loss of spirituality or a failure to aspire to its higher levels is a tragic thing.

Jesus the Perfect Example of Self-Mastery

Evidences of the achievement of self-mastery in Jesus' life are found throughout the scriptures. For example, after his baptism Jesus went into the wilderness for forty days, during which time he fasted and prayed. The King James Version says that Jesus went into the wilderness "to be tempted of the devil" (Matthew 4:1). The Joseph Smith Translation, being more spiritually attuned, gives us a different perspective. It says that Jesus went into the wilderness to fast and "to be with God." It was after he had "communed with God" that Jesus successfully resisted the temptations of the devil. (See JST, Matthew 4:1–2.) The Savior's communion with his Father, made possible by his fasting and prayers, strengthened him spiritually.

Consider another episode in Jesus' life. In Galilee the disciples tried to cast out an evil spirit, and they could not. The Savior, however, was successful in doing so. When the disciples asked Jesus why they had failed, he explained that they didn't have enough faith. He also said that evil spirits of that type "goeth not out but by prayer and fasting." (See Matthew 17:14–21.) Jesus' success in casting out that evil spirit demonstrates that he had the necessary faith developed by prayer and fasting.

Spiritual strength and self-mastery are rooted in personal prayer. The record says that before choosing the Twelve, Jesus prayed all night unto his Father (see Luke 6:12–13). Why would he have done that if it were not necessary for his spiritual well-being? No doubt such prayer would aid him in choosing the Twelve in accordance with his Father's will. At the time of his greatest ordeal in the Garden of Gethsemane, when he bled at every pore and took upon himself the sins of mankind, he prayed. And then, as the scriptural account tells us, "there appeared an angel unto him from heaven, strengthening him." (See Luke 22:41–43.) Elder Bruce R. McConkie suggested in his writings that Adam might have been that angel; for who else could have more appropriately offered strength to Jesus at this time?[4] What I want to emphasize here is *how* the Savior received this spiritual strength: He got it through prayer and fasting. We have every reason to believe that much of Jesus' spiritual power—the power by which he calmed the storm, walked on the water, turned water into wine, healed the sick, raised the dead, fed the five thousand, forgave sins, and so forth—came to him as a result of his triumphant struggles to overcome the drag of mortality. His attainment and development of spiritual power came through his deliberate effort and from his receiving strength from his Father.

Thus, for the Savior the cost of our redemption was his complete obedience and dedication to the Father's will; he did not allow himself any deviation or straying from that path of obedience. In order to be able to save the world, he had to be the One who would be sinless, who would be perfect in his self-denial and his self-mastery. He had to become the person able to save himself as well as others. This Jesus did, as he worked out his own and our salvation, ultimately paying the highest price imaginable—the sacrifice of his own life.

Jesus Suffered and Gave His Life

The price of our redemption was so high that only a God could bring about our deliverance. Jesus Christ, through his voluntary atoning sacrifice, "purchased [us] with his own blood" (Acts 20:28; see also Hebrews 9:12). Jesus' saving mission was described by Jacob over five hundred years before the Savior's mortal ministry: "And he cometh into the world that he may save all men if they will hearken unto his voice; for behold, he suffereth the pains of all men, yea, the pains of every living creature, both men, women, and children, who belong to the family of Adam. And he suffereth this that the resurrection might pass upon all men, that all might stand before him at the great and judgment day." (2 Nephi 9:21–22.)

In Luke's account in the New Testament we read of Jesus' going into the Garden of Gethsemane and there working out an atonement for all mankind:

> And he came out, and went, as he was wont, to the mount of Olives; and his disciples also followed him.
>
> And when he was at the place, he said unto them, Pray that ye enter not into temptation.
>
> And he was withdrawn from them about a stone's cast, and kneeled down, and prayed,
>
> Saying, Father, if thou be willing, remove this cup from me: nevertheless not my will, but thine, be done.
>
> And there appeared an angel unto him from heaven, strengthening him.
>
> And being in an agony he prayed more earnestly: and his sweat was as it were great drops of blood falling down to the ground.
>
> And when he rose from prayer, and was come to his disciples, he found them sleeping for sorrow,

> And said unto them, Why sleep ye? rise and pray, lest ye enter into temptation. (Luke 22:39–46.)

It was in Gethsemane, on the slopes of the Mount of Olives, that Jesus made his perfect atonement by the shedding of his blood—more so than on the cross. We have a corroboration of that concept in the Doctrine and Covenants, wherein the Lord says:

> For behold, I, God, have suffered these things for all, that they might not suffer if they would repent;
>
> But if they would not repent they must suffer even as I;
>
> Which suffering caused myself, even God, the greatest of all, to tremble because of pain, and to bleed at every pore, and to suffer both body and spirit—and would that I might not drink the bitter cup, and shrink—
>
> Nevertheless, glory be to the Father, and I partook and finished my preparations unto the children of men.
>
> Wherefore, I command you again to repent, lest I humble you with my almighty power; and that you confess your sins, lest you suffer these punishments of which I have spoken, of which in the smallest, yea, even in the least degree you have tasted at the time I withdrew my Spirit. (D&C 19:16–20.)

I suppose that all of us have at some time or another done something that caused the Spirit to leave us; hence we felt low, we felt down, we felt alone. In each case, our losing the Spirit was the result of something we had done individually, not something someone else had done.

Now, let us consider the case of Jesus, who had the Holy Ghost all the days of his life (and the Holy Ghost is the Comforter). Indeed, the Savior had the help of the Holy Ghost from the time he was born. At every trial and at every endeavor and at every temptation, he had the strength of the Holy Ghost to be with him. But as he went into the Garden of Gethsemane and began to take upon him our sins, the Father withdrew the Spirit from him, and Jesus worked out the Atonement alone.[5] This withdrawal of the Spirit is the agony described by the Savior in the verses above, an agony which, as he told Martin Harris, "in the smallest, yea, even in the least degree you have tasted at the time I withdrew my Spirit." It appears that the Father withdrew the Spirit from his Son in the Garden of Gethsemane so that Jesus might tread the winepress alone (see D&C 133:50). Jesus alone is our Redeemer and Savior. He committed no sins; nothing he had done caused the Spirit to withdraw from him. It was *our* sins he carried and for which he suffered.

The Costs of Redemption for Mankind

Now to the question, What will it cost *us* to be redeemed?

First we should understand that mankind cannot prepare for redemption by acquiring knowledge alone or by just attending to a few rituals. It is true that gaining knowledge and performing ordinances are part of the process, but redemption comes to a person through a change of heart, through being born again and being sanctified by the Holy Ghost. Unless a person experiences this change of heart and spiritual rebirth, he is never quite ready for a righteous existence. In fact, he might not even desire such an existence. The Holy Ghost must touch and temper that person's spirit and disposition. Spirit must speak to spirit; that is, the Holy Spirit must act upon a person's spirit to purify his desires and actions.

In a related vein, Paul wrote to the Corinthians: "I was with you in weakness, and in fear, and in much trembling. And my speech and my preaching was not with enticing words of man's wisdom, but in demonstration of the Spirit and of power: that your faith should not stand in the wisdom of men, but in the power of God." (1 Corinthians 2:3–5.)

Every person needs experiences with the Spirit of God. Without them there is no genuine testimony, no conversion—only intellectual commitment. It is folly to think that salvation can come by assimilation of knowledge alone, for the natural man has too many insurmountable limitations.

Gaining knowledge is important, but it is different from being sanctified by the Holy Ghost and different from having a change of heart. We need light and truth, not just truth alone. Light is the contribution of the Holy Spirit, and such light is lacking in an intellectual experience alone.

Paul continued his explanation to the Corinthians with these words: "The natural man receiveth not the things of the Spirit of God: for they are foolishness unto him: neither *can* he know them [he didn't say "neither *does* he know them"; he said he *can't* know them], because they are spiritually discerned" (1 Corinthians 2:14). Attitudes, convictions, and viewpoints of eternal significance are planted in the soul by the Spirit, not by cold intellectual exercise. Again, gaining knowledge is absolutely essential, but it is not the thing that changes a natural man into a saint; only the Holy Ghost will do that, which is a cleansing as by fire. Thus we see that intellectual exercise is a complement to, but no substitute for, the workings of the Holy Ghost.

The Book of Mormon speaks eloquently of the mighty change of heart that must take place in the soul of a believer (see Alma 5:12–26). When a person has experienced this phenomenon, he or she is a changed person, a new creature because of faith. Such a person has "no more disposition to do evil" and cannot "look upon sin save it [be] with abhorrence" (Mosiah 5:2; Alma 13:12). The luster and the wisdom of the world lose some of their attraction, and the hope of redemption enlivens the soul. Without this change the struggles of mortality can become so great that one grows weary and neglects the work of the Lord. However, a person truly converted or changed will have the proper attitude about spiritual things, even if he lacks the detailed supporting knowledge.

Love the Agent of Conversion

To understand how the change of heart occurs, let us consider the experience of a man who became one of the greatest of the Lord's servants, the Apostle Paul. At first Paul was a stout fighter against the gospel of Jesus because he saw it was a threat to the religion of Judaism. The Lord struck him down by His power, physically blinded him for three days, and then healed him of his blindness. The initial shock was so great that Paul began to fall into line, and he became a willing follower and disciple of Jesus. (See Acts 8–9.) But the good effect of that original blow would not have lasted the rest of Paul's life were it not for the understanding he received and the change of heart he experienced through the operation of the Holy Spirit.

As he learned how the redemption wrought by Jesus Christ operates, Paul became aware that the Lord suffered for mankind because He loved them. Paul could feel that love that Jesus had for him, and thus it was not the fear of the Lord's physical power that made Paul completely devoted and dedicated to the Savior. To Timothy, Paul wrote:

> I thank Christ Jesus our Lord, who hath enabled me, for that he counted me faithful, putting me into the ministry;
>
> Who was before a blasphemer, and a persecutor, and injurious: but I obtained mercy, because I did it ignorantly in unbelief.

> And the grace of our Lord was exceeding abundant with faith and love which is in Christ Jesus.
>
> This is a faithful saying, and worthy of all acceptation, that Christ Jesus came into the world to save sinners; of whom I am chief.
>
> Howbeit for this cause I obtained mercy, that in me first Jesus Christ might shew forth all long-suffering, for a pattern to them which should hereafter believe on him to life everlasting. (1 Timothy 1:12–16.)

To Titus, Paul wrote that Jesus "gave *himself* for us." I think the emphasis here ought to be on the word *himself*. Jesus "gave *himself* for us, that he might redeem us from all iniquity, and purify unto himself a peculiar people" (Titus 2:14, italics added). And to the Galatians, Paul wrote: "I am crucified with Christ: nevertheless I live; yet not I, but Christ liveth in me: and the life which I now live in the flesh I live by the faith of the Son of God, who *loved* me, and gave *himself* for me" (Galatians 2:20, italics added).

Paul preached salvation by grace because he learned that Jesus, out of his infinite love for the entire human family, had made it possible for man to conquer the forces that would bring upon him death and unhappiness. In the scriptural sense, what man does is called "works," and what Jesus does for us is called "grace." Thus, Jesus does for us what we could *not* do for ourselves, and we are able to obtain salvation because of his grace.

What If There Were No Redeemer?

Finally, we turn to the question, What would have been the fate of mankind had there been no Redeemer? I have noticed that quite often when we talk about our Savior we talk principally about the resurrection and its attendant blessings, but we rarely talk about what our circumstances would have been if there had been no atonement by Jesus.

I remember when, during a discussion in a class many years ago when I was a teenager, one of the students asked the teacher what would have become of our spirits if there had been no redemption made by Jesus. The teacher responded: "Well, I do not know what would have happened to our spirits, but I give it as my guess that, if there had been no atonement made by Jesus, we would still go on to whatever degree of glory we had merited. But we would have to go there as spirits without bodies, because Jesus brought to pass the resurrection, and if there were no resurrection we would have no bodies.''

None of us in the class knew enough about the gospel to know if that was the right answer. But some time later, while serving a mission, I was reading in the book of 2 Nephi when I realized that if Jacob had been in that earlier class meeting he would have said something like this: ''Now, wait a minute. This is what the atonement of Jesus does for us: It not only brings the body forth from the grave but also redeems the spirit from what otherwise would have been an endless, miserable condition with the devil.'' Or, in other words, if Jesus Christ had not performed the infinite atonement, every man, woman, and child—everybody who belongs to the family of Adam—would have become a son of perdition.

Here is Jacob's explanation as recorded in the Book of Mormon. Speaking of the Atonement, he stated:

> It must needs be an infinite atonement—save it should be an infinite atonement this corruption could not put on incorruption. Wherefore, the first judgment which came upon man must needs have remained to an endless duration. And if so, this flesh must have laid down to rot and to crumble to its mother earth, to rise no more.
>
> O the wisdom of God, his mercy and grace! For behold, if the flesh should rise no more [that is, if there were no resurrection of the body] our spirits must become subject to that angel who fell from before the presence of the Eternal God, and became the devil, to rise no more.
>
> And our spirits must have become like unto him, and we become devils, angels to a devil, to be shut out from the presence of our God, and to remain with the father of lies, in misery, like unto himself. . . .
>
> O how great the goodness of our God, who prepareth a way for our escape from the grasp of this awful monster; yea, that monster, death and hell, which I call the death of the body, and also the death of the spirit. (2 Nephi 9:7–10.)

Recall what Jesus said: ''I am come that they might have life, and that they might have it more abundantly'' (John 10:10). When we understand the alternative—what our fate would have been without the Savior—the preceding words have altogether new and deeper meaning. The more abundant life promised by Jesus refers not only to a resurrected, endless life with a body but also to a better quality of life both now and in the hereafter. It's the joy of a celestial life compared with the misery and disappointment of hell.

Jesus' unique situation, the important fact that he alone is the Savior for all mankind, and the truth that without him all is lost are borne out in several scriptures. For example, Jesus said, "I am the way, the truth, and the life: no man cometh unto the Father, but by me" (John 14:6). Peter, testifying of Jesus Christ before a council of Jews, said it this way: "Neither is there salvation in any other: for there is none other name under heaven given among men, whereby we must be saved" (Acts 4:12). Peter made this declaration *after* the atonement and resurrection of Jesus had already been accomplished, but in the Book of Mormon we find the same doctrine spoken many hundred years *before* Jesus was born (see 2 Nephi 31:21; Mosiah 3:17; 4:8; 5:8). We must realize that there never was any other name, even before Christ's mission in mortality, by which salvation could be obtained. He always has been the only Savior for all of mankind, and he always will be. There are no alternatives, no backup men, no substitute plans.

As we have mentioned previously in this chapter, the consequences of the fall of Adam were both physical and spiritual. Had Jesus not done what he did in his atonement, nothing the rest of us could ever do would make up for the loss. The Savior's words regarding the vine and the branches are appropriate in this context:

> I am the true vine, and my Father is the husbandman.
>
> Every branch in me that beareth not fruit he taketh away: and every branch that beareth fruit, he purgeth it, that it may bring forth more fruit.
>
> Now ye are clean through the word which I have spoken unto you.
>
> Abide in me, and I in you. As the branch cannot bear fruit of itself, except it abide in the vine; no more can ye, except ye abide in me.
>
> I am the vine, ye are the branches: He that abideth in me, and I in him, the same bringeth forth much fruit: for without me ye can do nothing. (John 15:1–5.)

The message of the gospel is that Jesus has broken the bands of death and hell. The resurrection of Jesus Christ is the greatest proclamation of all time, but the Savior's triumph affects more than the life of the physical body. For the faithful there is not only a resurrection of the dead body to everlasting life but also a redemption of the spirit from unhappiness to a state of eternal bliss and a fulness of joy. All of this has been made possible through the atoning blood of Jesus Christ, which he shed in Gethsemane, through his death upon the cross, and through his rising from the grave with a perfect resurrected body.

Quite often I find when I talk to students about the Savior, some of them wonder if there was an alternate plan; they seem to be asking, "What if Jesus had failed?" Now, not intending to cast aspersions on these students, I think that that question typifies one of the tools the devil used in the premortal life. I think he not only "guaranteed" salvation without effort for everybody but also probably went around saying something like this: "Now look, if you allow yourselves to be born into this world subject to the fall of Adam, subject to sin and to death, and if Jesus doesn't come through, then you have lost your salvation." That is true; that is what *would* have been the case. If Jesus had not performed the infinite atonement, we all would have become sons of perdition, and he would have also.

I can almost hear Lucifer in that premortal sphere saying, "Are you going to put all of your faith in Jesus?" And those spirits who were not strong in their faith were thus prompted by the devil to wonder, to doubt, and to think to themselves, "Well, I don't know if I want to trust Jesus or not. What if he fails?" Such a thought is just about like going tracting without purse or scrip but having ten dollars in your shoe just in case. That is not faith. During our premortal life, having faith in Jesus Christ meant that we *knew* he would not let us down. That is why the gospel is called the "good news." The good news is that there is a redemption for mankind and that Jesus successfully performed the Atonement in order to bring that redemption about.

Conclusion

What was the price of redemption? According to the scriptures the price that Jesus paid was that he gave of himself completely, not even withholding his life; he shed his blood and died on the cross for the sins of the world; he paid for a broken law—a debt we were unable to pay for ourselves. He would not have done this unless he loved us. The costs to us are minor in comparison: we are to love him, believe on his name, repent of our sins, be baptized in water, keep his commandments, and love one another. This doesn't just mean refraining from wrongdoing, but in the larger sense it means deliberately going about doing good and building up the kingdom. No person will do this consistently unless he has the same kind of love in his heart that Jesus had. We need the mighty change of heart that comes from the Holy Ghost.

We cannot fully appreciate the doctrine of redemption if we do not accept and understand the doctrine of the Fall. Moreover, if we take away from the plan of salvation the concept of the pre-earth life, the doctrine of the fall of Adam, and the doctrine of the atoning blood of Jesus Christ, then we make of the gospel simply a system of ethics. And that will not do. The gospel is related to ethics, but it is so much more than that. Like Alma, I rejoice in the coming of our Lord Jesus Christ. I am so glad he came.

> Yea, and the voice of the Lord, by the mouth of angels, doth declare it unto all nations; yea, doth declare it, that they may have glad tidings of great joy; yea, and he doth sound these glad tidings among all his people, yea, even to them that are scattered abroad upon the face of the earth; wherefore they have come unto us.
>
> And [the gospel is] made known unto us in plain terms, that we may understand, that we cannot err; and this because of our being wanderers in a strange land; therefore, we are thus highly favored. (Alma 13:22–23.)

Thus given the price of our redemption, we see that our relationship with the Savior is not casual; it is not optional. It is absolute and critical. Without him there would be no salvation, no redemption, no resurrection, and no happiness. All mankind must take upon themselves his name. Salvation is to triumph over everything that would destroy the happiness and the well-being of man—sin, fear, unhappiness, jealousy, death, and the devil. It is the Lord's purpose to help us achieve this triumph (see Moses 1:39). President J. Reuben Clark, Jr., said:

> You know, I believe that the Lord will help us. I believe if we go to him, he will give us wisdom, if we are living righteously. I believe he will answer our prayers. I believe that our Heavenly Father wants to save every one of his children. I do not think he intends to shut any of us off because of some slight transgression, some slight failure to observe some rule or regulation. There are the great elementals that we must observe, but he is not going to be captious about the lesser things.

> I believe that his juridical concept of his dealings with his children could be expressed in this way: I believe that in his justice and mercy he will give us the maximum reward for our acts, give us all that he can give, and in the reverse, I believe that he will impose upon us the minimum penalty which it is possible for him to impose.[6]

May we obtain the full benefit of our Savior's love and appreciate what he has done to redeem us. To ignore him is the greatest form of ingratitude. To fail to obey his commandments is the greatest of all mistakes. To follow him and to serve him are the greatest happiness.

Notes

1. See John E. Steinmueller, *A Companion to Scripture Studies. . . .* 3 vols. (New York: J. F. Wagner, Inc., 1941–43), 3:34–35.
2. Orson Pratt, "The Pre-existence of Man," *The Seer* 1 (April 1853): 54–56.
3. *Lectures on Faith* 5:2.
4. See Bruce R. McConkie, *The Mortal Messiah*, 4 vols. (Salt Lake City: Deseret Book Co., 1979–81), 4:124–25.
5. See Brigham Young, in *Journal of Discourses* 3:205–6.
6. J. Reuben Clark, Jr., in Conference Report, October 1953, p. 84.

APPENDIX

Sources of the selected writings in this volume are as follows:

Chapter 1: From the *Ensign* 17 (January 1987): 22–27.
Chapter 2: From the *Ensign* 9 (July 1979): 40–45.
Chapter 3: From an address given at the eighteenth annual Sidney B. Sperry Symposium, 28 October 1989.
Chapter 4: From *The Seventh Annual Church Educational System Religious Educators' Symposium on the Old Testament* (Salt Lake City: The Church of Jesus Christ of Latter-day Saints, 1983), pp. 118–21.
Chapter 5: From an address given as part of a BYU Lecture Series at the time of the Ramses II exhibit, 18 December 1985.
Chapter 6: From *The Ninth Annual Sidney B. Sperry Symposium, The Book of Mormon* (Provo, Utah: Brigham Young University Press, 1981), pp. 18–27; *The Sixth Annual Church Educational System Religious Educators' Symposium on the Book of Mormon* (Salt Lake City: The Church of Jesus Christ of Latter-day Saints, 1982), pp. 55–58; and *The Tenth Annual Church Educational System Religious Educators' Symposium on the Book of Mormon* (Salt Lake City: The Church of Jesus Christ of Latter-day Saints, 1986), pp. 86–90.
Chapter 7: From *The Third Annual Church Educational System Religious Educators' Symposium on the Old Testament* (Salt Lake City: The Church of Jesus Christ of Latter-day Saints, 1979), pp. 204–12.
Chapter 8: From *Pearl of Great Price Symposium* (Provo, Utah: Religious Instruction, Brigham Young University, 1975), pp. 14–27 (updated).
Chapter 9: From *The Joseph Smith Translation: The Restoration of Plain and Precious Things*, ed. Monte S. Nyman and Robert L. Millet (Provo, Utah: Religious Studies Center, Brigham Young University, 1985), pp. 271–89.
Chapter 10: From the *Ensign* 13 (January 1983): 57–64.
Chapter 11: From a lecture given to the faculty in Religious Education at Brigham Young University, 20 February 1987.
Chapter 12: From a manuscript dated 20 June 1988.

Chapter 13: From an informal address given to the faculty in Religious Education at Brigham Young University, 19 February 1988.

Chapter 14: From an address presented at a Book of Mormon symposium sponsored by the Division of Continuing Education, Brigham Young University, May 1989, and a lecture given to the faculty in Religious Education at Brigham Young University, 16 February 1990.

Chapter 15: From a presentation given at the Church Educational System Symposium for Religious Educators, 11 August 1988.

Chapter 16: From *The Sixth Annual Church Educational System Religious Educators' Symposium on the Book of Mormon* (Salt Lake City: The Church of Jesus Christ of Latter-day Saints, 1982), pp. 52–54.

Chapter 17: From a lecture given to the faculty in Religious Education at Brigham Young University, 17 February 1989.

Chapter 18: From *The Eleventh Annual Sidney B. Sperry Symposium, The New Testament* (Provo, Utah: Brigham Young University Press, 1983), pp. 157–68, and *Brigham Young University 1984–85 Devotional and Fireside Speeches* (Provo, Utah: Brigham Young University, University Publications, 1985), pp. 42–48.

SUBJECT INDEX

SCRIPTURE INDEX

OLD TESTAMENT

Psalms

Ecclesiastes

Isaiah

Jeremiah

Ezekiel

Jonah

Micah

Zechariah

NEW TESTAMENT

Matthew

Mark

BOOK OF MORMON

DOCTRINE AND COVENANTS

PEARL OF GREAT PRICE

Moses

Abraham

Joseph Smith—History

Articles of Faith